Common Stocks and Uncommon Profits and Other Writings by Philip A. Fisher

Philip A. Fisher

John Wiley & Sons, Inc.
New York • Chichester • Brisbane • Toronto • Singapore

Copyright © 1996 by Philip A. Fisher
Published by John Wiley & Sons, Inc.

Common Stocks and Uncommon Profits, was previously published in 1958 by Harper & Brothers, and then in 1960 by PSR Publications. *Conservative Investors Sleep Well* was previously published in 1975 by Business Classics. *Developing an Investment Philosophy* was previously published in 1980 by the Financial Analysts Society and Business Classics.

Library of Congress Cataloging-in-Publication Data:

Fisher, Philip A.
    Common stocks and uncommon profits and other writings / by Philip A. Fisher.
        p.   cm. — (Wiley investment classic)
    Originally published: Common stocks and uncommon profits. Harper & Brothers, 1958.
    Includes index.
    ISBN 0-471-11928-8 (cloth : alk. paper). — ISBN 0-471-11927-X (pbk. : alk. paper)
    1. Stocks.   2. Investments.   I. Fisher, Philip A. Common stocks and uncommon profits.   II. Title.   III. Series.
HG4661.F5   1996
332.83'223—dc20   95-51449
                                                                         CIP

Printed in the United States of America

10 9 8 7 6 5 4 3 2

Common Stocks and
Uncommon Profits and Other
Writings by Philip A. Fisher

WILEY INVESTMENT CLASSICS

CONTENTS

*This book is dedicated
to all investors, large and small,
who do NOT adhere to the philosophy:
"I have already made up my mind,
don't confuse me with facts."*

CONTENTS

INTRODUCTION

WHAT I LEARNED FROM MY FATHER'S WRITINGS

Kenneth L. Fisher

It took me about fifteen years to understand *Common Stocks and Uncommon Profits*. When I first read the book, it made darned little sense. I was eight. It was a waste of the start of a perfectly good summer vacation. Too many big words—needed a dictionary—ugh. When it comes to smarts, I was a slow starter, toward the tail end of my school class. But it was my father's book, and I was proud of him. I had heard at school and from neighbors and had seen in the local paper that this book was a big splash. It was supposed to be the very first investment book ever to have made the *New York Times* bestseller list, whatever that meant. It was my absolute duty to read it. So I did. And when completed, the fact was, I was glad to be through and free for the summer.

Who knew that I would later go on to found a large investment management firm, write my own books, and become the tenth longest-running columnist in *Forbes* magazine's formidable seventy-nine-year history, spanning hundreds of columns over more than a decade, including annual "Best of the Year" investment book reviews? And, yes, maybe it helped that I could say I'd read my first investment book when I was eight, even if I didn't understand it.

The book next crossed my mind seriously at age twenty as I faced college graduation. Father had offered to let me work with him and my older brother. It was a bit more convoluted, but that's the gist. A job. Anxious, but skeptical, I wanted to "check it out," to see if this job thing was really an opportunity. So, I read *Common Stocks and Uncommon Profits* again. There were only a few words I didn't understand this time.

Reading about father's fifteen points to look for in a stock, I wondered if I could apply them to a local stock. If so, in my mind, it affirmed the benefit of working with my father.

Well, it didn't work. There was a local publicly traded lumber stock, Pacific Lumber, that looked like a good profit opportunity. But the few folks I approached weren't impressed with some kid-sleuth seeking competitive detail who was clearly ill-prepared to analyze or do anything with it. I didn't even know how to ask the questions. After getting shut down for facts by the first few folks I approached, I gave up. But it showed me that I needed quite a bit of polishing.

Working for my father was a bumpy ride, somewhat like my first professional stock purchase—a reverse "ten bagger"—it fell from ten to one. I've told you all this only so you can see that even a kid in his twenties, who wasn't all that bright, and who made lots of mistakes, could go on and in just a few years learn to use this book's principles fairly effectively. I did, so anyone can. You can.

Applying the fifteen points in *Common Stocks and Uncommon Profits* was an over-and-over, real-world experience linked to "scuttlebutt"—all aimed at researching one stock here, another there. It worked. I will not here recount the successes it helped me achieve early in my career. But I gained material career momentum discovering a handful of stocks I could have known about only through scuttlebutt and the fifteen points. I could understand generally where a firm fit into the world and how it would or wouldn't prosper. If it wouldn't, what might its hiccups be? I soon understood why my college try at the fifteen points failed. The craft is in the scuttlebutt, which, like all craft, takes time to learn. The art is in seeing the signs of things that indicate the fifteen points. It's the difference between learning to play the piano (craft) and then composing (art). You probably won't compose until you're pretty competent at playing. In almost any field, you can learn the craft by repetition, but not otherwise. You may appreciate the art without any ability to create it yourself, or after mastering the craft, you may turn yourself into an artist.

My father's goals and mine have never been quite the same. But this book works for his or mine. He was a growth stock investor. It was simply who he was. Still is. I was always a value guy. A different cat. He wanted stock in a firm that could grow and grow and grow, and the stock could be bought at a reasonable price and virtually never be sold. I wanted a stock that was dirt cheap because it was better than its bad image.

My point: scuttlebutt and the fifteen points work for growth and value stocks. Take point number four: an above-average sales organization is as important, or maybe more so, to a value firm without great natural sales momentum behind it as it is to one with the wind to its back. Ditto for point five about a worthwhile profit margin. For example, in a commodity type business, without natural growth, it is true that market share, relative production costs, and long-term profit margins all tend to be pretty tightly linked. Good management gains market share and lowers relative production costs, often by introducing enhanced production technology (the application of technology rather than the production of it). Bad management simply but irregularly lower margins until they disappear. Hence, in 1976 I discovered Nucor, a tiny low-cost steel vendor—great management, innovative technology, lower production costs, high relative market share in tiny steel niches, gaining market share and adding niches. I bought it as a value guy; my father promptly bought Nucor as a growth guy. Same fifteen points.

I think my father, who was fifty-one and a bit of an eclectic genius and already very successful when this book came out, failed to see how the understanding of the craft, which had come to him slowly and intuitively over the years, would take time for a neophyte to learn. The scuttlebutt chapter is only three pages long. But they are among the book's most important pages. It is clear to me, in retrospect, that my father simply skipped the craft part of what otherwise might have been in the book. He just assumed it.

Over the years, I applied this process to lots of stocks on an individual basis, gaining great insights. The key? Focus on customers, competitors, and suppliers. The craft I described in my first book, *Super Stocks* (Dow Jones-Irwin 1984), including how to do it and several real-world examples. But again, this is all craft. Whenever you ask, you get answers. The art is to get more questions—and the right questions—flowing from the answers you receive. I've seen people who rigidly run down a standard question list, regardless of the responses they get. That isn't art. You ask. He or she answers. What question best flows from the answer? And so on. When you can do that well on a real-time basis, you are a composer; an artist; a creative, investigative investor.

I went with my father about a jillion times to visit companies between 1972 and 1982. I worked for him only for a year, but we did lots of things together after that. In looking at companies, he always prepared questions in advance, typed on yellow pages with space in between so he could scribble notes. He always wanted to be prepared, and he wanted the company to know he was prepared so they would appreciate him. And he used the questions as a sort of outline of topics to be covered. It was also a great backup in case the conversation went bad, and cold, which occasionally it did. Then he could get things back on course instantly with one of his prepared questions. But his very best questions always popped out of his mind, unprepared, never having been written down in advance because they were the angle he picked up on the fly, as he heard an answer to a lesser question. Those creative questions were the art. It is what, in my mind, made his querying great.

My firm has applied the fifteen points and scuttlebutt to firms of most varieties, although primarily smaller, beat-up ones. Retailers, technology of various forms, service firms, concrete, steel, specialty chemicals, consumer products, gambling, you name it. It hasn't always been the final decisive phenomena that compelled me or the firm, but it added value. While contemplating on a large scale, and attempting to get at hundreds of stocks yearly, my firm mass-produced the process into one we called Twelve-Call, run off an operations manual with remote-location workers doing telephone interviews of customers, competitors, and suppliers. It isn't as powerful as doing it yourself on a single stock, but it lets us cover lots of ground. My point is that the fifteen points and scuttlebutt are worthwhile whether used exactly as my father originally envisioned them or on an altered, more superficial but more mass-spectrum basis.

Now, don't get the idea that the only worthwhile parts of *Common Stocks and Uncommon Profits* are scuttlebutt and the fifteen points. It's just that I think they are the jewels. There are smaller sparkles, too, bits of wisdom well worn. For example, by 1990 I'd been a professional for eighteen years and fairly successful. I'd been a *Forbes* columnist for six years. Enter Saddam Hussein. As the threat of war grew, investors grew timid. The market buckled. I've studied history a lot and written two financial history books. The history as I saw it said, "buy." But I hadn't lived that much history. One weekend, I buttressed my resolve by reviewing Chapter 8, "Five Don'ts for Investors" and Chapter 9, "Five More Don'ts for Investors." And I knew that the war scare had to be a market buying opportunity. From it, along with some of my economic forecasting, came my well-timed late 1990 "buy" columns. Timing that right when most others were bearish helped secure my long-term place in *Forbes*, for which I've long been grateful.

You will find lots of other jewels of your own in these pages that may do as much for you as they have for me. But an important concluding point to make on *Common Stocks and Uncommon Profits* is to note its sheer fundamentalness. It is fundamental. Not only does it teach true fundamentals of investing, but it has been a fundamental part of the training of a lot of leading investment practitioners. For many years it has been part of the curriculum in the investment class at the Stanford Graduate School of Business. Students of all forms passed through Stanford, read the book, and went on to become some of the nation's leading investors. The book's breadth was broader than that. For example, Warren Buffett has long credited my father and *Common Stocks and Uncommon Profits* as being fundamental to the development of his investment philosophy. Want to see a touch of it? Read the first of my father's "Don'ts" in Chapter 9: "Don't overstress diversification." You get quickly to the source of one key cornerstone of Buffettism. You get it from the same place Buffett first did.

Not much of great importance to market fundamentalism changed between the writing of my father's first book and that of *Conservative Investors Sleep Well*. But a lot of water went under the bridge. A huge bull market, a huge bear market, 1958 to 1974—lots of fads and fancies. It was time, in my mind, for Philip A. Fisher to tell the world again about what was what. With no modesty, I say that without my goading he never would have written *Conservative Investors Sleep Well*. I was just a young twerp then, but I was pesky and I could get him to do things better than almost anyone. As you read his introduction to it, you see that I made up the title and "contributed many other matters, including part of the basic conception of what lies herein."

What he doesn't tell you, and never would out of grace for my benefit, is that it wasn't planned that way. He and I talked the content over, and in the name of ease for him, originally it was supposed to be a coauthored book. I was to write the first draft based on our agreed-upon content, and he would polish it up. That way it wouldn't take too much of his time. It was partly a way to get him to commit the time. Wrong. I did such a truly lousy job on the first draft that he had to scrap the whole thing and start over, leading it to be a sole-authorship and a book that is vastly better for you and a great credit to him. My written contributions would have wasted your time and discredited him.

I think Chapter 6's Motorola section is vintage Phil Fisher. In it, he shows why Motorola, which others then didn't like so well, is a great firm. It's tough to read this section and not appreciate that it was a true quality company. But look what happened afterward. The stock has since appreciated twenty-fold. That is, in twenty-one years, a dollar became twenty dollars, compounding at fifteen-plus percent per year, before dividends—and all in a safe, well-managed firm, incurring no brokerage costs year to year, no mutual fund operating expense ratios, and not much effort for a true believer. Would anyone actually hold one stock for all those twenty-one years? Well, I'm here to tell you for a certainty that one Philip A. Fisher did, as his largest personal holding. All this while the S&P 500 rose a mere seven-fold. And that is and was what Phil Fisher was all about. Finding great companies that he could really know and holding them for a long, long, long time while the stock appreciated phenomenally. *Conservative Investors Sleep Well* is simply the best treatise I know on how to buy and hold growth without taking much risk.

People often ask me about my relationship with my father. And because he is weird, and I'm weird, and often they are weird, I sometimes give weird answers. For example, when they ask, as they often do, what experience from my memories with my father is my favorite, I always answer, "The next one." They may try to pin me down with something like, "Well, weren't there favorite moments when you were younger?" I readily admit that there were. He was the world's greatest bedtime storyteller, and his stories had absolutely nothing at all to do with the stock market. As a small child I loved every moment—and folks like the growing legions of Buffett-philes hate that answer. They want some notion about researching some stock. But there was never really a lot of emotion about that. It was just work. So, then, in frustration, I'm often asked, "Well, if you could distill advice from your father down to a single sentence what would it be?" I'd say, "Read his writings and try to live them out." And that is what this book can do for you.

Part One

COMMON STOCKS
AND UNCOMMON
PROFITS

PREFACE

The publication of a new book in the field of investment may well require some explanatory statement from its author. The following remarks will therefore have to be somewhat personal in order to supply an adequate explanation for my venturing to offer another book on this subject to the investing public.

After one year in Stanford University's then brand-new Graduate School of Business Administration, I entered the business world in May 1928. I went to work for, and twenty months later was made the head of, the statistical department of one of the main constituent units of the present Crocker-Anglo National Bank of San Francisco. Under today's nomenclature I would have been called a security analyst.

Here I had a ringside seat at the incredible financial orgy that culminated in the autumn of 1929 as well as the period of adversity that followed. My observations led me to believe that there was a magnificent opportunity on the West Coast for a specialized investment counseling firm that would make itself the direct antithesis of that ancient but uncomplimentary description of certain stockbrokers—men who know the price of everything and the value of nothing.

On March first 1931, I started Fisher & Co. which, at that time, was an investment counseling business serving the general public but with its interests centered largely around a few growth companies. This activity prospered. Then came World War II. For three and a half years, while I was engaged in various desk jobs for the Army Air Force, I spent part of such spare time as I had in reviewing both the successful and, more particularly, the unsuccessful investment actions that I had taken and that I had seen others take during the preceding ten years. I began seeing certain investment principles emerge from this review which were different from some of those commonly accepted as gospel in the financial community.

When I returned to civilian life I decided to put these principles into practice in a business atmosphere as little disturbed by side issues as possible. Instead of serving the general public, Fisher & Co. for over eleven years has never served more than a dozen clients at one time. Most of these clients have remained the same during this period. Instead of being mainly interested in major capital appreciation, all Fisher & Co. activity has been focused upon this one objective. I am aware that these past eleven years have been a period of generally rising stock prices during which anyone engaged in such activities should have made good profits. Nevertheless by the degree to which these funds have consistently forged ahead of the generally recognized indices of the market as a whole, I find that following these principles has justified itself even more thoroughly in the post-war period than was the case in the ten pre-war years when I was only partially applying them. Perhaps even more significant, they have been no less rewarding during those of these years when the general market was static or declining than when it was sharply advancing.

In studying the investment record both of myself and others, two matters were significant influences in causing this book to be written. One, which I mention several times elsewhere, is the need for patience if big profits are to be made from investment. Put another way, it is often easier to tell what will happen to the price of a stock than how much time will elapse before it happens. The other is the inherently deceptive nature of the stock market. Doing what everybody else is doing at the moment, and therefore what you have an almost irresistible urge to do, is often the wrong thing to do at all.

For these reasons over the years I have found myself explaining in great detail to the owners of the funds I manage the principles behind one or another action I have taken. Only in this way would they have enough understanding of why I was acquiring some, to them, totally unknown security so that there would be no impulse to dispose of it before enough time had elapsed for the purchase to begin justifying itself in market quotations.

Gradually the desire arose to compile these investment principles and have a printed record to which I could point. This resulted in the first groping toward organizing this book. Then I began thinking of the many people, most of them owners of far smaller funds than those belonging to the handful of individuals it is my business to serve, who have come to me over the years and asked how they as small investors could get started off on the right path.

I thought of the difficulties of the army of small investors who have unintentionally picked up all sorts of ideas and investment notions that can prove expensive over a period of years, possibly because they had never been exposed to the challenge of more fundamental concepts. Finally I thought of the many discussions I have had with another group also vitally interested in these matters, although from a different standpoint. These are the corporate presidents, financial vice presidents and treasurers of publicly owned companies, many of whom show a deep interest in learning as much as possible about these matters.

I concluded there was need for a book of this sort. I decided such a book would have an informal presentation in which I would try to address you, the reader, in the first person. I would use much the same language and many of the same examples and analogies that I have employed in presenting the same concepts to those whose funds I manage. I hope my frankness, at times my bluntness, will not cause offense. I particularly hope that you will conclude the merit of the ideas I present may outweigh my defects as a writer.

PHILIP A. FISHER

San Mateo, California
September 1957

1

CLUES FROM THE PAST

Y ou have some money in the bank. You decide you would like to buy some common stock. You may have reached this decision because you desire to have more income than you would if you used these funds in other ways. You may have reached it because you want to grow with America. Possibly you think of earlier years when Henry Ford was starting the Ford Motor Company or Andrew Mellon was building up the Aluminum Company of America, and you wonder if you could not discover some young enterprise which might today lay the groundwork for a great fortune for you, too. Just as likely you are more afraid than hopeful and want to have a nest egg against a rainy day. Consequently, after hearing more and more about inflation, you desire something which will be safe and yet protected from further shrinkage in the buying power of the dollar.

Probably your real motives are a mixture of a number of these things, influenced somewhat by knowing a neighbor who has made some money in the market and, possibly, by receiving a pamphlet in the mail explaining just why Midwestern Pumpernickel is now a bargain. A single basic motive lies behind all this, however. For one reason or another, through one method or another, you buy common stocks in order to make money.

Therefore, it seems logical that before even thinking of buying any common stock the first step is to see how money has been most successfully made in the past. Even a casual glance at American stock market history will show that two very different methods have been used to amass spectacular fortunes. In the nineteenth century and in the early part of the twentieth century, a number of big fortunes and many small ones were made largely by betting on the business cycle. In a period when an unstable banking system caused recurring boom and bust, buying stocks in bad times and selling them in good had strong elements of value. This was particularly true for those with good financial connections who might have some advance information about when the banking system was becoming a bit strained.

But perhaps the most significant fact to be realized is that even in the stock market era which started to end with the coming of the Federal Reserve System in 1913 and became history with the passage of the securities and exchange legislation in the early days of the Roosevelt administration, those who used a different method made far more money and took far less risk. Even in those earlier times, finding the really outstanding companies and staying with them through all the fluctuations of a gyrating market proved far more profitable to far more people than did the more colorful practice of trying to buy them cheap and sell them dear.

If this statement appears surprising, further amplification of it may prove even more so. It may also provide the key to open the first door to successful investing. Listed on the various stock exchanges of the nation today are not just a few, but scores of companies in which it would have been possible to invest, say, $10,000 somewhere between twenty-five and fifty years ago and today have this purchase represent anywhere from $250,000 to several times this amount. In other words, within the lifetime of most investors and within the period in which their parents could have acted for nearly all of them, there were available scores of opportunities to lay the groundwork for substantial fortunes for oneself or one's children. These opportunities did not require purchasing on a particular day at the bottom of a great panic. The shares of these companies were available year after year at prices that were to make this kind of profit possible. What was required was the ability to distinguish these relatively few companies with outstanding investment possibilities from the much greater number whose future would vary all the way from the moderately successful to the complete failure.

Are there opportunities existing today to make investments that in the years ahead will yield corresponding percentage gains? The answer to this question deserves rather detailed attention. If it be in the affirmative, the path for making real profits through common stock investment starts to become clear. Fortunately, there is strong evidence indicating that the opportunities of today are not only as good as those of the first quarter of this century but are actually much better.

One reason for this is the change that has occurred during this period in the fundamental concept of corporate management and the corresponding changes in handling corporate affairs that this has brought about. A generation ago, heads of a large corporation were usually members of the owning family. They regarded the corporation as a personal possession. The interests of outside stockholders were largely ignored. If any consideration at all was given to the problem of management continuity—that is, of training younger men to step into the shoes of those whose age might make them no longer available—the motive was largely that of taking care of a son or a nephew who would inherit the job. Providing the best available talent to protect the average stockholder's investment was seldom a matter in the forefront of the minds of management. In that age of autocratic personal domination, the tendency of aging management was to resist innovation or improvement and frequently to refuse even to listen to suggestions or criticism. This is a far cry from today's constant competitive search to find ways of doing things better. Today's top corporate management is usually engaged in continuous self-analysis and, in a never-ending search for improvement, frequently even goes outside its own organization by consulting all sorts of experts in its effort to get good advice.

In former days there was always great danger that the most attractive corporation of the moment would not continue to stay ahead in its field or, if it did, that the insiders would grab all the benefits for themselves. Today, investment dangers like these, while not entirely a thing of the past, are much less likely to prove a hazard for the careful investor.

One facet of the change that has come over corporate management is worthy of attention. This is the growth of the corporate research and engineering laboratory—an occurrence that would hardly have benefited the stockholder if it had not been accompanied by corporate management's learning a parallel technique whereby this research could be made a tool to open up a golden harvest of ever-growing profits to the stockholder. Even today, many investors seem but slightly aware of how fast this development has come, how much further it is almost certainly going, and its impact on basic investment policy.

Actually, even by the late 1920's, only a half dozen or so industrial corporations had significant research organizations. By today's standards, their size was small. It was not until the fear of Adolf Hitler accelerated this type of activity for military purposes that industrial research really started to grow.

It has been growing ever since. A survey made in the spring of 1956, published in *Business Week* and a number of other McGraw-Hill trade publications, indicated that in 1953 private corporate expenditures for research and development were about $3.7 billion. By 1956 they had grown to $5.5 billion and present corporate planning called for this to be running at the rate of better than $6.3 billion by 1959. Equally startling, this survey indicated that by 1959, or in just three years, a number of our leading industries expect to get from 15 per cent to more than 20 per cent of their total sales from products which were not in commercial existence in 1956.

In the spring of 1957 the same source made a similar survey. If the totals revealed in 1956 were startling in their significance, those revealed just one year later might be termed explosive. Research expenditures were up 20 per cent from the previous year's total to $7.3 billion! This represents almost a 100 per cent growth in four years. It means the actual growth in twelve months was $1 billion more than only a year before had been expected as the total growth that would occur in the ensuing thirty-six months. Meanwhile, anticipated research expenditures in 1960 were estimated at $9 billion! Furthermore, all manufacturing industries, rather than just a few selected industries as represented in the earlier survey, expected that 10 per cent of 1960 sales would be from products not yet in commercial existence only three years before. For certain selected industries, this percentage—from which sales representing merely new model and style changes had been excluded—was several times higher.

The impact of this sort of thing on investment can hardly be overstated. The cost of this type of research is becoming so great that the corporation which fails to handle it wisely from a commercial standpoint may stagger under a crushing burden of operating expense. Furthermore, there is no quick and easy yardstick for either management or the investor to measure the profitability of research. Just as even the ablest professional baseball player cannot expect to get a hit much more often than one out of every three times he comes to bat, so a sizable number of research projects, governed merely by the law of averages, are bound to produce nothing profitable at all. Furthermore, by pure chance, an abnormal number of such unprofitable projects may happen to be bunched together in one particular span of time in even the best-run commercial laboratory. Finally, it is apt to take from seven to eleven years from the time a project is first conceived until it has a significant favorable effect on corporate earnings. Therefore, even the most profitable of research projects is pretty sure to be a financial drain before it eventually adds to the stockholder's profit.

But if the cost of poorly organized research is both high and hard to detect, the cost of too little research may be even higher. During the next few years, the introduction of many kinds of new materials and new types of machinery will steadily narrow the market for thousands of companies, possibly entire industries, which fail to keep pace with the times. So will such major changes in basic ways of doing things as will be brought about by the adoption of electronic computers for the keeping of records and the use of irradiation for industrial processing. However, other companies will be alert to the trends and will maneuver to make enormous sales gains from such awareness. The managements of certain of such companies may continue to maintain the highest standards of efficiency in handling their day-to-day operations while using equally good judgment in keeping ahead of the field on these matters affecting the long-range future. Their fortunate stockholders, rather than the proverbial meek, may well inherit the earth.

In addition to these influences of the changed outlook in corporate management and the rise of research, there is a third factor likewise tending to give today's investor greater opportunities than those existing in most past periods. Later in this book—in those sections dealing with when stocks should be bought and sold—it would seem more appropriate to discuss what, if any, influence the business cycle should have on investment policies. But discussion of one segment of this subject seems called for at this point. This is the greater advantage in owning certain types of common stocks, as a result of a basic policy change that has occurred within the framework of our federal government, largely since 1932.

Both prior to and since that date, regardless of how little they had to do with bringing it about, both major parties took and usually received credit for any prosperity that might occur when they were in power. Similarly, they were usually blamed by both the opposition and the general public if a bad slump occurred. However, prior to 1932 there would have been serious question from the responsible leadership of either party as to whether there was any moral justification or even political wisdom in deliberately running a huge deficit in order to buttress ailing segments of business. Fighting unemployment by methods far more costly than the opening of bread lines and soup kitchens would not have been given serious consideration, regardless of which party might have been in office.

Since 1932 all that is reversed. The Democrats may or may not be less concerned with a balanced federal budget than the Republicans. However, from President Eisenhower on down, with the possible exception of former Secretary of the Treasury Humphrey, the responsible Republican leadership has said again and again that if business should really turn down they would not hesitate to lower taxes or make whatever other deficit-producing moves were necessary to restore prosperity and eliminate unemployment. This is a far cry from the doctrines that prevailed prior to the big depression.

Even if this change in policy had not become generally accepted, certain other changes have occurred that would produce much the same results, though possibly not so quickly. The income tax only became legal during the Wilson administration. It was not a major influence on the economy until the 1930's. In earlier years, much of the federal revenue came from customs duties and similar excise sources. These fluctuated moderately with the level of prosperity but as a whole were fairly stable. Today, in contrast, about 80 per cent of the federal revenue comes from corporate and personal income taxes. This means that any sharp decline in the general level of business causes a corresponding decline in federal revenue.

Meanwhile, various devices such as farm price supports and unemployment compensation have become imbedded in our laws. At just the time that a business decline would be greatly reducing the federal government's income, expenditures in these fields made mandatory by legislation would cause governmental expenses to mount sharply. Add to this the definite intention of reversing any unfavorable business trend by cutting taxes, building more public works, and lending money to various hard-pressed business groups, and it becomes increasingly plain that if a real depression were to occur the federal deficit could easily run at a rate of $25 to $30 billion per annum. Deficits of this type would produce further inflation in much the same way that the deficits resulting from wartime expenditures produced the major price spirals of the postwar period.

This means that when a depression does occur it is apt to be shorter than some of the great depressions of the past. It is almost bound to be followed by enough further inflation to produce the type of general price rise that in the past has helped certain industries and hurt others. With this general economic background, the menace of the business cycle may well be as great as it ever was for the stockholder in the financially weak or marginal company. But to the stockholder in the growth company with sufficient financial strength or borrowing ability to withstand a year or two of hard times, a business decline under today's economic conditions represents far more a temporary shrinking of the market value of his holdings than the basic threat to the very existence of the investment itself that had to be reckoned with prior to 1932.

Another basic financial trend has resulted from this built-in inflationary bias having become imbedded so deeply in both our laws and our accepted concepts of the economic duties of government. Bonds have become undesirable investments for the strictly long-term holdings of the average individual investor. The rise in interest rates that had been going on for several years gained major momentum in the fall of 1956. With high-grade bonds subsequently selling at the lowest prices in twenty-five years, many voices in the financial community were raised to advocate switching from stocks which were selling at historically high levels into such fixed-income securities. The abnormally high yield of bonds over dividend return on stocks—in relation to the ratio that normally prevails—would appear to have given strong support to the soundness of this policy. For the short term, such a policy sooner or later may prove profitable. As such, it might have great appeal for those making short- or medium-term investments—that is, for "traders" with the acuteness and sense of timing to judge when to make the necessary buying and selling moves. This is because the coming of any significant business recession is almost certain to cause an easing of money rates and a corresponding rise in bond prices at a time when equity quotations are hardly likely to be buoyant. This leads us to the conclusion that high-grade bonds may be good for the speculator and bad for the long-term investor. This seems to run directly counter to all normally accepted thinking on this subject. However, any understanding of the influences of inflation will show why this is likely to be the case.

In its letter of December 1956, the First National City Bank of New York furnished a table showing the worldwide nature of the depreciation in the purchasing power of money that occurred in the ten years from 1946 to 1956. Sixteen of the major nations of the free world were included in this table. In every one of them the value of money significantly declined. These declines ranged from a minimum in Switzerland, where at the end of the ten-year period money would buy 85 per cent of what could be purchased ten years before, to the other extreme in Chile, where in ten years it had lost 95 per cent of its former value. In the United States this decline amounted to 29 per cent and in Canada to 35 per cent. This means that in the United States the annual rate of monetary depreciation during the period was 3.4 per cent, and in Canada it was 4.2 per cent. In contrast, the yield offered by United States Government bonds bought at the beginning of the period, which admittedly was one of rather low interest rates, was only 2.19 per cent. This means that the holder of this type of high-grade, fixed-income security actually received negative interest (or loss) of better than 1 per cent per annum if the real value of his money is considered.

Suppose, however, that instead of acquiring bonds at the rather low rates that prevailed at the beginning of this period, the investor could have bought them at the rather high interest rates that prevailed ten years later. The First National City Bank of New York in the same article also supplied figures on this matter. At the end of the period covered in the article, they estimated the return on United States Government bonds at 3.27 per cent, which still would leave no return whatever, actually a slight loss, on the investment. However, six months after this article was written, interest rates had risen sharply, and were above 3.5 per cent. How would the investor actually have fared if he had had the opportunity at the beginning of this period to invest with the highest returns that have prevailed in over a quarter of a century? In the great majority of cases he would still have gotten no real return on his investment. In many instances he would have had an actual loss. This is because nearly all such bond purchasers would have had to pay at least a

20 per cent income tax on the interest received before the genuine rate of their return on the investment could have been calculated. In many cases the bondholder's tax would have been at a considerably higher rate, since only the first $2000 to $4000 of taxable income qualifies at this 20 per cent level. Similarly, if an investor had purchased tax-free municipal bonds at this all-time high, the somewhat lower interest rate that these tax-free securities carry would again not have provided any real return on his investment.

Of course, these figures are only conclusive for this one ten-year period. They do indicate, however, that these conditions are worldwide and therefore not too likely to be reversed by political trends in any one country. What is really important concerning the attractiveness of bonds as long-term investments is whether a similar trend can be expected in the period ahead. It seems to me that if this whole inflation mechanism is studied carefully it becomes clear that major inflationary spurts arise out of wholesale expansions of credit, which in turn result from large government deficits greatly enlarging the monetary base of the credit system. The huge deficit incurred in winning World War II laid such a base. The result was that prewar bondholders who have maintained their positions in fixed-income securities have lost over half the real value of their investments.

As already explained, our laws, and more importantly our accepted beliefs of what should be done in a depression, make one of two courses seem inevitable. Either business will remain good, in which event outstanding stocks will continue to out-perform bonds, or a significant recession will occur. If this happens, bonds should temporarily out-perform the best stocks, but a train of major deficit-producing actions will then be triggered that will cause another major decline in the true purchasing power of bond-type investments. It is almost certain that a depression will produce further major inflation; the extreme difficulty of determining when in such a disturbing period bonds should be sold makes me believe that securities of this type are, in our complex economy, primarily suited either to banks, insurance companies and other institutions that have dollar obligations to offset against them, or to individuals with short-term objectives. They do not provide for sufficient gain to the long-term investor to offset this probability of further depreciation in purchasing power.

Before going further, it might be well to summarize briefly the various investment clues that can be gleaned from a study of the past and from a comparison of the major differences, from an investment standpoint, between the past and the present. Such a study indicates that the greatest investment reward comes to those who by good luck or good sense find the occasional company that over the years can grow in sales and profits far more than industry as a whole. It further shows that when we believe we have found such a company we had better stick with it for a long period of time. It gives us a strong hint that such companies need not necessarily be young and small. Instead, regardless of size, what really counts is a management having both a determination to attain further important growth and an ability to bring its plans to completion. The past gives us a further clue that this growth is often associated with knowing how to organize research in the various fields of the natural sciences so as to bring to market economically worthwhile and usually interrelated product lines. It makes clear to us that a general character-istic of such companies is a management that does not let its preoccu-pation with long-range planning prevent it from exerting constant vig-ilance in performing the day-to-day tasks of ordinary business outstandingly well. Finally, it furnishes considerable assurance that in spite of the very many spectacular investment opportunities that existed twenty-five or fifty years ago, there are probably even more such oppor-tunities available today.

2

WHAT "SCUTTLEBUTT" CAN DO

As a general description of what to look for, all this may be helpful. But as a practical guide for finding outstanding investments, it obviously contributes relatively little. Granted that this furnishes a broad outline of the type of investment that should be sought, how does the investor go about finding the specific company which might open the way to major appreciation?

One way that immediately suggests itself is logical but rather impractical. This is to find someone who is sufficiently skilled in the various facets of management to examine each subdivision of a company's organization and by detailed investigation of its executive personnel, its production, its sales organization, its research, and each of its other major functions, form a worthwhile conclusion as to whether the particular company has outstanding potentialities for growth and development.

Such a method may appear sensible. Unfortunately there are several reasons why it usually will not serve the average investor very well. In the first place, there are only a few individuals who have the necessary degree of top management skill to do a job of this kind. Most of them are busy at top-level and high-paying management jobs. They have neither the time nor the inclination to occupy themselves in this way. Furthermore, if they were so inclined, it is doubtful if many of the real growth companies of the nation would allow someone outside their own organization to have all the data necessary to make an informed decision. Some of the knowledge gained in this way would be too valuable to existing or potential competition to permit its being passed on to anyone having no responsibility to the company furnishing the data.

Fortunately, there is another course which the investor can pursue. If properly handled, this method will provide the clues that are needed to find really outstanding investments. For lack of a better term, I shall call this way of proceeding the "scuttlebutt" method.

As this method is spelled out in detail in the pages that follow, the average investor will have one predominant reaction. This is that regardless of how beneficial this "scuttlebutt" method may be to someone else, it is not going to be helpful to him, because he just won't have much chance to apply it. I am aware that most investors are not in a position to do for themselves much of what is needed to get the most from their investment funds. Nevertheless I think they should thoroughly understand just what is needed and why. Only in this way are they in a position to select the type of professional advisor who can best help them. Only in this way can they adequately evaluate the work of that advisor. Furthermore, when they understand not only what can be accomplished, but also how it can be accomplished, they may be surprised at how from time to time they may be in a position to enrich and make more profitable the worthwhile work already being done for them by their investment advisors.

The business "grapevine" is a remarkable thing. It is amazing what an accurate picture of the relative points of strength and weakness of each company in an industry can be obtained from a representative cross-section of the opinions of those who in one way or another are concerned with any particular company. Most people, particularly if they feel sure there is no danger of their being quoted, like to talk about the field of work in which they are engaged and will talk rather freely about their competitors. Go to five companies in an industry, ask each of them intelligent questions about the points of strength and weakness of the other four, and nine times out of ten a surprisingly detailed and accurate picture of all five will emerge.

However, competitors are only one and not necessarily the best source of informed opinion. It is equally astonishing how much can be learned from both vendors and customers about the real nature of the people with whom they deal. Research scientists in universities, in government, and in competitive companies are another fertile source of worthwhile data. So are executives of trade associations.

In the case of trade association executives especially, but to a great extent the other groups as well, it is impossible to lay too much stress on the importance of two matters. The inquiring investor must be able to make clear beyond any doubt that his source of information will never be revealed. Then he must scrupulously live up to this policy. Otherwise, the danger of getting an informant into trouble is obviously so great that unfavorable opinions just do not get passed along.

There is still one further group which can be of immense help to the prospective investor in search of a bonanza company. This group, however, can be harmful rather than helpful if the investor does not use good judgment and does not do plenty of cross-checking with others to verify his own judgment as to the reliability of what is told him. This group consists of former employees. Such people frequently have a real inside view in regard to their former employer's strength and weakness. Equally important, they will usually talk freely about them. But enough such former employees may, rightly or wrongly, feel they were fired without good cause or left because of a justified grievance that it is always important to check carefully into why employees left the company being studied. Only then is it possible to determine the degree of prejudice that may exist and to allow for it in considering what the former employee has to say.

If enough different sources of information are sought about a company, there is no reason to believe that each bit of data obtained should agree with each other bit of data. Actually, there is not the slightest need for this to happen. In the case of really outstanding companies, the preponderant information is so crystal-clear that even a moderately experienced investor who knows what he is seeking will be able to tell which companies are likely to be of enough interest to him to warrant taking the next step in his investigation. This next step is to contact the officers of the company to try and fill out some of the gaps still existing in the investor's picture of the situation being studied.

3

WHAT TO BUY

THE FIFTEEN POINTS TO LOOK FOR IN A COMMON STOCK

What are these matters about which the investor should learn if he is to obtain the type of investment which in a few years might show him a gain of several hundred per cent, or over a longer period of time might show a correspondingly greater increase? In other words, what attributes should a company have to give it the greatest likelihood of attaining this kind of results for its shareholders?

There are fifteen points with which I believe the investor should concern himself. A company could well be an investment bonanza if it failed fully to qualify on a very few of them. I do not think it could come up to my definition of a worthwhile investment if it failed to qualify on many. Some of these points are matters of company policy; others deal with how efficiently this policy is carried out. Some of these points concern matters which should largely be determined from information obtained from sources outside the company being studied, while others are best solved by direct inquiry from company personnel. These fifteen points are:

POINT 1. Does the company have products or services with sufficient market potential to make possible a sizable increase in sales for at least several years?

It is by no means impossible to make a fair one-time profit from companies with a stationary or even a declining sales curve. Operating economies resulting from better control of costs can at times create enough improvement in net income to produce an increase in the market price of a company's shares. This sort of one-time profit is eagerly sought by many speculators and bargain hunters. It does not offer the degree of opportunity, however, that should interest those desiring to make the greatest possible gains from their investment funds.

Neither does another type of situation which sometimes offers a considerably larger degree of profit. Such a situation occurs when a changed condition opens up a large increase in sales for a period of a very few years, after which sales stop growing. A large-scale example of this is what happened to the many radio set manufacturers with the commercial development of television. A huge increase in sales occurred for several years. Now that nearly 90 per cent of United States homes that are wired for electricity have television sets, the sales curve is again static. In the case of a great many companies in the industry, a large profit was made by those who bought early enough. Then as the sales curve leveled out, so did the attractiveness of many of these stocks.

Not even the most outstanding growth companies need necessarily be expected to show sales for every single year larger than those of the year before. In another chapter I will attempt to show why the normal intricacies of commercial research and the problems of marketing new products tend to cause such sales increases to come in an irregular series of uneven spurts rather than in a smooth year-by-year progression. The vagaries of the business cycle will also have a major influence on year-to-year comparisons. Therefore growth should not be judged on an annual basis but, say, by taking units of several years each. Certain companies give promise of greater than normal growth not only for the next several-year period, but also for a considerable time beyond that.

Those companies which decade by decade have consistently shown spectacular growth might be divided into two groups. For lack of better terms I will call one group those that happen to be both "fortunate and able" and the other group those that are "fortunate because they are able." A high order of management ability is a must for both groups. No company grows for a long period of years just because it is lucky. It must have and continue to keep a high order of business skill, otherwise it will not be able to capitalize on its good fortune and to defend its competitive position from the inroads of others.

The Aluminum Company of America is an example of the "fortunate and able" group. The founders of this company were men with great vision. They correctly foresaw important commercial uses for their new product. However, neither they nor anyone else at that time could foresee anything like the full size of the market for aluminum products that was to develop over the next seventy years. A combination of technical developments and economies, of which the company was far more the beneficiary than the instigator, was to bring this about. Alcoa has and continues to show a high order of skill in encouraging and taking advantage of these trends. However, if background conditions, such as the perfecting of airborne transportation, had not caused influences completely beyond Alcoa's control to open up extensive new markets, the company would still have grown—but at a slower rate.

The Aluminum Company was fortunate in finding itself in an even better industry than the attractive one envisioned by its early management. The fortunes made by many of the early stockholders of this company who held on to their shares is of course known to everyone. What may not be so generally recognized is how well even relative newcomers to the stockholder list have done. When I wrote the original edition, Alcoa shares were down almost 40 per cent from the all-time high made in 1956. Yet at this "low" price the stock showed an increase in value of almost 500 per cent over not the low price, but the median average price at which it could have been purchased in 1947, just ten years before.

Now let us take Du Pont as an example of the other group of growth stocks—those which I have described as "fortunate because they are able." This company was not originally in the business of making nylon, cellophane, lucite, neoprene, orlon, milar, or any of the many other glamorous products with which it is frequently associated in the public mind and which have proven so spectacularly profitable to the investor. For many years Du Pont made blasting powder. In time of peace its growth would largely have paralleled that of the mining industry. In recent years, it might have grown a little more rapidly than this as additional sales volume accompanied increased activity in road building. None of this would have been more than an insignificant fraction of the volume of business that has developed, however, as the company's brilliant business and financial judgment teamed up with superb technical skill to attain a sales volume that is now exceeding two billion dollars each year. Applying the skills and knowledge learned in its original powder business, the company has successfully launched product after product to make one of the great success stories of American industry.

The investment novice taking his first look at the chemical industry might think it is a fortunate coincidence that the companies which usually have the highest investment rating on many other aspects of their business are also the ones producing so many of the industry's most attractive growth products. Such an investor is confusing cause and effect to about the same degree as the unsophisticated young lady who returned from her first trip to Europe and told her friends what a nice coincidence it was that wide rivers often happened to flow right through the heart of so many of the large cities. Studies of the history of corporations such as Du Pont or Dow or Union Carbide show how clearly this type of company falls into the "fortunate because they are able" group so far as their sales curve is concerned.

Possibly one of the most striking examples of these "fortunate because they are able" companies is General American Transportation. A little over fifty years ago when the company was formed, the railroad equipment industry appeared a good one with ample growth prospects. In recent years few industries would appear to offer less rewarding prospects for continued growth. Yet when the altered outlook for the railroads began to make the prospects for the freight car builders increasingly less appealing, brilliant ingenuity and resourcefulness kept this company's income on a steady uptrend. Not satisfied with this, the management started taking advantage of some of the skills and knowledge learned in its basic business to go into other unrelated lines affording still further growth possibilities.

A company which appears to have sharply increasing sales for some years ahead may prove to be a bonanza for the investor regardless of whether such a company more closely resembles the "fortunate and able" or the "fortunate because it is able" type. Nevertheless, examples such as General American Transportation make one thing clear. In either case the investor must be alert as to whether the management is and continues to be of the highest order of ability; without this, the sales growth will not continue.

Correctly judging the long-range sales curve of a company is of extreme importance to the investor. Superficial judgment can lead to wrong conclusions. For example, I have already mentioned radio-television stocks as an instance where instead of continued long-range growth there was one major spurt as the homes of the nation acquired television sets. Nevertheless, in recent years certain of these radio-television companies have shown a new trend. They have used their electronic skills to build up sizable businesses in other electronic fields such as communication and automation equipment. These industrial and, in some cases, military electronic lines give promise of steady growth for many years to come. In a few of these companies, such as Motorola for example, they already are of more importance than the television operation. Meanwhile, certain new technical developments afford a possibility that in the early 1960's current model television sets will appear as awkward and obsolete as the original wall-type crank-operated hand telephones appear today.

One potential development, color television, has possibly been overdiscounted by the general public. Another is a direct result of transistor development and printed circuitry. It is a screen-type television with sets that would be little different in size and shape from the larger pictures we now have on our walls. The present bulky cabinet would be a thing of the past. Should such developments obtain mass commercial acceptance, a few of the technically most skillful of existing television companies might enjoy another major spurt in sales even larger and longer lasting than that which they experienced a few years ago. Such companies would find this spurt superimposed on a steadily growing industrial and military electronics business. They would then be enjoying the type of major sales growth which should be the first point to be considered by those desiring the most profitable type of investments.

I have mentioned this example not as something which is sure to happen, but rather as something which could easily happen. I do so because I believe that in regard to a company's future sales curve there is one point that should always be kept in mind. If a company's management is outstanding and the industry is one subject to technological change and development research, the shrewd investor should stay alert to the possibility that management might handle company affairs so as to produce in the future exactly the type of sales curve that is the first step to consider in choosing an outstanding investment.

Since I wrote these words in the original edition, it might be interesting to note, not what "is sure to happen" or "may happen," but what has happened in regard to Motorola. We are not yet in the early 1960's, the closest time to which I refer as affording a possibility of developing television models that will obsolete those of the 1950's. This has not happened nor is it likely to do so in the near future. But in the meanwhile let us see what an alert management has done to take advantage of technological change to develop the type of upward sales curve that I stated was the first requisite of an outstanding investment.

Motorola has made itself an outstanding leader in the field of two-way electronic communications that started out as a specialty for police cars and taxicabs, and now appears to offer almost unlimited growth. Trucking companies, owners of delivery fleets of all types, public utilities, large construction projects, and pipe lines are but a few of the users of this type of versatile equipment. Meanwhile, after several years of costly developmental effort, the company has established a semi-conductor (transistor) division on a profitable basis which appears headed toward obtaining its share of the fabulous growth trend of that industry. It has become a major factor in the new field of stereophonic phonographs and is obtaining an important and growing new source of sales in this way. By a rather unique style tie-in with a leading national furniture manu-facturer (Drexel), it has significantly increased its volume in the higher-priced end of its television line. Finally, through a small acquisition it is just getting into the hearing-aid field and may develop other new spe-cialties as well. In short, while some time in the next decade important major stimulants may cause another large spurt in its original radio-television lines, this has not happened yet nor is it likely to happen soon. Yet management has taken advantage of the resources and skills within the organization again to put this company in line for growth. Is the stock market responding to this? When I finished writing the original edition, Motorola was 45½. Today it is 122.

When the investor is alert to this type of opportunity, how profitable may it be? Let us take an actual example from the industry we have just been discussing. In 1947 a friend of mine in Wall Street was making a survey of the infant television industry. He studied approximately a dozen of the principal set producers over the better part of a year. His conclusion was that the business was going to be competitive, that there were going to be major shifts in position between the leading concerns, and that certain stocks in the industry had speculative appeal. However, in the process of this survey it developed that one of the great shortages was the glass bulb for the picture tube. The most successful producer appeared to be Corning Glass Works. After further examination of the technical and research aspects of Corning Glass Works it became ap-parent that this company was unusually well qualified to produce these glass bulbs for the television industry. Estimates of the possible market indicated that this would be a major source of new business for the company. Since prospects for other product lines seemed generally favorable, this analyst recommended the stock for both individual and institutional investment. The stock at that time was selling at about 20. It has since been split 2½-for-1 and ten years after his purchase was selling at over 100, which was the equivalent of a price of 250 on the old stock.

POINT 2. Does the management have a determination to continue to develop products or processes that will still further increase total sales potentials when the growth potentials of currently attractive product lines have largely been exploited?

Companies which have a significant growth prospect for the next few years because of new demand for existing lines, but which have neither policies nor plans to provide for further developments beyond this may provide a vehicle for a nice one-time profit. They are not apt to provide the means for the consistent gains over ten or twenty-five years that are the surest route to financial success. It is at this point that scientific research and development engineering begin to enter the picture. It is largely through these means that companies improve old products and develop new ones. This is the usual route by which a management not content with one isolated spurt of growth sees that growth occurs in a series of more or less continuous spurts.

The investor usually obtains the best results in companies whose engineering or research is to a considerable extent devoted to products having some business relationship to those already within the scope of company activities. This does not mean that a desirable company may not have a number of divisions, some of which have product lines quite different from others. It does mean that a company with research centered around each of these divisions, like a cluster of trees each growing additional branches from its own trunk, will usually do much better than a company working on a number of unrelated new products which, if successful, will land it in several new industries unrelated to its existing business.

At first glance Point 2 may appear to be a mere repetition of Point 1. This is not the case. Point 1 is a matter of fact, appraising the degree of potential sales growth that now exists for a company's product. Point 2 is a matter of management attitude. Does the company now recognize that in time it will almost certainly have grown up to the potential of its present market and that to continue to grow it may have to develop further new markets at some future time? It is the company that has both a good rating on the first point and an affirmative attitude on the second that is likely to be of the greatest investment interest.

POINT 3. How effective are the company's research and development efforts in relation to its size?

For a large number of publicly-owned companies it is not too difficult to get a figure showing the number of dollars being spent each year on research and development. Since virtually all such companies report their annual sales total, it is only a matter of the simplest mathematics to divide the research figure by total sales and so learn the per cent of each sales dollar that a company is devoting to this type of activity. Many professional investment analysts like to compare this research figure for one company with that of others in the same general field. Sometimes they compare it with the average of the industry, by averaging the figures of many somewhat similar companies. From this, conclusions are drawn both as to the importance of a company's research effort in relation to competition and the amount of research per share of stock that the investor is getting in a particular company.

Figures of this sort can prove a crude yardstick that may give a worthwhile hint that one company is doing an abnormal amount of research or another not nearly enough. But unless a great deal of further knowledge is obtained, such figures can be misleading. One reason for this is that companies vary enormously in what they include or exclude as research and development expense. One company will include a type of engineering expense that most authorities would not consider genuine research at all, since it is really tailoring an existing product to a particular order—in other words, sales engineering. Conversely, another company will charge the expense of operating a pilot plant on a completely new product to production rather than research. Most experts would call this a pure research function, since it is directly related to obtaining the know-how to make a new product. If all companies were to report research on a comparable accounting basis, the relative figures on the amount of research done by various well-known companies might look quite different from those frequently used in financial circles.

In no other major subdivision of business activity are to be found such great variations from one company to another between what goes in as expense and what comes out in benefits as occurs in research. Even among the best-managed companies this variation seems to run in a ratio of as much as two to one. By this is meant some well-run companies will get as much as twice the ultimate gain for each research dollar spent as will others. If averagely-run companies are included, this variation between the best and the mediocre is still greater. This is largely because the big strides in the way of new products and processes are no longer the work of a single genius. They come from teams of highly trained men, each with a different specialty. One may be a chemist, another a solid state physicist, a third a metallurgist and a fourth a mathematician. The degree of skill of each of these experts is only part of what is needed to produce outstanding results. It is also necessary to have leaders who can coordinate the work of people of such diverse backgrounds and keep them driving toward a common goal. Consequently, the number or prestige of research workers in one company may be overshadowed by the effectiveness with which they are being helped to work as a team in another.

Nor is a management's ability to coordinate diverse technical skills into a closely-knit team and to stimulate each expert on that team to his greatest productivity the only kind of complex coordination upon which optimum research results depend. Close and detailed coordination between research workers on each developmental project and those thoroughly familiar with both production and sales problems is almost as important. It is no simple task for management to bring about this close relationship between research, production, and sales. Yet unless this is done, new products as finally conceived frequently are either not designed to be manufactured as cheaply as possible, or, when designed, fail to have maximum sales appeal. Such research usually results in products vulnerable to more efficient competition.

Finally there is one other type of coordination necessary if research expenditures are to attain maximum efficiency. This is coordination with top management. It might perhaps better be called top management's understanding of the fundamental nature of commercial research. Development projects cannot be expanded in good years and sharply curtailed in poor ones without tremendously increasing the total cost of reaching the desired objective. The "crash" programs so loved by a few top managements may occasionally be necessary but are often just expensive. A crash program is what occurs when important elements of the research personnel are suddenly pulled from the projects on which they have been working and concentrated on some new task which may have great importance at the moment but which, frequently, is not worth all the disruption it causes. The essence of successful commercial research is that only tasks be selected which promise to give dollar rewards of many times the cost of the research. However, once a project is started, to allow budget considerations and other extraneous factors outside the project itself to curtail or accelerate it invariably expands the total cost in relation to the benefits obtained.

Some top managements do not seem to understand this. I have heard executives of small but successful electronic companies express surprisingly little fear of the competition of one of the giants of the industry. This lack of worry concerning the ability of the much larger company to produce competitive products is not due to lack of respect for the capabilities of the larger company's individual researchers or unawareness of what might otherwise be accomplished with the large sums the big company regularly spends on research. Rather it is the historic tendency of this larger company to interrupt regular research projects with crash programs to attain the immediate goals of top management that has produced this feeling. Similarly, some years ago I heard that while they desired no publicity on the matter for obvious reasons, an outstanding technical college quietly advised its graduating class to avoid employment with a certain oil company. This was because top management of that company had a tendency to hire highly skilled people for what would normally be about five-year projects. Then in about three years the company would lose interest in the particular project and abandon it, thereby not only wasting their own money but preventing those employed from gaining the technical reputation for accomplishment that otherwise might have come to them.

Another factor making proper investment evaluation of research even more complex is how to evaluate the large amount of research related to defense contracts. A great deal of such research is frequently done not at the expense of the company doing it, but for the account of the federal government. Some of the subcontractors in the defense field also do significant research for the account of the contractors whom they are supplying. Should such totals be appraised by the investor as being as significant as research done at a company's own expense? If not, how should it be valued in relation to company-sponsored research? Like so many other phases in the investment field, these matters cannot be answered by mathematical formulae. Each case is different.

The profit margin on defense contracts is smaller than that of non-government business, and the nature of the work is often such that the contract for a new weapon is subject to competitive bidding from government blueprints. This means that it is sometimes impossible to build up steady repeat business for a product developed by government-sponsored research in a way that can be done with privately sponsored research, where both patents and customer goodwill can frequently be brought into play. For reasons like these, from the standpoint of the investor there are enormous variations in the economic worth of different government-sponsored research projects, even though such projects might be roughly equal in their importance so far as the benefits to the defense effort are concerned. The following theoretical example might serve to show how three such projects might have vastly different values to the investor:

One project might produce a magnificent new weapon having no non-military applications. The rights to this weapon would all be owned by the government and, once invented, it would be sufficiently simple to manufacture that the company which had done the research would have no advantage over others in bidding for a production contract. Such a research effort would have almost no value to the investor.

Another project might produce the same weapon, but the technique of manufacturing might be sufficiently complex that a company not participating in the original development work would have great difficulty trying to make it. Such a research project would have moderate value to the investor since it would tend to assure continuous, though probably not highly profitable, business from the government.

Still another company might engineer such a weapon and in so doing might learn principles and new techniques directly applicable to its regular commercial lines, which presumably show a higher profit margin. Such a research project might have great value to the investor. Some of the most spectacularly successful companies of the recent past have been those that show a high order of talent for finding complex and technical defense work, the doing of which provides them at government expense with know-how that can legitimately be transferred into profitable non-defense fields related to their existing commercial activities. Such companies are providing the government the research results the defense authorities vitally need. However, at the same time they are obtaining, at little or no cost, related non-defense research benefits which otherwise they would probably be paying for themselves. This factor may well have been one of the reasons for the spectacular investment success of Texas Instruments, Inc., which in four years rose nearly 500 per cent from the price of 5¼ at which it traded when first listed on the New York Stock Exchange in 1953; it may also have contributed, in the same period, to the even greater 700 per cent rise experienced by Ampex shareholders from the time this company's shares were first offered to the public in the same year.

Finally, in judging the relative investment value of company research organizations, another type of activity must be evaluated. This is something which ordinarily is not considered as developmental research at all—the seemingly unrelated field of market research. Market research may be regarded as the bridge between developmental research and sales. Top management must be alert against the temptation to spend significant sums on the research and development of a colorful product or process which, when perfected, has a genuine market but one too small to be profitable. By too small to be profitable I mean one that never will enjoy a large enough sales volume to get back the cost of the research, much less a worthwhile profit for the investor. A market research organization that can steer a major research effort of its company from one project which if technically successful would have barely paid for itself, to another which might cater to so much broader a market that it would pay out three times as well, would have vastly increased the value to its stockholders of that company's scientific manpower.

If quantitative measurements—such as the annual expenditures on research or the number of employees holding scientific degrees—are only a rough guide and not the final answer to whether a company has an outstanding research organization, how does the careful investor obtain this information? Once again it is surprising what the "scuttlebutt" method will produce. Until the average investor tries it, he probably will not believe how complete a picture will emerge if he asks intelligent questions about a company's research activities of a diversified group of research people, some from within the company and others engaged in related lines in competitive industries, in universities, and in government. A simpler and often worthwhile method is to make a close study of how much in dollar sales or net profits has been contributed to a company by the results of its research organization during a particular span, such as the prior ten years. An organization which in relation to the size of its activities has produced a good flow of profitable new products during such a period will probably be equally productive in the future as long as it continues to operate under the same general methods.

POINT 4. Does the company have an above-average sales organization?

In this competitive age, the products or services of few companies are so outstanding that they will sell to their maximum potentialities if they are not expertly merchandised. It is the making of a sale that is the most basic single activity of any business. Without sales, survival is impossible. It is the making of repeat sales to satisfied customers that is the first benchmark of success. Yet, strange as it seems, the relative efficiency of a company's sales, advertising, and distributive organizations receives far less attention from most investors, even the careful ones, than do production, research, finance, or other major subdivisions of corporate activity.

There is probably a reason for this. It is relatively easy to construct simple mathematical ratios that will provide some sort of guide to the attractiveness of a company's production costs, research activity, or financial structure in comparison with its competitors. It is a great deal harder to make ratios that have even a semblance of meaning in regard to sales and distribution efficiency. In regard to research we have already seen that such simple ratios are far too crude to provide anything but the first clues as to what to look for. Their value in relation to production and the financial structure will be discussed shortly. However, whether or not such ratios have anything like the value frequently placed upon them in financial circles, the fact remains that investors like to lean upon them. Because sales effort does not readily lend itself to this type of formulae, many investors fail to appraise it at all in spite of its basic importance in determining real investment worth.

Again, the way out of this dilemma lies in the use of the "scuttlebutt" technique. Of all the phases of a company's activity, none is easier to

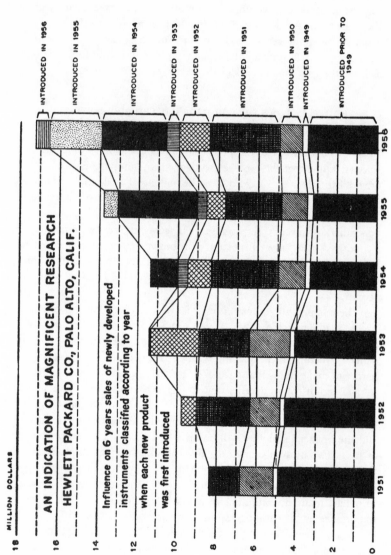

AN INDICATION OF MAGNIFICENT RESEARCH

HEWLETT PACKARD CO., PALO ALTO, CALIF.

Influence on 6 years sales of newly developed instruments classified according to year when each new product was first introduced

learn about from sources outside the company than the relative efficiency of a sales organization. Both competitors and customers know the answers. Equally important, they are seldom hesitant to express their views. The time spent by the careful investor in inquiring into this subject is usually richly rewarded.

I am devoting less space to this matter of relative sales ability than I did to the matter of relative research ability. This does not mean that I consider it less important. In today's competitive world, many things are important to corporate success. However, outstanding production, sales, and research may be considered the three main columns upon which such success is based. Saying that one is more important than another is like saying that the heart, the lungs, or the digestive tract is the most important single organ for the proper functioning of the body. All are needed for survival, and all must function well for vigorous health. Look around you at the companies that have proven outstanding investments. Try to find some that do not have both aggressive distribution and a constantly improving sales organization.

I have already referred to the Dow Chemical Company and may do so several times again, as I believe this company, which over the years has proven so rewarding to its stockholders, is an outstanding example of the ideal conservative long-range investment. Here is a company which in the public mind is almost synonymous with outstandingly successful research. However, what is not as well known is that this company selects and trains its sales personnel with the same care as it handles its research chemists. Before a young college graduate becomes a Dow salesman, he may be invited to make several trips to Midland so that both he and the company can become as sure as possible that he has the background and temperament that will fit him into their sales organization. Then, before he so much as sees his first potential customer, he must undergo specialized training that occasionally lasts only a few weeks but at times continues for well over a year to prepare him for the more complex selling jobs. This is but the beginning of the training he will receive; some of the company's greatest mental effort is devoted to seeking and frequently finding more efficient ways to solicit from, service, and deliver to the customer.

Are Dow and the other outstanding companies in the chemical industry unique in this great attention paid to sales and distribution? Definitely not. In another and quite different industry, International Business Machines is a company which has (speaking conservatively) handsomely rewarded its owners. An IBM executive recently told me that the average salesman spends a third of his entire time training in company sponsored schools! To a considerable degree this amazing ratio results from an attempt to keep the sales force abreast of a rapidly changing technology. Nevertheless I believe it one more indication of the weight that most successful companies give to steadily improving their sales arm. A one-time profit can be made in the company which because of manufacturing or research skill obtains some worthwhile business without a strong distribution organization. However, such companies can be quite vulnerable. For steady long-term growth a strong sales arm is vital.

POINT 5. Does the company have a worthwhile profit margin?

Here at last is a subject of importance which properly lends itself to the type of mathematical analysis which so many financial people feel is the backbone of sound investment decisions. From the standpoint of the investor, sales are only of value when and if they lead to increased profits. All the sales growth in the world won't produce the right type of investment vehicle if, over the years, profits do not grow correspondingly. The first step in examining profits is to study a company's profit margin, that is, to determine the number of cents of each dollar of sales that is brought down to operating profit. The wide variation between different companies, even those in the same industry, will immediately become apparent. Such a study should be made, not for a single year, but for a series of years. It then becomes evident that nearly all companies have broader profit margins—as well as greater total dollar profits—in years when an industry is unusually prosperous. However, it also becomes clear that the marginal companies—that is, those with the smaller profit margins—nearly always increase their profit margins by a considerably greater percentage in the good years than do the lower-cost companies, whose profit margins also get better but not to so great a degree. This usually causes the weaker companies to show a greater percentage increase in earnings in a year of abnormally good business than do the stronger companies in the same field. However, it should also be remembered that these earnings will decline correspondingly more rapidly when the business tide turns.

For this reason I believe that the greatest long-range investment profits are never obtained by investing in marginal companies. The only reason for considering a long-range investment in a company with an abnormally low profit margin is that there might be strong indications that a fundamental change is taking place within the company. This would be such that the improvement in profit margins would be occurring for reasons other than a temporarily expanded volume of business. In other words, the company would not be marginal in the true sense of the word, since the real reason for buying is that efficiency or new products developed within the company have taken it out of the marginal category. When such internal changes are taking place in a corporation which in other respects pretty well qualifies as the right type of long-range investment, it may be an unusually attractive purchase.

So far as older and larger companies are concerned, most of the really big investment gains have come from companies having relatively broad profit margins. Usually they have among the best such margins in their industry. In regard to young companies, and occasionally older ones, there is one important deviation from this rule—a deviation, however, that is generally more apparent than real. Such companies will at times deliberately elect to speed up growth by spending all or a very large part of the profits they would otherwise have earned on even more research or on even more sales promotion than they would otherwise be doing. What is important in such instances is to make absolutely certain that it is actually still further research, still further sales promotion, or still more of any other activity which is being financed today so as to build for the future, that is the real cause of the narrow or non-existent profit margin.

The greatest care should be used to be sure that the volume of the activities being credited with reducing the profit margin is not merely the volume of these activities needed for a good rate of growth, but actually represents even more research, sales promotion, etc., than this. When this happens, the research company with an apparently poor profit margin may be an unusually attractive investment. However, with the exception of companies of this type in which the low profit margin is being deliberately engineered in order to further accelerate the growth rate, investors desiring maximum gains over the years had best stay away from low profit-margin or marginal companies.

POINT 6. What is the company doing to maintain or improve profit margins?

The success of a stock purchase does not depend on what is generally known about a company at the time the purchase is made. Rather it depends upon what gets to be known about it after the stock has been bought. Therefore it is not the profit margins of the past but those of the future that are basically important to the investor.

In the age in which we live, there seems to be a constant threat to profit margins. Wages and salary costs go up year by year. Many companies now have long-range labor contracts calling for still further increases for several years ahead. Rising labor costs result in corresponding increases in raw materials and supplies. The trend of tax rates, particularly real estate and local tax rates, also seems to be steadily increasing.

Against this background, different companies are going to have different results in the trend of their profit margins. Some companies are in the seemingly fortunate position that they can maintain profit margins simply by raising prices. This is usually because they are in industries in which the demand for their products is abnormally strong or because the selling prices of competitive products have gone up even more than their own. In our economy, however, maintaining or improving profit margins in this way usually proves a relatively temporary matter. This is because additional competitive production capacity is created. This new capacity sufficiently outbalances the increased gain so that, in time, cost increases can no longer be passed on as price increases. Profit margins then start to shrink.

A striking example of this is the abrupt change that occurred in the fall of 1956, when the aluminum market went in a few weeks from a condition of short supply to one of aggressive competitive selling. Prior to that time aluminum prices rose about with costs. Unless demand for the product should grow even faster than production facilities, future price increases will occur less rapidly. Similarly the persistent disinclination of some of the largest steel producers to raise prices of certain classes of scarce steel products to "all the market would bear" may in part reflect long-range thinking about the temporary nature of broad profit margins that arise from no other cause than an ability to pass on increased costs by higher selling prices.

The long-range danger of this is perhaps best illustrated by what happened to the leading copper producers during this same second half of 1956. These companies used considerable self-restraint, even going so far as to sell under world prices in an attempt to keep prices from going too high. Nevertheless, copper rose sufficiently to curtail demand and attract new supply. Aggravated by curtailed Western European consumption resulting from the closing of the Suez Canal, the situation became quite unbalanced. It is probable that 1957 profit margins were noticeably poorer than would have been the case if those of 1956 had not been so good. When profit margins of a whole industry rise because of repeated price increases, the indication is not a good one for the long-range investor.

In contrast, certain other companies, including some within these same industries, manage to improve profit margins by far more ingenious means than just raising prices. Some companies achieve great success by maintaining capital-improvement or product-engineering departments. The sole function of such departments is to design new equipment that will reduce costs and thus offset or partially offset the rising trend of wages. Many companies are constantly reviewing procedures and methods to see where economies can be brought about. The accounting function and the handling of records has been a particularly fertile field for this sort of activity. So has the transportation field. Shipping costs have risen more than most expenses because of the larger percentage of labor costs in most forms of transportation as compared to most types of manufacturing. Using new types of containers, heretofore unused methods of transportation, or even putting in branch plants to avoid cross-hauling, have all cut costs for alert companies.

None of these things can be brought about in a day. They all require close study and considerable planning ahead. The prospective investor should give attention to the amount of ingenuity of the work being done on new ideas for cutting costs and improving profit margins. Here the "scuttlebutt" method may prove of some value, but much less so than direct inquiry from company personnel. Fortunately, this is a field about which most top executives will talk in some detail. The companies which are doing the most successful work along this line are very likely to be the ones which have built up the organization with the know-how to continue to do constructive things in the future. They are extremely likely to be in the group offering the greatest long-range rewards to their shareholders.

POINT 7. Does the company have outstanding labor
and personnel relations?

Most investors may not fully appreciate the profits from good labor relations. Few of them fail to recognize the impact of bad labor relations.
The effect on production of frequent and prolonged strikes is obvious to
anyone making even the most cursory review of corporate financial
statements.

However, the difference in the degree of profitability between a company with good personnel relations and one with mediocre personnel
relations is far greater than the direct cost of strikes. If workers feel that
they are fairly treated by their employer, a background has been laid
wherein efficient leadership can accomplish much in increasing productivity per worker. Furthermore, there is always considerable cost in training each new worker. Those companies with an abnormal labor turnover
have therefore an element of unnecessary expense avoided by better-
managed enterprises.

But how does the investor properly judge the quality of a company's
labor and personnel relations? There is no simple answer. There is no
set yardstick that will apply in all cases. About the best that can be done
is to look at a number of factors and then judge from the composite
picture.

In this day of widespread unionization, those companies that still
have no union or a company union probably also have well above average
labor and personnel relations. If they did not, the unions would have
organized them long ago. The investor can feel rather sure, for example,
that Motorola, located in highly unionized Chicago, and Texas Instruments, Inc., in increasingly unionized Dallas, have convinced at least an
important part of their work force of the company's genuine desire and
ability to treat its employees well. Lack of affiliation with an international
union can only be explained by successful personnel policies in instances
of this sort.

On the other hand, unionization is by no means a sign of poor labor
relations. Some of the companies with the very best labor relations are
completely unionized, but have learned to get along with their unions
with a reasonable degree of mutual respect and trust. Similarly, while a
record of constant and prolonged strikes is a good indication of bad labor
relations, the complete absence of strikes is not necessarily a sign of

fundamentally good relations. Sometimes the company with no strikes is too much like the henpecked husband. Absence of conflict may not mean a basically happy relationship so much as fear of the consequences of conflict.

Why do workers feel unusually loyal to one employer and resentful of another? The reasons are often so complex and difficult to trace that for the most part the investor may do better to concern himself with comparative data showing how workers feel, rather than with an attempt to appraise each part of the background causing them to feel that way. One series of figures that indicates the underlying quality of labor and personnel policies is the relative labor turnover in one company as against another in the same area. Equally significant is the relative size of the waiting list of job applicants wanting to work for one company as against others in the same locality. In an area where there is no labor surplus, companies having an abnormally long list of personnel seeking to enter their employ are usually companies that are desirable for investment from the standpoint of good labor and personnel relations.

Nevertheless, beyond these general figures there are a few specific details the investor might notice. Companies with good labor relations usually are ones making every effort to settle grievances quickly. The small individual grievances that take long to settle and are not considered important by management are ones that smoulder and finally flare up seriously. In addition to appraising the methods set up for settling grievances, the investor might also pay close attention to wage scales. The company that makes above-average profits while paying above-average wages for the area in which it is located is likely to have good labor relations. The investor who buys into a situation in which a significant part of earnings comes from paying below-standard wages for the area involved may in time have serious trouble on his hands.

Finally the investor should be sensitive to the attitude of top management toward the rank and file employees. Underneath all the fine-sounding generalities, some managements have little feeling of responsibility for, or interest in, their ordinary workers. Their chief concern is that no greater share of their sales dollar go to lower echelon personnel than the pressure of militant unionism makes mandatory. Workers are readily hired or dismissed in large masses, dependent on slight changes in the company's sales outlook or profit picture. No feeling of responsibility exists for the hardships this can cause to the families affected.

Nothing is done to make ordinary employees feel they are wanted, needed, and part of the business picture. Nothing is done to build up the dignity of the individual worker. Managements with this attitude do not usually provide the background for the most desirable type of investment.

POINT 8. Does the company have outstanding executive relations?

If having good relations with lower echelon personnel is important, creating the right atmosphere among executive personnel is vital. These are the men whose judgment, ingenuity, and teamwork will in time make or break any venture. Because the stakes for which they play are high, the tension on the job is frequently great. So is the chance that friction or resentment might create conditions whereby top executive talent either does not stay with a company or does not produce to its maximum ability if it does stay.

The company offering greatest investment opportunities will be one in which there is a good executive climate. Executives will have confidence in their president and/or board chairman. This means, among other things, that from the lowest levels on up there is a feeling that promotions are based on ability, not factionalism. A ruling family is not promoted over the heads of more able men. Salary adjustments are reviewed regularly so that executives feel that merited increases will come without having to be demanded. Salaries are at least in line with the standard of the industry and the locality. Management will bring outsiders into anything other than starting jobs only if there is no possibility of finding anyone within the organization who can be promoted to fill the position. Top management will recognize that wherever human beings work together, some degree of factionalism and human friction will occur, but will not tolerate those who do not cooperate in team play so that such friction and factionalism is kept to an irreducible minimum. Much of this the investor can usually learn without too much direct questioning by chatting about the company with a few executives scattered at different levels of responsibility. The further a corporation departs from these standards, the less likely it is to be a really outstanding investment.

POINT 9. **Does the company have depth to its management?**

A small corporation can do extremely well and, if other factors are right, provide a magnificent investment for a number of years under really able one-man management. However, all humans are finite, so even for smaller companies the investor should have some idea of what can be done to prevent corporate disaster if the key man should no longer be available. Nowadays this investment risk with an otherwise outstanding small company is not as great as it seems, in view of the recent tendency of big companies with plenty of management talent to buy up outstanding smaller units.

However, companies worthy of investment interest are those that will continue to grow. Sooner or later a company will reach a size where it just will not be able to take advantage of further opportunities unless it starts developing executive talent in some depth. This point will vary between companies, depending on the industry in which they are engaged and the skill of the one-man management. It usually occurs when annual sales totals reach a point somewhere between fifteen and forty million dollars. Having the right executive climate, as discussed in Point 8, becomes of major investment significance at this time.

Those matters discussed in Point 8 are, of course, needed for development of proper management in depth. But such management will not develop unless certain additional policies are in effect as well. Most important of these is the delegation of authority. If from the very top on down, each level of executives is not given real authority to carry out assigned duties in as ingenious and efficient a manner as each individual's ability will permit, good executive material becomes much like healthy young animals so caged in that they cannot exercise. They do not develop their faculties because they just do not have enough opportunity to use them.

Those organizations where the top brass personally interfere with and try to handle routine day-to-day operating matters seldom turn out to be the most attractive type of investments. Cutting across the lines of authority which they themselves have set up frequently results in well-meaning executives significantly detracting from the investment caliber of the companies they run. No matter how able one or two bosses may be in handling all this detail, once a corporation reaches a certain size executives of this type will get in trouble on two fronts. Too much detail will have arisen for them to handle. Capable people just are not being developed to handle the still further growth that should lie ahead.

Another matter is worthy of the investor's attention in judging whether a company has suitable depth in management. Does top management welcome and evaluate suggestions from personnel even if, at times, those suggestions carry with them adverse criticism of current management practices? So competitive is today's business world and so great the need for improvement and change that if pride or indifference prevent top management from exploring what has frequently been found to be a veritable gold mine of worthwhile ideas, the investment climate that results probably will not be the most suitable one for the investor. Neither is it likely to be one in which increasing numbers of vitally needed younger executives are going to develop.

POINT 10. How good are the company's cost analysis and accounting controls?

No company is going to continue to have outstanding success for a long period of time if it cannot break down its over-all costs with sufficient accuracy and detail to show the cost of each small step in its operation. Only in this way will a management know what most needs its attention. Only in this way can management judge whether it is properly solving each problem that does need its attention. Furthermore, most successful companies make not one but a vast series of products. If the management does not have a precise knowledge of the true cost of each product in relation to the others, it is under an extreme handicap. It becomes almost impossible to establish pricing policies that will insure the maximum obtainable over-all profit consistent with discouraging undue competition. There is no way of knowing which products are worthy of special sales effort and promotion. Worst of all, some apparently successful activities may actually be operating at a loss and, unknown to management, may be decreasing rather than swelling the total of over-all profits. Intelligent planning becomes almost impossible.

In spite of the investment importance of accounting controls, it is usually only in instances of extreme inefficiency that the careful investor will get a clear picture of the status of cost accounting and related activities in a company in which he is contemplating investment. In this sphere, the "scuttlebutt" method will sometimes reveal companies that are really deficient. It will seldom tell much more than this. Direct inquiry of company personnel will usually elicit a completely sincere reply that the cost data are entirely adequate. Detailed cost sheets will often be shown in support of the statement. However, it is not so much the existence of detailed figures as their relative accuracy which is important. The best that the careful investor usually can do in this field is to recognize both the importance of the subject and his own limitations in making a worthwhile appraisal of it. Within these limits he usually can only fall back on the general conclusion that a company well above average in most other aspects of business skill will probably be above average in this field, too, as long as top management understands the basic importance of expert accounting controls and cost analysis.

POINT 11. **Are there other aspects of the business, somewhat peculiar to the industry involved, which will give the investor important clues as to how outstanding the company may be in relation to its competition?**

By definition, this is somewhat of a catch-all point of inquiry. This is because matters of this sort are bound to differ considerably from each other—those which are of great importance in some lines of business can, at times, be of little or no importance in others. For example, in most important operations involving retailing, the degree of skill a company has in handling real estate matters—the quality of its leases, for instance—is of great significance. In many other lines of business, a high degree of skill in this field is less important. Similarly, the relative skill with which a company handles its credits is of great significance to some companies of minor or no importance to others. For both these matters, our old friend the "scuttlebutt" method will usually furnish the investor with a pretty clear picture. Frequently his conclusions can be checked against mathematical ratios such as comparative leasing costs per dollar of sales, or ratio of credit loss, if the point is of sufficient importance to warrant careful study.

In a number of lines of business, total insurance costs mount to an important per cent of the sales dollar. At times this can matter enough so that a company with, say, a 35 per cent lower overall insurance cost than a competitor of the same size will have a broader margin of profit.

In those industries where insurance is a big enough factor to affect earnings, a study of these ratios and a discussion of them with informed insurance people can be unusually rewarding to the investor. It gives a supplemental but indicative check as to how outstanding a particular management may be. This is because these lower insurance costs do not come solely from a greater skill in handling insurance in the same way, for example, as skill in handling real estate results in lower than average leasing costs. Rather they are largely the reflection of over-all skill in handling people, inventory, and fixed property so as to reduce the over-all amount of accident, damage, and waste and thereby make these lower costs possible. An index of insurance costs in relation to the coverage obtained points out clearly which companies in a given field are well run.

Patents are another matter having varying significance from company to company. For large companies, a strong patent position is usually a point of additional rather than basic strength. It usually blocks off certain subdivisions of the company's activities from the intense competition that might otherwise prevail. This normally enables these segments of the company's product lines to enjoy wider profit margins than would otherwise occur. This in turn tends to broaden the average of the entire line. Similarly, strong patent positions may at times give a company exclusive rights to the easiest or cheapest way of making a particular product. Competitors must go a longer way round to get to the same place, thereby giving the patent owner a tangible competitive advantage although frequently a small one.

In our era of widespread technical know-how it is seldom that large companies can enjoy more than a small part of their activities in areas sheltered by patent protection. Patents are usually able to block off only a few rather than all the ways of accomplishing the same result. For this reason many large companies make no attempt to shut out competition through patent structure, but for relatively modest fees license competition to use their patents and in return expect the same treatment from these licensees. Influences such as manufacturing know-how, sales and service organization, customer good will, and knowledge of customer problems are depended on far more than patents to maintain a competitive position. In fact, when large companies depend chiefly on patent protection for the maintenance of their profit margin, it is usually more a sign of investment weakness than strength. Patents do not run on indefinitely. When the patent protection is no longer there, the company's profit may suffer badly.

The young company just starting to develop its production, sales, and service organization, and in the early stages of establishing customer good will is in a very different position. Without patents its products might be copied by large entrenched enterprises which could use their established channels of customer relationship to put the small young competitor out of business. For small companies in the early years of marketing unique products or services, the investor should therefore closely scrutinize the patent position. He should get information from qualified sources as to how broad the protection actually may be. It is one thing to get a patent on a device. It may be quite another to get protection that will prevent others from making it in a slightly different way. Even here, however, engineering that is constantly improving the product can prove considerably more advantageous than mere static patent protection.

For example, a few years ago when it was a much smaller organization than as of today, a young West Coast electronic manufacturer had great success with a new product. One of the giants of the industry made what was described to me as a "Chinese copy" and marketed it under its well-known trade name. In the opinion of the young company's designer, this large competitor managed to engineer all the small company's engineering mistakes into the model along with the good points. The large company's model came out at just the time the small manufacturer introduced its own improved model with the weak points eliminated. With a product that was not selling, the large company withdrew from the field. As has been true many times before and since, it is the constant leadership in engineering, not patents, that is the fundamental source of protection. The investor must be at least as careful not to place too much importance on patent protection as to recognize its significance in those occasional places where it is a major factor in appraising the attractiveness of a desirable investment.

POINT 12. Does the company have a short-range or long-range outlook in regard to profits?

Some companies will conduct their affairs so as to gain the greatest possible profit right now. Others will deliberately curtail maximum immediate profits to build up good will and thereby gain greater over-all profits over a period of years. Treatment of customers and vendors gives frequent examples of this. One company will constantly make the sharpest possible deals with suppliers. Another will at times pay above contract price to a vendor who has had unexpected expense in making delivery, because it wants to be sure of having a dependable source of needed raw materials or high quality components available when the market has turned and supplies may be desperately needed. The difference in treatment of customers is equally noticeable. The company that will go to special trouble and expense to take care of the needs of a regular customer caught in an unexpected jam may show lower profits on the particular transaction, but far greater profits over the years.

The "scuttlebutt" method usually reflects these differences in policies quite clearly. The investor wanting maximum results should favor companies with a truly long-range outlook concerning profits.

POINT 13. In the foreseeable future will the growth of the company require sufficient equity financing so that the larger number of shares then outstanding will largely cancel the existing stockholders' benefit from this anticipated growth?

The typical book on investment devotes so much space to a discussion on the corporation's cash position, corporate structure, percentage of capitalization in various classes of securities, etc. that it may well be asked why these purely financial aspects should not be given more than the amount of space devoted to this one point out of a total of fifteen. The reason is that it is the basic contention of this book that the intelligent investor should not buy common stocks simply because they are cheap but only if they give promise of major gain to him.

Only a small percentage of all companies can qualify with a high rating for all or nearly all of the other fourteen points listed in this discussion. Any company which can so qualify could easily borrow money, at prevailing rates for its size company, up to the accepted top percentage of debt for that kind of business. If such a company needed more cash once this top debt limit has been reached—always assuming of course that it qualifies at or near the top in regard to further sales growth, profit margins, management, research, and the various other points we are now considering—it could still raise equity money at some price, since investors are always eager to participate in ventures of this sort.

Therefore, if investment is limited to outstanding situations, what really matters is whether the company's cash plus further borrowing ability is sufficient to take care of the capital needed to exploit the prospects of the next several years. If it is, and if the company is willing to borrow to the limit of prudence, the common stock investor need have no concern as to the more distant future. If the investor has properly appraised the situation, any equity financing that might be done some years ahead will be at prices so much higher than present levels that he need not be concerned. This is because the near-term financing will have produced enough increase in earnings, by the time still further financing is needed some years hence, to have brought the stock to a substantially higher price level.

If this borrowing power is not now sufficient, however, equity financing becomes necessary. In this case, the attractiveness of the investment depends on careful calculations as to how much the dilution resulting from the greater number of shares to be outstanding will cut into the benefits to the present common stockholder that will result from the increased earnings this financing makes possible. This equity dilution is just as mathematically calculable when the dilution occurs through the issuance of senior securities with conversion features as when it occurs through the issuance of straight common stock. This is because such conversion features are usually exercisable at some moderate level above the market price at the time of issuance—usually from 10 to 20 per cent. Since the investor should never be interested in small gains of 10 to 20 per cent, but rather in gains which over a period of years will be closer to ten or a hundred times this amount, the conversion price can usually be ignored and the dilution calculated upon the basis of complete conversion of the new senior issue. In other words, it is well to consider that all senior convertible issues have been converted and that all warrants, options, etc. have been exercised when calculating the real number of common shares outstanding.

If equity financing will be occurring within several years of the time of common stock purchase, and if this equity financing will leave common stockholders with only a small increase in subsequent per-share earnings, only one conclusion is justifiable. This is that the company has a management with sufficiently poor financial judgment to make the common stock undesirable for worthwhile investment. Unless this situation prevails, the investor need not be deterred by purely financial considerations from going into any situation which, because of its high rating on the remaining fourteen points covered, gives promise of being outstanding. Conversely, from the standpoint of making maximum profits over the years, the investor should never go into a situation with a poor score on any of the other fourteen points, merely because of great financial strength or cash position.

POINT 14. Does the management talk freely to investors about its affairs when things are going well but "clam up" when troubles and disappointments occur?

It is the nature of business that in even the best-run companies unexpected difficulties, profit squeezes, and unfavorable shifts in demand for their products will at times occur. Furthermore, the companies into which the investor should be buying if greatest gains are to occur are companies which over the years will constantly, through the efforts of technical research, be trying to produce and sell new products and new processes. By the law of averages, some of these are bound to be costly failures. Others will have unexpected delays and heartbreaking expenses during the early period of plant shake-down. For months on end, such extra and unbudgeted costs will spoil the most carefully laid profit forecasts for the business as a whole. Such disappointments are an inevitable part of even the most successful business. If met forthrightly and with good judgment, they are merely one of the costs of eventual success. They are frequently a sign of strength rather than weakness in a company.

How a management reacts to such matters can be a valuable clue to the investor. The management that does not report as freely when things are going badly as when they are going well usually "clams up" in this way for one of several rather significant reasons. It may not have a program worked out to solve the unanticipated difficulty. It may have become panicky. It may not have an adequate sense of responsibility to its stockholders, seeing no reason why it should report more than what may seem expedient at the moment. In any event, the investor will do well to exclude from investment any company that withholds or tries to hide bad news.

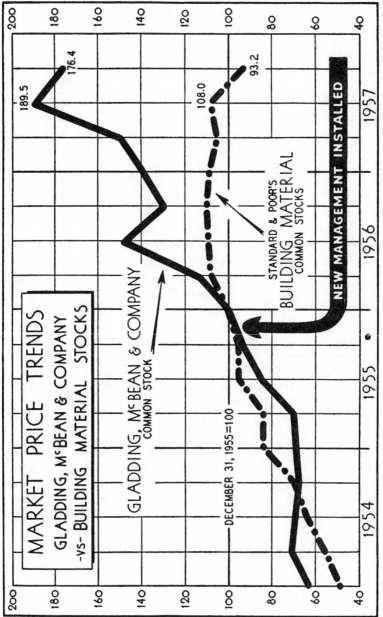

MARKET PRICE TRENDS
GLADDING, McBEAN & COMPANY
-vs- BUILDING MATERIAL STOCKS

GLADDING, McBEAN & COMPANY
COMMON STOCK

DECEMBER 31, 1955=100

STANDARD & POOR'S
BUILDING MATERIAL
COMMON STOCKS

NEW MANAGEMENT INSTALLED

189.5   176.4

108.0   93.2

1954   1955   1956   1957

Chart work courtesy Standard & Poor's Corporation

POINT 15. Does the company have a management of
unquestionable integrity?

The management of a company is always far closer to its assets than is
the stockholder. Without breaking any laws, the number of ways in
which those in control can benefit themselves and their families at the
expense of the ordinary stockholder is almost infinite. One way is to put
themselves—to say nothing of their relatives or in-laws—on the payroll
at salaries far above the normal worth of the work performed. Another
is to own properties they sell or rent to the corporation at above market
rates. Among smaller corporations this is sometimes hard to detect, since
controlling families or key officers at times buy and lease real estate to
such companies, not for purposes of unfair gain but in a sincere desire
to free limited working capital for other corporate purposes.

Another method for insiders to enrich themselves is to get the corporation's vendors to sell through certain brokerage firms which perform
little if any service for the brokerage commissions involved but which
are owned by these same insiders and relatives or friends. Probably most
costly of all to the investor is the abuse by insiders of their power of
issuing common stock options. They can pervert this legitimate method
of compensating able management by issuing to themselves amounts of
stock far beyond what an unbiased outsider might judge to represent a
fair reward for services performed.

There is only one real protection against abuses like these. This is to
confine investments to companies the managements of which have a
highly developed sense of trusteeship and moral responsibility to their
stockholders. This is a point concerning which the "scuttlebutt" method
can be very helpful. Any investment may still be considered interesting
if it falls down in regard to almost any other one of the fifteen points
which have now been covered, but rates an unusually high score in regard
to all the rest. Regardless of how high the rating may be in all other
matters, however, if there is a serious question of the lack of a strong
management sense of trusteeship for stockholders, the investor should
never seriously consider participating in such an enterprise.

4

WHAT TO BUY

APPLYING THIS TO YOUR OWN NEEDS

T he average investor is not a specialist in the field of investment. If a man, he usually gives but a tiny fraction of the time or mental effort to handling his investments that he devotes to his own work. If a woman, the time and effort given to investments is equally small compared to that devoted to her normal duties. The result is that the typical investor has usually gathered a good deal of the half-truths, misconceptions, and just plain bunk that the general public has gradually accumulated about successful investing.

One of the most widespread and least accurate of such ideas is the popular conception of what traits are needed to be an investment wizard. If a public opinion poll were taken on this subject, I suspect John Q. Public's composite picture of such an expert would be an introverted, bookish individual with an accounting-type mind. This scholastic-like investment expert would sit all day in undisturbed isolation poring over vast quantities of balance sheets, corporate earning statements, and trade statistics. From these, his superior intellect and deep understanding of figures would glean information not available to the ordinary mortal. This type of cloistered study would yield invaluable knowledge about the location of magnificent investments.

Like so many other widespread misconceptions, this mental picture has just enough accuracy to make it highly dangerous for anyone wanting to get the greatest long-range benefit from common stocks.

As already pointed out in the discussion of the fifteen points to be considered if a major investment winner is to be selected by any means other than pure luck, a few of these matters are largely determined by cloistered mathematical calculation. Furthermore, as mentioned near the beginning of this book, there is more than one method by which an investor, if sufficiently skilled, can over the years make some money—occasionally even really worthwhile money—through investment. The purpose of this book is not to point out every way such money can be made. Rather it is to point out the best way. By the best way is meant the greatest total profit for the least risk. The type of accounting-statistical activity which the general public seems to visualize as the heart of successful investing will, if enough effort be given it, turn up some apparent bargains. Some of these may be real bargains. In the case of others there may be such acute business troubles lying ahead, yet not discernible from a purely statistical study, that instead of being bargains they are actually selling at prices which in a few years will have proven to be very high.

Meanwhile, in the case of even the genuine bargain, the degree by which it is undervalued is usually somewhat limited. The time it takes to get adjusted to its true value is frequently considerable. So far as I have been able to observe, this means that over a time sufficient to give a fair comparison—say five years—the most skilled statistical bargain hunter ends up with a profit which is but a small part of the profit attained by those using reasonable intelligence in appraising the business characteristics of superbly managed growth companies. This, of course, is after charging the growth stock investor with losses on ventures which did not turn out as expected, and charging the bargain hunter for a proportionate amount of bargains that just didn't turn out.

The reason why the growth stocks do so much better is that they seem to show gains in value in the hundreds of per cent each decade. In contrast, it is an unusual bargain that is as much as 50 per cent undervalued. The cumulative effect of this simple arithmetic should be obvious.

At this point, the potential investor may have to start revising his ideas about the amount of time needed to locate the right investments for his purpose, to say nothing of the characteristics he must have if he is to find them. Perhaps he looked forward to spending a few hours each week in the comfort of his home, studying scads of written material which he felt would unlock the door to worthwhile profits. He just does not have the time to seek out, cultivate, and talk with all the various people it might be wise to contact if he wants to handle his common stock investments to his optimum benefit. Perhaps he does have the time. He still may not have the inclination and personality to seek out and chat with a group of people, most of whom he previously had not known very well if at all. Furthermore, it is not enough just to chat with them; it is necessary to arouse their interest and their confidence to a point where they will tell what they know. The successful investor is usually an individual who is inherently interested in business problems. This results in his discussing such matters in a way that will arouse the interest of those from whom he is seeking data. Naturally he must have reasonably good judgment or all the data he gets will avail him nothing.

An investor may have the time, inclination, and judgment but still be blocked from getting maximum results in the handling of his common stocks. The matter of geography is also a factor. An investor, for example, living in or near Detroit would have opportunities for learning about automotive accessory and parts companies that would not be available to one equally diligent or able in Oregon. But so many major companies and industries are today organized on a nation-wide basis with distribution, if not manufacturing, centers in most key cities, that investors living in larger industrial centers or their suburbs usually have ample opportunities to practice the art of finding at least a few outstanding long-range investments. This unfortunately is not equally true for those living in rural areas remote from such centers.

However, the rural investor or the overwhelming majority of other investors who may not have the time, inclination, or ability to uncover outstanding investments for themselves are by no means barred from making such investments because of this. Actually, the investor's work is so specialized and so intricate that there is no more reason why an individual should handle his own investments than that he should be his own lawyer, doctor, architect, or automobile mechanic. He should perform these functions if he has special interest in and skill at the particular field. Otherwise, he definitely should go to an expert.

What is important is that he know enough of the principles involved so that he can pick a real expert rather than a hack or a charlatan. In some ways it is easier for a careful layman to pick an outstanding investment advisor than, say, a comparably superior doctor or lawyer. In other ways it is much harder. It is harder because the investment field has developed much more recently than most comparable specialties. As a result mass ideas have not yet crystallized to the point where there is an accepted line of demarcation between true knowledge and mumbo-jumbo. There are not as yet the barriers to weed out the ignorant and the incompetent in the financial field that exist, for example, in the fields of law or medicine. Even among some of the so-called authorities on investment, there is still enough lack of agreement on the basic principles involved that it is as yet impossible to have schools for training investment experts comparable to the recognized schools for teaching law or medicine. This makes even more remote the practicability of government authorities licensing those having the necessary background of knowledge to guide others in investments in a manner comparable to the way our states license the practicing of law or medicine. It is true that many of our states do go through the form of licensing investment advisors. However in such instances only known dishonesty or financial insolvency, rather than a lack of training or skill, provides the basis for denying a license.

All this probably results in a higher percentage of incompetence among financial advisors than may exist in fields such as law and medicine. However, there are compensating factors that can enable an individual with no personal expertness in investments to pick a capable financial advisor more easily than a comparably outstanding doctor or lawyer. Finding out which physician had lost the smallest percentage of his practice through deaths would not be a good way to pick a superb doctor. Neither would a corresponding box score of cases won and lost show the relative skill of attorneys. Fortunately, most medical treatments are not matters of immediate life or death, and a good lawyer will frequently avoid going into litigation at all.

In the investment advisor's case it is quite different, however. There is a score board that, after enough time has elapsed, should pretty much reflect that advisor's investment skill. In occasional cases it may take as much as five years for investments to demonstrate their real merit. Usually it does not take that long. It would normally be foolhardy for anyone to entrust his savings to the skill of a so-called advisor who, working either for himself or others, had less than five years experience. Therefore, in the case of investments, there is no reason why those trying to pick a professional advisor should not demand to see a fair cross-section of results obtained for others. Those results, compared to a record of security prices for the same period of time, give a real clue to the advisor's ability.

Two more steps are then necessary before an investor should make final determination of the individual or organization to which he will delegate the important responsibility for his funds. One is the obvious step of being certain of that advisor's complete and unquestioned honesty. The other step is more complex. A financial advisor may have obtained far above average results during a period of falling prices not because of skill but because he always keeps a large part of the funds he manages in, let us say, high-grade bonds. At another time, after a long period of rising prices, another advisor may have obtained above-average results because of a tendency to go into risky, marginal companies. As explained in the discussion of profit margins, such companies usually do well only in such a period and subsequently do rather poorly. Still a third advisor might do well in both such periods because of a tendency to try to guess what the security markets are going to do. This can produce magnificent results for a while, but is almost impossible to continue indefinitely.

Before selecting an advisor, an investor should learn from that advisor the nature of his basic concept of financial management. He should then only accept an advisor with concepts fundamentally the same as the investor's own. Naturally, I believe that the concepts expressed in this book are those which fundamentally should govern. Many, reared in the old-time financial atmosphere of "buy them when they are cheap and sell them when they are high," would strongly disagree with this conclusion.

Assuming an investor desires the type of huge, long-range gain which I believe should be the objective of nearly all common stock purchases, there is one matter which he must decide for himself whether he uses an investment advisor or handles his own affairs. It is a decision which must be made because the type of stocks which qualify most satisfactorily under the previously discussed fifteen points can vary considerably among themselves in their investment characteristics.

At one end of the scale are large companies which in spite of outstanding prospects of major further growth are so financially strong, with roots going so deep into the economic soil, that they qualify under the general classification of "institutional stocks." This means that insurance companies, professional trustees, and similar institutional buyers will buy them. They will do so because they feel that, while they may misjudge market prices and could lose a part of their original investment should they be forced to sell such stocks at a time of lower quotations, they are avoiding the greater danger of loss they could suffer if they bought into a company that subsequently fell from its present competitive position.

The Dow Chemical Company, Du Pont, and International Business Machines are good examples of this type of growth stock. In Chapter One I mentioned the totally insignificant return available from high-grade bonds during the ten-year period 1946 to 1956. At the close of this period, each of these three stocks—Dow, Du Pont, and IBM—had a value approximately five times what it sold for at the beginning of the period. Nor during these ten years did their holders suffer from the standpoint of current income. Dow, for example, is almost notorious for the low rate of return it customarily pays on current market price. Yet the investor who bought Dow at the start of this period would at the end of it be doing well from the standpoint of current income. Although Dow at the time of purchase would only have provided a return of about 2½ per cent (this was a period when yields on all stocks were high), just ten years later it had increased dividends or split stock so many times that the investor would have been enjoying a dividend return of between 8 and 9 per cent on the price of his investment ten years earlier. More significantly, the ten-year period covered is not an unusual one for companies of the caliber of these three. Decade after decade, with only occasional interruptions from such one-time influences as the great 1929–1932 bear market or World War II, these stocks have given almost fabulous performance.

At the other end of the scale, also of extreme interest for the right sort of long-range investment, are small and frequently young companies which may only have total sales of from one to six or seven million dollars per annum, but which also have products that might bring a sensational future. To qualify under the fifteen points already described, such companies will usually have a combination of outstanding business management and equally capable scientific personnel who are pioneering in a new or economically promising field. The Ampex Corporation at the time the stock was first offered to the public in 1953 might serve as a good example of this type of company. Within four years the value of this stock had increased over seven-fold.

Between these two extremes lie a host of other promising growth companies varying all the way from those as young and risky as was Ampex in 1953 to those as strong and well entrenched as are Dow, Du Pont and IBM today. Assuming it is time to buy at all (see the next chapter), which type should the investor buy?

The young growth stock offers by far the greatest possibility of gain. Sometimes this can mount up to several thousand per cent in a decade. But making at least an occasional investment mistake is inevitable even for the most skilled investor. It should never be forgotten that if such a mistake is made in this type of common stock, every dollar put into the investment can be lost. In contrast, if the stock is bought according to the rules described in the next chapter, any losses that might occur in the older and more established growth stocks should be temporary, resulting from a period of unanticipated decline in the stock market as a whole. The long-range gain in value of this class of big company growth stock will, over the years, be considerably less than that of the small and usually younger enterprise. Nevertheless it will mount to thoroughly worthwhile totals. Even in the most conservative of the growth stocks it should run to at least several times the original investment.

Therefore, for anyone risking a stake big enough to be of real significance to himself or his family, the rule to follow should be rather obvious. It is to put "most" of his funds into the type of company which, while perhaps not as large as a Dow, Du Pont or an International Business Machines, at least comes closer to that type of stock than to the small young company. Whether this "most" be 60 per cent or 100 per cent of total investments varies with the needs or requirements of each individual. A widow with a half million dollars of total assets and no children might put all her funds in the more conservative class of growth stocks. Another widow with a million dollars to invest and three children for whom she would like to increase her assets—to a degree that would not, however, jeopardize her scale of living—might well put up to 15 per cent of her assets in carefully selected small young companies. A businessman with a wife, two children, a present investment worth $400,000, and an income big enough to save $10,000 per annum after taxes might put all his present $400,000 into the more conservative type growth companies but venture the $10,000 of new savings each year on the more risky half of the investment scale.

In all these cases, however, the gain in value over the years of the more conservative group of stocks should be enough to outweigh even complete loss of all funds put into the more risky type. Meanwhile, if properly selected, the more risky type could significantly increase the total capital gain. Equally important if this happens, these young risky companies will by that time have reached a point in their own development where their stocks will no longer be carrying anything like the former degree of risk but may even have progressed to a status where institutions have begun buying them.

The problems of the small investor are somewhat more difficult. The large investor can often completely ignore the matter of dividend returns in his endeavor to employ all his funds in situations affording maximum growth potential. After his funds are so invested he may still obtain from them sufficient dividends either to take care of his desired standard of living or to enable him to attain this standard if the dividend income is added to his other regular earning power. Most small investors cannot live on the return on their investment no matter how high a yield is obtained, since the total value of their holdings is not great enough. Therefore for the small investor the matter of current dividend return usually comes down to a choice between a few hundred dollars a year starting right now, or the chance of obtaining an income many times this few hundred dollars a year at a later date.

Before reaching a decision on this crucial point, there is one matter which the small investor should face squarely. This is that the only funds he should consider using for common stock investment are funds that are truly surplus. This does not mean using all funds that remain over and above what he needs for everyday living expense. Except in the most unusual circumstances, he should have a backlog of several thousand dollars, sufficient to take care of illnesses or other unexpected contingencies, before attempting to buy anything with as much intrinsic risk as a common stock. Similarly, funds already set aside for some specific future purpose, such as sending a child through college, should never be risked in the stock market. It is only after taking care of matters of this sort that he should consider common stock investment.

The objective which the small investor then has for this surplus becomes somewhat a matter of personal choice and of his particular circumstances, including the size and nature of his other income. A young man or woman, or an older investor with children or other heirs of whom he or she is particularly fond, may be willing to sacrifice a dividend income of, say, $30 or $40 a month in order to obtain an income ten times that size in fifteen years. In contrast, an elderly person with no close heirs would naturally prefer a larger immediate income. Similarly, a person earning a relatively small income and with heavy financial obligations might have no choice but to provide for immediate needs.

However, for the great majority of small investors, the decision on the importance of immediate income is one of personal choice. It probably is largely dependent on the psychology of each individual investor. My own purely personal view is that a small amount of additional income (after taxes) palls in comparison to an investment that in the years ahead could bring me a sizable income and, in time, might make my children really wealthy. Others may feel quite differently about this. It is to the large investor, and to the small investor who feels as I do on this subject and desires an intelligent approach to the principles that have made this kind of results possible, that the procedures set forth in this book are presented.

The success which any particular individual will have in applying these principles to his own investments will depend on two things. One is the degree of skill with which he applies them. The other is, of course, the matter of good fortune. In an age when an unforeseeable discovery might happen tomorrow in a research laboratory in no way connected with the company in which the investment has been made, and in an age when five years from now that unrelated research development could result in either tripling or cutting in half the profits of this investment, good fortune obviously can play a tremendous part so far as any one investment is concerned. This is why even the medium-sized investor has an advantage over those of very small means. This element of good or bad fortune will largely average out if several well-selected investments are chosen.

However, for both large and small investors who prefer far greater income some years from now to maximum possible return today, it is well to remember that during the past thirty-five years numerous studies have been made by various financial authorities. These have compared the results obtained from the purchase of common stocks which afford a high dividend yield with those obtained from the purchase of low-yield stocks of companies that have concentrated on growth and the reinvestment of assets. As far as I know, every one of these studies has shown the same trend. The growth stocks, over a five- or ten-year span, have proven spectacularly better so far as their increase in capital value is concerned.

More surprising, in the same time span such stocks have usually so increased their dividends that, while still paying a low return in relation to the enhanced value at which they were by then selling, they were by this time paying a greater dividend return on the original investment than were the stocks selected for yield alone. In other words, the growth stocks had not only shown a marked superiority in the field of capital appreciation. Given a reasonable time, they had grown to a point where they showed superiority in the matter of dividend return as well.

5

WHEN TO BUY

The preceding chapters attempted to show that the heart of successful investing is knowing how to find the minority of stocks that in the years ahead will have spectacular growth in their per-share earnings. Therefore, is there any reason to divert time or mental effort from the main issue? Does not the matter of when to buy become of relatively minor importance? Once the investor is sure he has definitely found an outstanding stock, isn't any time at all a good time to buy it? The answer to this depends somewhat on the investor's objective. It also depends on his temperament.

Let us take an example. With the ease of hindsight it can be made the most extreme example in modern financial history. This would be the purchase of several superbly selected enterprises in the summer of 1929 or just before the greatest stock market crash of American history. In time such a purchase would have turned out well. But twenty-five years later it would provide a much smaller percentage gain than would have been the case if, having done the hardest part of the job in selecting his companies properly, an investor had made the small extra effort needed to understand a few simple principles about the timing of growth stocks.

In other words, if the right stocks are bought and held long enough they will always produce some profit. Usually they will produce a handsome profit. However, to produce close to the maximum profit, the kind of spectacular profit defined earlier, some consideration must be given to timing.

The conventional method of timing when to buy stocks is, I believe, just as silly as it appears on the surface to be sensible. This method is to marshal a vast mass of economic data. From these data conclusions are reached as to the near- and medium-term course of general business. More sophisticated investors will usually form opinions about the future course of money rates as well as business activity. Then, if their forecasts for all these matters indicate no major worsening of background conditions, the conclusion is that the desired stock may be bought. It sometimes appears that dark clouds are forming on the horizon. Then those who use this generally accepted method will postpone or cancel purchases they otherwise would make.

My objection to this approach is not that it is unreasonable in theory. It is that in the current state of human knowledge about the economics which deal with forecasting future business trends, it is impossible to apply this method in practice. The chances of being right are not good enough to warrant such methods being used as a basis for risking the investment of savings. This may not always be the case. It might not even be the case five or ten years from now. At present, able men are attempting to harness electronic computers to establish "input-output" series of sufficient intricacy that perhaps at some future date it may be possible to know with a fair degree of precision what the coming business trends will be.

When, if ever, such developments occur, the art of common stock investment may have to be radically revised. Until they occur, however, I believe that the economics which deal with forecasting business trends may be considered to be about as far along as was the science of chemistry during the days of alchemy in the Middle Ages. In chemistry then, as in business forecasting now, basic principles were just beginning to emerge from a mysterious mass of mumbo-jumbo. However, chemistry had not reached a point where such principles could be safely used as a basis for choosing a course of action.

Occasionally, as in 1929, the economy gets so out of line that speculative enthusiasm for the future runs to unprecedented proportions. Even in our present state of economic ignorance, it is possible to make a pretty accurate guess as to what will occur. However, I doubt if the years when it is safe to do this have averaged much more than one out of ten. They may be even rarer in the future.

The typical investor is so used to having economic forecasts made for him that he may start by trusting too strongly the dependability of such forecasts. If so, I suggest that he look over a file of the back issues of the *Commercial & Financial Chronicle* for any year he may choose since the end of World War II. As a matter of fact it might pay him to look over such a file even though he is aware of the fallibility of these forecasts. Regardless of the year he selects he will find, among other material, a sizable number of articles in which leading economic and financial authorities give their views of the outlook for the period ahead. Since the editors of this journal appear to select their material so as to give the ablest available presentations of both optimistic and pessimistic opinions, it is not surprising that opposing forecasts will be found in any such series of back issues. What is surprising is the degree by which such experts disagree with each other. Even more surprising is how strong and convincing some of the arguments were bound to seem at the time they were written. This is particularly true of some of the forecasts that turned out to be most wrong.

The amount of mental effort the financial community puts into this constant attempt to guess the economic future from a random and probably incomplete series of facts makes one wonder what might have been accomplished if only a fraction of such mental effort had been applied to something with a better chance of proving useful. I have already compared economic forecasting with chemistry in the days of alchemy. Perhaps this preoccupation with trying to do something which apparently cannot yet be done properly permits another comparison with the Middle Ages.

That was a period when most of the western world lived in an environment of unnecessary want and human suffering. This was largely because the considerable mental ability of the period was devoted to fruitless results. Consider what might have been accomplished if half as much thought had been given to fighting hunger, disease, and greed as was devoted to debating such points as the number of angels that could balance on the head of a pin. Perhaps just part of the collective intelligence nowadays employed in the investment community's attempt to guess the future trend of the business cycle could produce spectacular results if it were harnessed to more productive purposes.

If, then, conventional studies of the near-term economic prospect do not provide the right method of approach to the proper timing of buying, what does provide it? The answer lies in the very nature of growth stocks themselves.

At the risk of being repetitious, let us review for a moment some of the basic characteristics of outstandingly desirable investments, as discussed in the preceding chapter. These companies are usually working in one way or another on the very frontiers of scientific technology. They are developing various new products or processes from the laboratory through the pilot plant to the early stages of commercial production. All of this costs money in varying amounts. All of it is a drain on other profits of the business. Even in the early stage of commercial production the extra sales expense involved in building sufficient volume for a new product to furnish the desired margin of profit is such that the out-of-pocket losses at this stage of development may be greater than they were during the pilot-plant period.

From the standpoint of the investor there are two aspects of all this that have particular significance. One of these is the impossibility of depending on any sure time table in the development cycle of a new product. The other is that even for the most brilliantly-managed enterprises, a percentage of failures is part of the cost of doing business. In a sport, such as baseball, even the most outstanding league champions will have dropped some percentage of their scheduled games.

The point in the development of a new process that is perhaps worth the closest scrutiny from the standpoint of timing the buying of common stocks is that at which the first full-scale commercial plant is about to begin production. In a new plant for even established processes or products, there will probably be a shake-down period of six to eight weeks that will prove rather expensive. It takes this long to get the equipment adjusted to the required operating efficiency and to weed out the inevitable "bugs" that seem to occur in breaking in modern intricate machinery. When the process is really revolutionary, this expensive shake-down period may extend far beyond the estimate of even the most pessimistic company engineer. Furthermore, when problems finally do get solved, the weary stockholder still cannot look forward to immediate profits. There are more months of still further drain while even more of the company's profits from older lines are being ploughed back into special sales and advertising efforts to get the new product accepted.

It may be that the company making all this effort is having such growth in revenue from other and older products that the drain on profits is not noticed by the average stockholder. Frequently, however, just the opposite happens. As word first gets out about a spectacular new product in the laboratory of a well-run company, eager buyers bid up the price of that company's shares. When word comes of successful pilot-plant operation, the shares go still higher. Few think of the old analogy that operating a pilot plant is like driving an automobile over a winding country road at ten miles per hour. Running a commercial plant is like driving on that same road at 100 miles per hour.

Then when month after month difficulties crop up in getting the commercial plant started, these unexpected expenses cause per-share earnings to dip noticeably. Word spreads that the plant is in trouble. Nobody can guarantee when, if ever, the problems will be solved. The former eager buyers of the stock become discouraged sellers. Down goes the price of the stock. The longer the shake-down lasts the more market quotations sag. At last comes the good news that the plant is finally running smoothly. A two-day rally occurs in the price of the stock. However, in the following quarter when special sales expenses have caused a still further sag in net income, the stock falls to the lowest price in years. Word passes all through the financial community that the management has blundered.

At this point the stock might well prove a sensational buy. Once the extra sales effort has produced enough volume to make the first production scale plant pay, normal sales effort is frequently enough to continue the upward movement of the sales curve for many years. Since the same techniques are used, the placing in operation of a second, third, fourth, and fifth plant can nearly always be done without the delays and special expenses that occurred during the prolonged shake-down period of the first plant. By the time plant Number Five is running at capacity, the company has grown so big and prosperous that the whole cycle can be repeated on another brand new product without the same drain on earnings percentage-wise or the same downward effect on the price of the company's shares. The investor has acquired at the right time an investment which can grow for him for many years.

In the original edition I then used the following words to describe an example of this type of opportunity. I used an example that was still fairly recent at that time. I said:

"Immediately prior to the 1954 congressional elections, certain investment funds took advantage of this type of situation. For several years before this time, American Cyanamid shares had sold in the market at a considerably lower price-earning ratio than most of the other major chemical companies. I believe this was because the general feeling in the financial community was that, while the Lederle division represented one of the world's most outstanding pharmaceutical organizations, the relatively larger industrial and agricultural chemical activities constituted a hodge-podge of expensive and inefficient plants flung together in the typical 'stock market' merger period of the booming 1920's. These properties were generally considered anything but a desirable investment.

"Largely unnoticed was the fact that a new management was steadily but without fanfare cutting production costs, eliminating dead wood, and streamlining the organization. What was noticed was that this company was 'making a huge bet'—making a major capital expenditure, for a company its size, in a giant new organic chemical plant at Fortier, Louisiana. So much complex engineering was designed into this plant that it should have surprised no one when the plant lagged many months behind schedule in reaching the break-even point. As the problems at Fortier continued, however, the situation added to the generally unfavorable light in which American Cyanamid shares were then being regarded. At this stage, in the belief a buying point was at hand, the funds to which I have already referred acquired their holdings at an average price of 45¾. This would be 22⅞ on the present shares as a result of a 2-for-1 stock split which occurred in 1957.

"What has happened since? Sufficient time has elapsed for the company to begin getting the benefits of some of the management activities that were creating abnormal costs in 1954. Fortier is now profitable. Earnings have increased from $1.48 per (present) common share in 1954 to $2.10 per share in 1956 and promise to be slightly higher in 1957, a year in which most chemical (though not pharmaceutical) profits have run behind those of the year before. At least as important, 'Wall Street' has come to realize that American Cyanamid's industrial and agricultural chemical activities are worthy of institutional investment. As a result, the price-earnings ratio of these shares has changed noticeably. A 37 per cent increase in earnings that has taken place in somewhat under three years has produced a gain in market value of approximately 85 per cent."

Since writing these words, the financial community's steady upgrading of the status of American Cyanamid appears to have continued. With earnings for 1959 promising to top the previous all-time peak of $2.42 in 1957, the market price of these shares has steadily advanced. It now is about 60, representing a gain of about 70 per cent in earning power and 163 per cent in market value in the five years since the shares referred to in the first edition were acquired.

I would like to end the discussion of American Cyanamid on this happy note. However, in the preface to this revised edition I stated I intended to make this revision an honest record and not the most favorable sounding record it might appear plausible to present. You may have noticed that in the original edition I referred to this 1954 purchase of Cyanamid stock by "certain funds"; these funds are no longer retaining the shares, which were sold in the spring of 1959 at an average price of about 49. This was of course significantly below the current market but still represented a profit of about 110 per cent.

The size of the profit had nothing whatsoever to do with the decision to sell. There were two motives behind this decision. One was that the long-range outlook for another company appeared even better. You will find this discussed in the next chapter as one of the valid reasons for selling. While not enough time has yet passed to give conclusive proof one way or the other, so far comparative market quotations for both stocks appear to have warranted this move.

However, there was a second motive behind this switch of investments which hindsight may prove to be less creditable. This was concern that in relation to the most outstanding of competitive companies, American Cyanamid's chemical (in contrast to its pharmaceutical) business was not making as much progress in broadening profit margins and establishing profitable new lines as had been hoped. Concern over these factors was accentuated by uncertainty over the possible costs of the company's attempt to establish itself in the acrylic fiber business in the highly competitive textile industry. This reasoning may prove to be correct and still could turn out to have been the wrong investment decision, because of bright prospects in the Lederle, or pharmaceutical, division. These prospects have become more apparent since the shares were sold. The possibilities for a further sharp jump in Lederle earning power in the medium-term future center around 1) a new and quite promising antibiotic, and 2) in time a sizable market for an oral "live" polio vaccine, a field in which this company has been a leader. These developments make it problematic and a matter that only the future will decide as to whether this decision to dispose of Cyanamid shares may not have been an investment mistake. Because studying possible mistakes can be even more rewarding than reviewing past successes, I am going to suggest—even at the risk of appearing presumptuous—that anyone seriously interested in bettering his investment technique mark these last several paragraphs and reread them after having read the coming chapter on "When to Sell."

Now let me turn to the next and more recent example of this type of purchasing opportunity which I cited in the original edition. I said:

"A somewhat similar situation may be occurring in the second half of 1957 in the case of the Food Machinery and Chemical Corporation. A few large institutional buyers have liked these shares for some time. Many more, however, seem to feel that in spite of some elements of interest they want evidence concerning certain matters before acquiring shares. To understand this attitude it is necessary to go into some of the background.

"Prior to World War II this company had confined its activities to a diversified line of machinery manufacture. As a result of brilliant management and equally brilliant developmental engineering, Food Machinery had become one of the spectacularly successful investments of the prewar period. Then during the war, in addition to going into the related line of ordnance manufacture at which the company has been comparably successful, the company built up a diversified chemical business. Reason for this was a desire to stabilize the cyclical tendency of the machinery business through the manufacture of consumable products, sales of which over the years could be continuously expanded through research in much the same manner as had been so successfully exploited in the machinery and ordnance divisions.

"By 1952, four separate companies had been acquired and were converted into four (now five) divisions. Combined they represent slightly less than half the total sales volume if ordnance activities are included, slightly more than half if only the normal non-defense activities are considered. Before and in the early acquisition years, these chemical units varied enormously. One was a leader in a rapidly growing field with broad profit margins and excellent technical prestige in the industry. Another suffered from obsolete plant, low margins, and poor morale. The average of all left much to be desired in comparison with the real leaders among chemical companies. In some cases there were intermediate products without basic raw materials. In others, there were plenty of low-profit raw materials, but few products with higher profit margins that could be built from these raw materials.

"The financial community reached some pretty definite conclusions on all this. The machinery divisions—with an internal growth rate of 9 to 10 per cent per annum (comparable to the chemical industry as a whole), with a demonstrated ability to design and sell ingenious and commercially worthwhile new products year after year, and with some of the lowest cost plants in their respective fields—represented the highest grade investment. However, until the chemical divisions could demonstrate broader over-all profit margins and other evidence of intrinsic quality, there was little desire to invest in this combined enterprise.

"Meanwhile, the management went aggressively to work to solve this problem. What did they do? Their first move was through internal promotions and external recruitments to build up a top management team. This new team spent money on modernizing old plant, developing new plant, and on research. Entirely aside from plant expenditures that are normally capitalized, it is impossible to undergo major modernization and plant expansion without running up current expenses as well. It is rather surprising that all the abnormal expenses that occurred in 1955, 1956, and 1957 did not cause reported chemical earnings to decline during that period. The fact that earnings held steady gives strong indication of the worth of what had already been done.

"In any event, if projects have been properly planned, the cumulative effect of those already completed must in time outweigh the abnormal expense of those still to come. Something of this sort might have happened as far back as 1956 if research expenditures in that year had not been increased about 50 per cent above the 1955 levels. This was done even though in 1955 these expenditures for chemical research were not far below the average of the industry, and those for machinery research were well above that of most segments of the machinery business. In spite of continuing this higher level of research, such an earning spurt was expected in the second half of 1957. At midyear the company's modernized chlorine cells at South Charleston, West Virginia, were scheduled to go on stream. Unexpected troubles, characteristic of the chemical industry but from which this company had been surprisingly free in most of its other modernization and expansion programs, indicate that it will be the first quarter of 1958 before this earning spurt will now occur.

"I suspect that until this earning betterment comes and chemical profit margins grow and continue to broaden for a period of time, the institutional buyer will generally fail to look beneath the surface and will largely stay away from this stock. If, as I suspect will happen, such a development manifests itself in 1958 and 1959, financial sentiment some time in that period will come around to recognizing the basic improvement in fundamentals that started several years before. At that time the stock, which may then continue to grow for years, will be selling at a price that has advanced partly because of the improvement in per-share earnings that had already occurred but even more because of the changed price-earnings ratio that results from a general reappraisal of the company's intrinsic quality."

I believe the record of the past two years emphatically validates these comments. Possibly the first general recognition of what had been happening beneath the surface came when in the depression-like year of 1958, a year when nearly all chemical and machinery companies showed a decided drop in earning power, Food Machinery reported profits at an all-time peak of $2.39 per share. This was moderately above the levels of the several preceding years when the general economy was at higher levels. It was a tip-off that the chemical divisions were at last being brought to a point where they could take their place along with the machinery end of the business as a highly desirable and not a marginal investment. While 1959 profits are not yet available as these words are written, the sharp gains in earning power reported for the first nine months over the corresponding period of 1958 give further assurance that the long period of reorganizing the chemical divisions is bearing rich fruit. The 1959 gains are perhaps particularly significant in that this is the year in which the ordnance division is in transition from its former principal product of an armored personnel and light equipment amphibious tank-like carrier made of steel, to an aluminum one that can be dropped from the air by parachute. This means that 1959 was the one year in the recent past or foreseeable future in which ordnance activities made no significant contribution to total earning power. Yet an important new earning peak was attained.

How is the market responding to all this? At the end of September

1957, when writing of the first edition was concluded, these shares were selling at 25¼. Today they are at 51, a gain of 102 per cent. It is beginning to look as though the financial sentiment I mentioned in the original edition is beginning "to recognize the basic improvement in fundamentals that started some years before."

Other events are confirming this trend and may give further impetus to it. In 1959 the McGraw-Hill Publications inaugurated a new custom. They decided each year to give an award for outstanding management achievement in the chemical industries. To determine the first winner of this honor they selected an unusually distinguished and informed panel of ten members. Four represented leading university graduate schools of business administration, three came from major investment institutions with heavy holdings in the chemical industry, and three were leading members of prominent chemical consulting firms. Twenty-two companies were nominated and fourteen submitted presentations. This award for management accomplishment did not go to one or another of the giants of the industry, the managements of several of which, with very good reason, are highly respected in Wall Street. Instead it went to the Chemical Divisions of the Food Machinery Corporation which, two years before, had been regarded by most and is still regarded by many institutional stock buyers as a rather undesirable investment!

Why is a matter of this sort of major importance to long-range investors? First, it gives strong assurance that, plus or minus the trend of general business activity, the earnings of such a company will grow for years to come. Informed chemical businessmen would not give this kind of award in the industry to a company that did not have the research departments to keep developing worthwhile new products and the chemical engineers to produce them profitably. Secondly, this type of award will leave its impression on the investment community. Nothing is more desirable for stockholders than the influence on share prices of an upward trend of earnings multiplied by a comparable upward trend in the way each dollar of such earnings is valued in the market place, as I mentioned in my concluding remarks about this company in the original edition.

Other matters besides the introduction of new products and the problems of starting complex plants can also open up buying opportunities in the unusual company. For example, a Middle Western electronic company was, among other things, well known for its unusual and excellent labor relations. It grew to a point where size alone forced some change in its method of handling employees. An unfortunate interplay of personalities caused friction, slow-down strikes, and low productivity in an enterprise heretofore known for its good labor relations and high labor productivity. At just this time the company made one of the very few mistakes it has made in judging the potential market for a new product. Earnings dropped precipitously and so did the price of the shares.

The unusually able and ingenious management made plans at once to correct this situation. While plans can be made in a matter of weeks, putting them into effect takes much longer. As results from these plans began coming through to earnings, the stock reached what might be called buying point A. However, it took about a year and a half before all the benefits could flow through to the profit statement. Toward the end of this period a second strike occurred, settlement of which was the last step needed to enable the company to restore competitive efficiency. This strike was not a long one. Nevertheless, while this short and relatively inexpensive strike was occurring, word went through the financial community that labor matters were going from bad to worse. In spite of heavy buying from officers of the company, the stock went lower. It did not stay lower for long. This proved to be another of the right sort of buying opportunities from the standpoint of timing, and might be called buying point B. Those who looked beneath the surface and saw what was really happening were able to buy, at bargain prices, a stock that may well grow for them for many years.

Let us see just how profitable it might have been if an investor had bought at either buying point A or buying point B. I do not intend to use the lowest price which a table of monthly price ranges would show that this stock reached in either period. This is because only a few hundred shares changed hands at the extreme low point. If an investor had bought at the absolute lows, it would have been more a matter of luck than anything else. Instead, I will use a figure moderately above the low in one case and several points above in the other. In each instance a good many thousand shares were available and changed hands at these levels. I will use only prices at which the shares could easily have been bought by anyone making a realistic study of the situation.

At buying point A the stock had slipped in just a few months by about 24 per cent from its former peak. Within about a year those who bought here would have had a gain in market value of between 55 per cent and 60 per cent. Then came the strike that produced buying point B. The stock dropped back almost 20 per cent. Strangely enough, it remained there for some weeks after the strike ended. At this time, a brilliant employee of a large investment trust explained to me that he knew how good the situation was and what was almost sure to happen. Nevertheless he would not recommend the purchase to his financial committee. He said certain of the members were sure to check with Wall Street friends and not only turn down his recommendation, but rebuke him for bringing to their attention a company with a sloppy management and hopeless labor relations!

As I write this not so many months later, the stock has already risen 50 per cent from buying point B. This means that it is now up over 90 per cent from buying point A. More important, the company's future looks brilliant, with every prospect that it will enjoy abnormal growth for years to come just as it did for some years before the combination of unusual and temporary unfortunate occurrences produced buying points A and B. Those who bought at either time got into the right sort of company at the right sort of time.

In short, the company into which the investor should be buying is the company which is doing things under the guidance of exceptionally able management. A few of these things are bound to fail. Others will from time to time produce unexpected troubles before they succeed. The investor should be thoroughly sure in his own mind that these troubles are temporary rather than permanent. Then if these troubles have produced a significant decline in the price of the affected stock and give promise of being solved in a matter of months rather than years, he will probably be on pretty safe ground in considering that this is a time when the stock may be bought.

All buying points do not arise out of corporate troubles. In industries such as chemical production, where large amounts of capital are required for each dollar of sales, another type of opportunity sometimes occurs. The mathematics of such situations are usually about like this: A new plant or plants will be erected for, say, $10 million. A year or two after these plants are in full-scale operation, the company's engineers will go over them in detail. They will come up with proposals for spending an additional, say, $1½ million. For this 15 per cent greater total capital investment the engineers will show how the output of the plants can be increased by perhaps 40 per cent of previous capacity.

Obviously, since the plants are already profitable and 40 per cent more output can be made and sold for only 15 per cent more capital cost, and since almost no additional general overhead is involved, the profit margin on this extra 40 per cent of output will be unusually good. If the project is large enough to affect the company's earnings as a whole, buying the company's shares just before this improvement in earning power has been reflected in the market price for these shares can similarly mean a chance to get into the right sort of company at the right time.

What is the common denominator of each of the examples just given? It is that a worthwhile improvement in earnings is coming in the right sort of company, but that this particular increase in earnings has not yet produced an upward move in the price of that company's shares. I believe that whenever this situation occurs the right sort of investment may be considered to be in a buying range. Conversely, when it does not occur, an investor will still in the long run make money if he buys into outstanding companies. However, he had then better have a somewhat greater degree of patience for it will take him longer to make this money and percentage-wise it will be a considerably smaller profit on his original investment.

Does this mean that if a person has some money to invest he should completely ignore what the future trend of the business cycle may be and invest 100 per cent of this fund the moment he has found the right stocks, as defined in Chapter Three, and located a good buying point, as indicated in this chapter? A depression might strike right after he has made his investment. Since a decline of 40 to 50 per cent from its peak is not at all uncommon for even the best stock in a normal business depression, is not completely ignoring the business cycle rather a risky policy?

I think this risk may be taken in stride by the investor who, for a considerable period of time, has already had the bulk of his stocks placed in well-chosen situations. If properly chosen, these should by now have already shown him some fairly substantial capital gains. But now, either because he believes one of his securities should be sold or because some new funds have come his way, such an investor has funds to purchase something new. Unless it is one of those rare years when speculative buying is running riot in the stock market and major economic storm signals are virtually screaming their warnings (as happened in 1928 and 1929), I believe this class of investor should ignore any guesses on the coming trend of general business or the stock market. Instead he should invest the appropriate funds as soon as the suitable buying opportunity arises.

In contrast to guessing which way general business or the stock market may go, he should be able to judge with only a small probability of error what the company into which he wants to buy is going to do in relation to business in general. Therefore he starts off with two advantages. He is making his bet upon something which he knows to be the case, rather than upon something about which he is largely guessing. Furthermore, since by definition he is only buying into a situation which for one reason or another is about to have a worthwhile increase in its earning power in the near or medium-term future, he has a second element of support. Just as his stock would have risen more than the average stock when this new source of earning power became recognized in the market place if business had remained good, so if by bad fortune he has made his new purchase just prior to a general market break this same new source of earnings should prevent these shares from declining quite as much as other stocks of the same general type.

However, many investors are not in the happy position of having a backlog of well-chosen investments bought comfortably below present prices. Perhaps this may be the first time they have funds to invest. Perhaps they may have a portfolio of bonds or relatively static non-growth stocks which at long last they desire to convert into shares that in the future will show them more worthwhile gains. If such investors get possession of new funds or develop a desire to convert to growth stocks after a prolonged period of prosperity and many years of rising stock prices, should they, too, ignore the hazards of a possible business depression? Such an investor would not be in a very happy position if, later on, he realized he had committed all or most of his assets near the top of a long rise or just prior to a major decline.

This does create a problem. However, the solution to this problem is not especially difficult—as in so many other things connected with the stock market it just requires an extra bit of patience. I believe investors in this group should start buying the appropriate type of common stocks just as soon as they feel sure they have located one or more of them. However, having made a start in this type of purchasing, they should stagger the timing of further buying. They should plan to allow several years before the final part of their available funds will have become invested. By so doing, if the market has a severe decline somewhere in this period, they will still have purchasing power available to take advantage of such a decline. If no decline occurs and they have properly selected their earlier purchases, they should have at least a few substantial gains on such holdings. This would provide a cushion so that if a severe decline happened to occur at the worst possible time for them—which would be just after the final part of their funds had become fully invested—the gains on the earlier purchases should largely, if not entirely, offset the declines on the more recent ones. No severe loss of original capital would therefore be involved.

There is an equally important reason why investors who have not already obtained a record of satisfactory investments, and who have enough funds to be able to stagger their purchases should do so. This is that such investors will have had a practical demonstration, prior to using up all their funds, that they or their advisors are sufficient masters of investment technique to operate with reasonable efficiency. In the event that such a record had not been attained, at least all of an investor's assets would not be committed before he had had a warning signal to revise his investment technique or to get someone else to handle such matters for him.

All types of common stock investors might well keep one basic thought in mind; otherwise the financial community's constant worry about and preoccupation with the danger of downswings in the business cycle will paralyze much worthwhile investment action. This thought is that here in the mid-twentieth century the current phase of the business cycle is but one of at least five powerful forces. All of these forces, either by influencing mass psychology or by direct economic operation, can have an extremely powerful influence on the general level of stock prices.

The other four influences are the trend of interest rates, the over-all governmental attitude toward investment and private enterprise, the long-range trend to more and more inflation, and—possibly most powerful of all—new inventions and techniques as they affect old industries. These forces are seldom all pulling stock prices in the same direction at the same time. Nor is any one of them necessarily going to be of vastly greater importance than any other for long periods of time. So complex and diverse are these influences that the safest course to follow will be the one that at first glance appears to be the most risky. This is to take investment action when matters you know about a specific company appear to warrant such action. Be undeterred by fears or hopes based on conjectures, or conclusions based on surmises.

6

WHEN TO SELL

AND WHEN NOT TO

There are many good reasons why an investor might decide to sell common stocks. He may want to build a new home or finance his son in a business. Any one of a number of similar reasons can, from the standpoint of happy living, make selling common stocks sensible. This type of selling, however, is personal rather than financial in its motive. As such it is well beyond the scope of this book. These comments are only designed to cover that type of selling that is motivated by a single objective—obtaining the greatest total dollar benefit from the investment dollars available.

I believe there are three reasons, and three reasons only, for the sale of any common stock which has been originally selected according to the investment principles already discussed. The first of these reasons should be obvious to anyone. This is when a mistake has been made in the original purchase and it becomes increasingly clear that the factual background of the particular company is, by a significant margin, less favorable than originally believed. The proper handling of this type of situation is largely a matter of emotional self-control. To some degree it also depends upon the investor's ability to be honest with himself.

Two of the important characteristics of common stock investment are the large profits that can come with proper handling, and the high degree of skill, knowledge, and judgment required for such proper handling. Since the process of obtaining these almost fantastic profits is so complex, it is not surprising that a certain percentage of errors in purchasing are sure to occur. Fortunately the long-range profits from really good common stocks should more than balance the losses from a normal percentage of such mistakes. They should leave a tremendous margin of gain as well. This is particularly true if the mistake is recognized quickly. When this happens, losses, if any, should be far smaller than if the stock bought in error had been held for a long period of time. Even more important, the funds tied up in the undesirable situation are freed to be used for something else which, if properly selected, should produce substantial gains.

However, there is a complicating factor that makes the handling of investment mistakes more difficult. This is the ego in each of us. None of us likes to admit to himself that he has been wrong. If we have made a mistake in buying a stock but can sell the stock at a small profit, we have somehow lost any sense of having been foolish. On the other hand, if we sell at a small loss we are quite unhappy about the whole matter. This reaction, while completely natural and normal, is probably one of the most dangerous in which we can indulge ourselves in the entire investment process. More money has probably been lost by investors holding a stock they really did not want until they could "at least come out even" than from any other single reason. If to these actual losses are added the profits that might have been made through the proper reinvestment of these funds if such reinvestment had been made when the mistake was first realized, the cost of self-indulgence becomes truly tremendous.

Furthermore this dislike of taking a loss, even a small loss, is just as illogical as it is natural. If the real object of common stock investment is the making of a gain of a great many hundreds per cent over a period of years, the difference between, say, a 20 per cent loss or a 5 per cent profit becomes a comparatively insignificant matter. What matters is not whether a loss occasionally occurs. What does matter is whether worthwhile profits so often fail to materialize that the skill of the investor or his advisor in handling investments must be questioned.

While losses should never cause strong self-disgust or emotional upset, neither should they be passed over lightly. They should always be reviewed with care so that a lesson is learned from each of them. If the particular elements which caused a misjudgment on a common stock purchase are thoroughly understood, it is unlikely that another poor purchase will be made through misjudging the same investment factors.

We come now to the second reason why sale should be made of a common stock purchased under the investment principles already outlined in Chapters Two and Three. Sales should always be made of the stock of a company which, because of changes resulting from the passage of time, no longer qualifies in regard to the fifteen points outlined in Chapter Three to about the same degree it qualified at the time of purchase. This is why investors should be constantly on their guard. It explains why it is of such importance to keep at all times in close contact with the affairs of companies whose shares are held.

When companies deteriorate in this way they usually do so for one of two reasons. Either there has been a deterioration of management, or the company no longer has the prospect of increasing the markets for its product in the way it formerly did. Sometimes management deteriorates because success has affected one or more key executives. Smugness, complacency, or inertia replace the former drive and ingenuity. More often it occurs because a new set of top executives do not measure up to the standard of performance set by their predecessors. Either they no longer hold to the policies that have made the company outstandingly successful, or they do not have the ability to continue to carry out such policies. When any of these things happen the affected stock should be sold at once, regardless of how good the general market may look or how big the capital gains tax may be.

Similarly it sometimes happens that after growing spectacularly for many years, a company will reach a stage where the growth prospects of its markets are exhausted. From this time on it will only do about as well as industry as a whole. It will only progress at about the same rate as the national economy does. This change may not be due to any deterioration of the management. Many managements show great skill in developing related or allied products to take advantage of growth in their immediate field. They recognize, however, that they do not have any particular advantage if they go into unrelated spheres of activity. Hence, if after years of being experts in a young and growing industry, times change and the company has pretty well exhausted the growth prospects of its market, its shares have deteriorated in an important way from the standards outlined under our frequently mentioned fifteen points. Such a stock should then be sold.

In this instance, selling might take place at a more leisurely pace than if management deterioration had set in. Possibly part of the holding might be kept until a more suitable investment could be found. However, in any event, the company should be recognized as no longer suitable for worthwhile investment. The amount of capital gains tax, no matter how large, should seldom prevent the switching of such funds into some other situation which, in the years ahead, may grow in a manner similar to the way in which this investment formerly grew.

There is a good test as to whether companies no longer adequately qualify in regard to this matter of expected further growth. This is for the investor to ask himself whether at the next peak of a business cycle, regardless of what may happen in the meantime, the comparative per-share earnings (after allowances for stock dividends and stock splits but not for new shares issued for additional capital) will probably show at least as great an increase from present levels as the present levels show from the last known peak of general business activity. If the answer is in the affirmative, the stock probably should be held. If in the negative, it should probably be sold.

For those who follow the right principles in making their original purchases, the third reason why a stock might be sold seldom arises, and should be acted upon only if an investor is very sure of his ground. It arises from the fact that opportunities for attractive investment are extremely hard to find. From a timing standpoint, they are seldom found just when investment funds happen to be available. If an investor has had funds for investment for quite a period of time and found few attractive situations into which to place these funds, he may well place some or all of them in a well-run company which he believes has definite growth prospects. However, these growth prospects may be at a slower average annual rate than may appear to be the case for some other seemingly more attractive situation that is found later. The already-owned company may in some other important aspects appear to be less attractive as well.

If the evidence is clear-cut and the investor feels quite sure of his ground, it will, even after paying capital gains taxes, probably pay him handsomely to switch into the situation with seemingly better prospects. The company that can show an average annual increase of 12 per cent for a long period of years should be a source of considerable financial satisfaction to its owners. However, the difference between these results and those that could occur from a company showing a 20 per cent average annual gain would be well worth the additional trouble and capital gains taxes that might be involved.

A word of caution may not be amiss, however, in regard to too readily selling a common stock in the hope of switching these funds into a still better one. There is always the risk that some major element in the picture has been misjudged. If this happens, the investment probably will not turn out nearly as well as anticipated. In contrast, an alert investor who has held a good stock for some time usually gets to know its less desirable as well as its more desirable characteristics. Therefore, before selling a rather satisfactory holding in order to get a still better one, there is need of the greatest care in trying to appraise accurately all elements of the situation.

At this point the critical reader has probably discerned a basic investment principle which by and large seems only to be understood by a small minority of successful investors. This is that once a stock has been properly selected and has borne the test of time, it is only occasionally that there is any reason for selling it at all. However, recommendations and comments continue to pour out of the financial community giving other types of reasons for selling outstanding common stocks. What about the validity of such reasons?

Most frequently given of such reasons is the conviction that a general stock market decline of some proportion is somewhere in the offing. In the preceding chapter I tried to show that postponing an attractive purchase because of fear of what the general market might do will, over the years, prove very costly. This is because the investor is ignoring a powerful influence about which he has positive knowledge through fear of a less powerful force about which, in the present state of human knowledge, he and everyone else is largely guessing. If the argument is valid that the purchase of attractive common stocks should not be unduly influenced by fear of ordinary bear markets, the argument against selling outstanding stocks because of these fears is even more impressive. All the arguments mentioned in the previous chapter equally apply here. Furthermore, the chance of the investor being right in making such sales is still further diminished by the factor of the capital gains tax. Because of the very large profits such outstanding stocks should be showing if they have been held for a period of years, this capital gains tax can still further accentuate the cost of making such sales.

There is another and even more costly reason why an investor should never sell out of an outstanding situation because of the possibility that an ordinary bear market may be about to occur. If the company is really a right one, the next bull market should see the stock making a new peak well above those so far attained. How is the investor to know when to buy back? Theoretically it should be after the coming decline. However, this presupposes that the investor will know when the decline will end. I have seen many investors dispose of a holding that was to show stupendous gain in the years ahead because of this fear of a coming bear market. Frequently the bear market never came and the stock went right on up. When a bear market has come, I have not seen one time in ten when the investor actually got back into the same shares before they had gone up above his selling price. Usually he either waited for them to go far lower than they actually dropped, or, when they were way down, fear of something else happening still prevented their reinstatement.

This brings us to another line of reasoning so often used to cause well-intentioned but unsophisticated investors to miss huge future profits. This is the argument that an outstanding stock has become overpriced and therefore should be sold. What is more logical than this? If a stock is overpriced, why not sell it rather than keep it?

Before reaching hasty conclusions, let us look a little bit below the surface. Just what is overpriced? What are we trying to accomplish? Any really good stock will sell and should sell at a higher ratio to current earnings than a stock with a stable rather than an expanding earning power. After all, this probability of participating in continued growth is obviously worth something. When we say that the stock is overpriced, we may mean that it is selling at an even higher ratio in relation to this expected earning power than we believe it should be. Possibly we may mean that it is selling at an even higher ratio than are other comparable stocks with similar prospects of materially increasing their future earnings.

All of this is trying to measure something with a greater degree of preciseness than is possible. The investor cannot pinpoint just how much per share a particular company will earn two years from now. He can at best judge this within such general and non-mathematical limits as "about the same," "up moderately," "up a lot," or "up tremendously." As a matter of fact, the company's top management cannot come a great deal closer than this. Either they or the investor should come pretty close in judging whether a sizable increase in average earnings is likely to occur a few years from now. But just how much increase, or the exact year in which it will occur, usually involves guessing on enough variables to make precise predictions impossible.

Under these circumstances, how can anyone say with even moderate precision just what is overpriced for an outstanding company with an unusually rapid growth rate? Suppose that instead of selling at twenty-five times earnings, as usually happens, the stock is now at thirty-five times earnings. Perhaps there are new products in the immediate future, the real economic importance of which the financial community has not yet grasped. Perhaps there are not any such products. If the growth rate is so good that in another ten years the company might well have quadrupled, is it really of such great concern whether at the moment the stock might or might not be 35 per cent overpriced? That which really matters is not to disturb a position that is going to be worth a great deal more later.

Again our old friend the capital gains tax adds its bit to these conclusions. Growth stocks which are recommended for sale because they are supposedly overpriced nearly always will cost their owners a sizable capital gains tax if they are sold. Therefore, in addition to the risk of losing a permanent position in a company which over the years should continue to show unusual further gains, we also incur a sizable tax liability. Isn't it safer and cheaper simply to make up our minds that momentarily the stock may be somewhat ahead of itself? We already have a sizable profit in it. If for a while the stock loses, say, 35 per cent of its current market quotation, is this really such a serious matter? Again, isn't the maintaining of our position rather than the possibility of temporarily losing a small part of our capital gain the matter which is really important?

There is still one other argument investors sometimes use to separate themselves from the profits they would otherwise make. This one is the most ridiculous of all. It is that the stock they own has had a huge advance. Therefore, just because it has gone up, it has probably used up most of its potential. Consequently they should sell it and buy something that hasn't gone up yet. Outstanding companies, the only type which I believe the investor should buy, just don't function this way. How they do function might best be understood by considering the following somewhat fanciful analogy:

Suppose it is the day you were graduated from college. If you did not go to college, consider it to be the day of your high school graduation;

from the standpoint of our example it will make no difference whatsoever. Now suppose that on this day each of your male classmates had an
urgent need of immediate cash. Each offered you the same deal. If you
would give them a sum of money equivalent to ten times whatever they
might earn during the first twelve months after they had gone to work,
that classmate would for the balance of his life turn over to you one
quarter of each year's earnings! Finally let us suppose that, while you
thought this was an excellent proposition, you only had spare cash on
hand sufficient to make such a deal with three of your classmates.

At this point, your reasoning would closely resemble that of the investor using sound investment principles in selecting common stocks.
You would immediately start analyzing your classmates, not from the
standpoint of how pleasant they might be or even how talented they
might be in other ways, but solely to determine how much money they
might make. If you were part of a large class, you would probably eliminate quite a number solely on the ground of not knowing them sufficiently well to be able to pass worthwhile judgment on just how financially proficient they actually would get to be. Here again, the analogy
with intelligent common stock buying runs very close.

Eventually you would pick the three classmates you felt would have
the greatest future earning power. You would make your deal with them.
Ten years have passed. One of your three has done sensationally. Going
to work for a large corporation, he has won promotion after promotion.
Already insiders in the company are saying that the president has his eye
on him and that in another ten years he will probably take the top job.
He will be in line for the large compensation, stock options, and pension
benefits that go with that job.

Under these circumstances, what would even the writers of stock market reports who urge taking profits on superb stocks that "have gotten
ahead of the market" think of your selling out your contract with this
former classmate, just because someone has offered you 600 per cent on
your original investment? You would think that anyone would need to
have his head examined if he were to advise you to sell this contract and
replace it with one with another former classmate whose annual earnings
still were about the same as when he left school ten years before. The
argument that your successful classmate had had his advance while the
advance of your (financially) unsuccessful classmate still lay ahead of him
would probably sound rather silly. If you know your common stocks

equally well, many of the arguments commonly heard for selling the good one sound equally silly.

You may be thinking all this sounds fine, but actually classmates are not common stocks. To be sure, there is one major difference. That difference increases rather than decreases the reason for never selling the outstanding common stock just because it has had a huge rise and may be temporarily overpriced. This difference is that the classmate is finite, may die soon and is sure to die eventually. There is no similar life span for the common stock. The company behind the common stock can have a practice of selecting management talent in depth and training such talent in company policies, methods, and techniques in a way which will retain and pass on the corporate vigor for generations. Look at Du Pont in its second century of corporate existence. Look at Dow years after the death of its brilliant founder. In this era of unlimited human wants and incredible markets, there is no limitation to corporate growth such as the life span places upon the individual.

Perhaps the thoughts behind this chapter might be put into a single sentence: If the job has been correctly done when a common stock is purchased, the time to sell it is—almost never.

7

THE HULLABALOO
ABOUT DIVIDENDS

T here is a considerable degree of twisted thinking and general acceptance of half truths about a number of aspects of common stock investments. However, whenever the significance and importance of dividends are considered, the confusion of the typical investor becomes little short of monumental.

This confusion and acceptance of half truths spreads over even to the choice of words customarily used in describing various types of dividend action. A corporation has been paying no dividend or a small one. Its president requests the board of directors to start paying a substantial dividend. This is done. In speaking of this action he or the board will often describe it by saying that the time had come to "do something" for stockholders. The inference is that by not paying or raising the dividend the company had been doing nothing for its stockholders. This could possibly be true. However, it certainly was not true just because no dividend action had been taken. It is possible that by spending earnings not as dividends but to build a new plant, to launch a new product line, or to install some major cost saving equipment in an old plant, the management might have been doing much more to benefit the stockholder than it would have been doing just by passing these earnings out as dividends. No matter what might be done with any earnings not passed on as dividends, increases in the dividend rate are invariably referred to as "favorable" dividend action. Possibly with greater reason, reduction or elimination of dividends is nearly always called "unfavorable."

One of the main reasons for the confusion about dividends in the public mind is the great variation between the amount of benefit, if any, that accrues to the stockholder each time earnings are not passed on to him but retained in the business. At times he is not benefited at all by such retained earnings. At others he is benefited only in a negative sense. If the earnings were not retained, his holdings would decrease in value. However, the retained earnings in no sense increase the value of his holdings, therefore, they seem of no benefit to him. Finally, in the many cases where the stockholder benefits enormously from retained earnings the benefits accrue in quite different proportions to different types of stockholders within the same company, thereby confusing investor thinking even more. In other words, each time earnings are not passed out as dividends, such action must be examined on its own merit to see exactly what is actually happening. It might pay to look a little below the surface here and discuss some of these differences in detail.

When do stockholders get no benefit from retained earnings? One way is when managements pile up cash and liquid assets far beyond any present or prospective needs of the business. The management might have no nefarious motive in doing this. Some executives get a sense of confidence and security from steadily piling up unneeded liquid reserves. They don't seem to realize they are buttressing their own feelings of security by not turning over to the stockholder wealth which he should be entitled to use in his own way and as he sees fit. Today there are tax laws which tend to curb this evil so that while it still occurs, it is no longer the factor which it once was.

There is another and more serious way in which earnings are frequently retained in the business without any significant benefit to stockholders. This occurs when substandard managements can get only a subnormal return on the capital already in the business, yet use the retained earnings merely to enlarge the inefficient operation rather than to make it better. What normally happens is that the management having in time built up a larger inefficient domain over which to rule usually succeeds in justifying bigger salaries for itself on the grounds that it is doing a bigger job. The stockholders end up with little or no profit.

Neither of these situations is likely to affect the investor who follows the concept discussed in this book. He is buying stocks because they are outstanding and not just because they are cheap. Managements with inefficient and substandard operations would fail to qualify under our fifteen points. Meanwhile, managements of the type that do qualify would almost certainly be finding uses for surplus cash and not just piling it up!

How can it happen that earnings retained in the business can be vitally needed yet have no possibility of increasing the value of the stockholder shares? This can occur in one of two ways. One way is when a change in custom or public demand forces each competitive company to spend money on so-called assets which in no sense increase the volume of business, but which would cause a loss of business if the expenditure had not been made. A retail store installing an expensive air conditioning system is a classic example of this sort of thing. After each competitive store has installed such equipment, no net increase in business will occur, yet any store which had not met the competitive move might find very few customers on a hot summer day. Since for some strange reason our accepted accounting system and the tax laws which are based on it make no differentiation between "assets" of this type and those which have actually increased the value of the business, the stockholder frequently thinks that he has been badly treated when earnings have not been passed out to him and yet he can see no increase in value coming to him from what was retained in the business.

The other and even more important way that retained earnings fail to produce increased profits results from an even more serious failure of our accepted accounting methods. In our world of rapid and major changes in the purchasing value of our money units, standard accounting proceeds as though the dollar were a fixed unit of value. Accountants say this is all accounting is supposed to do. This may very well be true; but if a balance sheet is supposed to have any relationship to the real values of the assets described thereon, the confusion that results seems about parallel to what would happen if engineers and scientists made their calculations in our three dimensional world by using only two dimensional plane geometry.

The depreciation allowance in theory should be enough to replace an existing asset when that asset is no longer economically usable. If the depreciation rate were properly calculated and the replacement cost of the asset remained unchanged over its useful life, this would happen. But with ever rising costs, the total accumulated depreciation is seldom enough to replace the outmoded asset. Therefore, additional sums must be retained from the earnings merely to make up the difference if the corporation is to continue to have what it had before.

This type of thing, while affecting all investors, usually affects holders of growth companies less than any other class. This is because the rate of acquiring new capital assets (as against merely replacing existing and about-to-be-retired assets) is usually so fast that more of the depreciation is on recently acquired assets installed at somewhere near today's values. A smaller percentage of it is for assets installed years ago at a fraction of today's costs.

It would be repetitious to go into detail concerning the cases where retaining earnings for building new plants and launching new products has proven of spectacular advantage to investors. However, consideration of how much one type of investor benefits in relation to another is worthy of careful consideration for two reasons. It is a matter about which there is always misunderstanding throughout the financial community. It is also a matter the proper understanding of which provides an easy key to evaluating the real significance of dividends.

Let us examine these misconceptions about who benefits most from dividends by taking a fictitious example. The well managed XYZ Corporation has had a steady growth in its earnings over the last several years. The dividend rate has remained the same. Consequently, whereas four years ago it took 50 per cent of earnings to pay the dividend, so much additional earning power has developed in these four years that paying the same dividend now requires only 25 per cent of this year's earnings. Some directors want to raise the dividend. Others point out that never before has the corporation had so many attractive places to invest their retained earnings. They further point out that only by maintaining rather than raising the rate will it be possible to exploit all the attractive opportunities available. Only in this way can the maximum growth be attained. At this point a lively discussion breaks out as to what course to follow.

Someone on this fictitious board of directors is then sure to state one of the financial community's most common half-truths about dividends. This is that if the XYZ Corporation does not raise its dividend, it will be favoring its large stockholders at the expense of its small ones. The theory behind this is that the big stockholder is presumably in the higher bracket. After paying taxes, the big stockholder can retain a much smaller percentage of his dividends than the small stockholder. Therefore he does not want the increased dividend, whereas the small stockholder does want it.

Actually, whether it is more to the interest of any individual XYZ Corporation stockholder to have the dividend raised or to have more funds ploughed back into the growth depends upon something quite different from the size of his income. It depends upon whether or not each stockholder is at the point where he is putting any part of his income aside for additional investment. Millions of stockholders in the lower income brackets are handling their affairs so that each year they put something, no matter how little, aside for additional investment. If they are doing this and if, as is likely to be the case, they are paying income tax, it is a matter of elementary arithmetic that the board of directors would be acting against their interests by raising the dividend at a time when all these worthwhile opportunities are available for using retained company earnings. In contrast, the raised dividend might be to the interest of a big stockholder who had urgent need of additional funds, a contingency not entirely unknown to those in high tax brackets.

Let us see just why all this is so. Almost anyone having enough surplus funds to own common stocks will probably also have enough income to be in at least the lowest tax bracket. Therefore, once he has used up his individual dividend exemption of $50, even the smallest stockholder will presumably have to pay as tax at least 20 per cent of any additional income he receives as dividends. In addition, he must pay a brokerage commission on any stock he buys. Because of odd lot charges, minimum commissions, etc. these costs run to a much larger percentage of the sums involved in small purchases than in large ones. This will bring the actual capital available for reinvestment well below 80 per cent of the amount received. If the shareholder is in a higher tax bracket, the percentage of a dividend increase which he can actually use for reinvestment becomes proportionately less.

There are, of course, certain special types of stockholders such as universities and pension funds that pay no income tax. There are also some individuals with dividend income less than the $50 individual exemption, although the total number of shares owned by this group appears to be small. For these special groups the equation is somewhat different. However, for the great majority of all stockholders, regardless of size, there is no avoiding this one basic fact about dividends. If they are saving any part of their income rather than spending it and if they have their funds invested in the right sort of common stocks, they are better off when the managements of such companies reinvest increased earnings than they would be if these increased earnings were passed on to them as larger dividends which they would have to reinvest themselves.

Nor is this advantage—having 100 per cent of such funds put to work for them in place of the smaller amount that would be available after income taxes and brokerage charges—the only one the stockholders get. Selecting the right common stock is not an easy or simple matter. If the company considering the dividends is a good one, the investor has already wisely done his task of selection. Therefore, he is usually running less risk in having this good management make the additional investment of these retained extra earnings than he would be running if he had to again risk serious error in finding some new and equally attractive investment for himself. The more outstanding the company considering whether to retain or pass on increased earnings, the more important this factor can become. This is why even the stockholder who does not pay income tax and who is not spending every bit of his income finds it almost as much to his interest as to the interest of his tax-paying counterpart to have such companies retain funds to take advantage of worthwhile new opportunities.

Measured against this background dividends begin to fall into true perspective. For those desiring the greatest benefit from the use of their funds, dividends begin rapidly to lose the importance that many in the financial community give them. This is as true for the conservative investor going into the institutional type growth stock as for those willing and able to take greater risks for greater gain. The opinion is sometimes expressed that a high dividend return is a factor of safety. The theory behind this is that since the high-yield stock is already offering an above-average return, it cannot be overpriced and is not likely to go down very much. Nothing could be farther from the truth. Every study I have seen on this subject indicates that far more of those stocks giving a bad performance price-wise have come from the high dividend-paying rather than the low dividend-paying group. An otherwise good management which increases dividends, and thereby sacrifices worthwhile opportunities for reinvesting increased earnings in the business, is like the manager of a farm who rushes his magnificent livestock to market the minute he can sell them rather than raising them to the point where he can get the maximum price above his costs. He has produced a little more cash right now but at a frightful cost.

I have commented about a corporation raising its dividend rather than about it paying any dividend at all. I am aware that while the occasional investor might not need any income, nearly all do. It is only in rare cases even among outstanding corporations that the opportunity for growth is so great that the management cannot afford to pay some part of earnings and still—through retaining the rest and through senior financing— obtain adequate cash to take advantage of worthwhile growth opportunities. Each investor must decide in relation to his own needs how much, if any, money to put into corporations with such abnormal growth factors that no dividends whatsoever are justified. What is most important, however, is that stocks are not bought in companies where the dividend pay-out is so emphasized that it restricts realizable growth.

This brings us to what is probably the most important but least discussed aspect of dividends. This is regularity or dependability. The wise investor will plan his affairs. He will look ahead to what he can or cannot do with his income. He may not care about immediately increasing income but he will want assurance against the decreased income and unexpected disruption of his plans that this can cause. Furthermore, he will want to make his own decisions between companies which should plough back a great part or all of their earnings and those that may grow at a good but slower rate and need to plough back a smaller proportion.

For these reasons, those who set wise policies on stockholder relations and those who enjoy the high price-earnings ratios for their shares which such policies help bring about usually avoid the muddled thinking that typifies so many corporate treasurers and financial vice presidents. They set a dividend policy and will not change it. They will let stockholders know what this policy is. They may substantially change the dividend but seldom the policy.

This policy will be based on the percentage of earnings that should be retained in the business for maximum growth. For younger and rapidly growing companies, it may be that no dividends at all will be paid for so many years. Then when assets have been brought to the point where the depreciation flow-back is greater, from 25 to 40 per cent of profits will be paid out to stockholders. For older companies this pay-out ratio will vary from company to company. However, in no case will the rough percentages govern the exact amount paid out; this would make each year's dividend different from that of the year before. This is just what stockholders do not want, since it makes impossible independent long-range planning on their part. What they desire is a set amount approximating these percentages and paid out regularly—quarterly, semiannually or annually, as the case may be. As earnings grow, the amount will occasionally be increased to bring the pay-out up to the former percentage. This, however, will only be done when a) funds are otherwise available for taking advantage of all the good opportunities for growth that the management is uncovering and b) there is every reason to believe that this new regular rate can be maintained from this time on, after allowing for all reasonable probabilities of a subsequent downturn in the business or the appearance of additional opportunities for growth.

The managements whose dividend policies win the widest approval among discerning investors are those who hold that a dividend should be raised with the greatest caution and only when there is great probability that it can be maintained. Similarly, only in the gravest of emergencies should such dividends be lowered. It is surprising how many corporate financial officers will approve the paying of one-shot extra dividends. They do this even though such unanticipated extra dividends almost always fail to leave a permanent impact on the market price of their shares—which should indicate how contrary such policies are to the desires of most long-range investors.

No matter how wise or foolish a dividend policy may be, a corporation can usually in time get an investor following which likes the particular policy, provided that the corporation follows the policy consistently. Many stockholders, whether it is to their best interests or not, still like a high rate of return. Others like a low rate. Others like none at all. Some like a very low rate combined with a small regular annual stock dividend. Others do not want this stock dividend preferring the low rate by itself. If a management selects one of these policies in line with its natural needs, it usually builds up a stockholder group which likes and comes to expect the continuation of such a policy. A wise management wishing to obtain investment prestige for its stock will respect that desire for continuity.

There is perhaps a close parallel between setting policy in regard to dividends and setting policy on opening a restaurant. A good restaurant man might build up a splendid business with a high-priced venture. He might also build up a splendid business with an attractive place selling the best possible meals at the lowest possible prices. Or he could make a success of Hungarian, Chinese, or Italian cuisine. Each would attract a following. People would come there expecting a certain kind of meal. However, with all his skill, he could not possibly build up a clientele if one day he served the costliest meals, the next day low-priced ones, and then without warning served nothing but exotic dishes. The corporation that keeps shifting its dividend policies becomes as unsuccessful in attracting a permanent shareholder following. Its shares do not make the best long-range investments.

As long as dividend policy is consistent, so that investors can plan ahead with some assurance, this whole matter of dividends is a far less important part of the investment picture than might be judged from the endless arguments frequently heard about the relative desirability of this dividend policy or that. The large groups in the financial community that would dispute this view fail to explain the number of stocks that have offered no prospect of anything but below-average yield for years ahead, yet which have done so well for their owners. Several examples of such stocks have already been mentioned. Another typical investment of this type is Rohm & Haas. This stock first became publicly available in 1949, when a group of investment bankers purchased a large block held by the Alien Property Custodian and reoffered it publicly. The public offering price was $41.25. At that time the stock was paying only $1.00 in dividends, supplemented by stock dividends. Many investors felt that in view of the low yield the stock was unattractive for conservative investment. Since this date, however, the company has continued to pay stock dividends, has raised the cash dividend at frequent intervals although the yield has remained very low, and the stock has sold well over 400. The original owner of Rohm & Haas has received stock dividends of 4 per cent each year from 1949 through 1955, and 3 per cent in 1956, so his capital gain has been well over ten-fold.

Actually dividend considerations should be given the least, not the most, weight by those desiring to select outstanding stocks. Perhaps the most peculiar aspect of this much-discussed subject of dividends is that those giving them the least consideration usually end up getting the best dividend return. Worthy of repetition here is that over a span of five to ten years, the best dividend results will come not from the high-yield stocks but from those with the relatively low yield. So profitable are the results of the ventures opened up by exceptional managements that while they still continue the policy of paying out a low proportion of current earnings, the actual number of dollars paid out progressively exceed what could have been obtained from high-yield shares. Why shouldn't this logical and natural trend continue in the future?

8

FIVE DON'TS FOR INVESTORS

1. Don't buy into promotional companies.

Close to the very heart of successful investing is finding companies which are developing new products and processes or exploiting new markets. Companies that have just started or are about to be started are frequently attempting to do just this. Many of them are formed to develop a colorful new invention. Many are started to participate in industries, such as electronics, in which there is great growth potential. Another large group is formed to discover mineral or other natural wealth—a field where the rewards for success can be outstanding. For these reasons, young companies not yet earning a profit on their operations may at first glance appear to be of investment value.

There is another argument which frequently increases interest. This is that by buying now when the first shares are offered to the public, there is a chance to "get in on the ground floor." The successful company is now selling at several times the price at which it was originally offered. Therefore why wait and have somebody else make all this money? Instead why not use the same methods of inquiry and judgment in finding the outstanding new enterprise now being promoted as can be used in finding the outstanding established corporation?

From the investment standpoint, I believe there is a basic matter which puts any company without at least two or three years of commercial operation and one year of operating profit in a completely different category from an established company—even one so small that it may not have more than a million dollars of annual sales. In the established company, all the major functions of the business are currently operating. The investor can observe the company's production, sales, cost accounting, management teamwork, and all the other aspects of its operations. Perhaps even more important, he can obtain the opinion of other qualified observers who are in a position to observe regularly some or all of these points of relative strength or weakness in the company under consideration. In contrast, when a company is still in the promotional stage, all an investor or anyone else can do is look at a blueprint and guess what the problems and the strong points may be. This is a much more difficult thing to do. It allows a much greater probability of error in the conclusions reached.

Actually, it is so difficult to do that no matter how skillful the investor, it makes it impossible to obtain even a fraction of the "batting average" for selecting outstanding companies that can be attained if judgment is confined to established operations. All too often, young promotional companies are dominated by one or two individuals who have great talent for certain phases of business procedure but are lacking in other equally essential talents. They may be superb salesmen but lack other types of business ability. More often they are inventors or production men, totally unaware that even the best products need skillful marketing as well as manufacture. The investor is seldom in a position to convince such individuals of the skills missing in themselves or their young organizations. Usually he is even less in a position to point out to such individuals where such talents may be found.

For these reasons, no matter how appealing promotional companies may seem at first glance, I believe their financing should always be left to specialized groups. Such groups have management talent available to bolster up weak spots as unfolding operations uncover them. Those who are not in a position to supply such talent and to convince new managements of the need of taking advantage of such help will find investing in promotional companies largely a disillusioning experience. There are enough spectacular opportunities among established companies that ordinary individual investors should make it a rule never to buy into a promotional enterprise, no matter how attractive it may appear to be.

2. Don't ignore a good stock just because it is traded "over the counter."

The attractiveness of unlisted stocks versus those listed on a stock exchange is closely related to the marketability of one group as against the other. Everyone should recognize the importance of marketability. Normally, most if not all buying should be confined to stocks which can be sold should a reason—either financial or personal—arise for such selling. However, some confusion seems to exist in the minds of investors as to what gives adequate protection in this regard and what does not. This in turn gives rise to even more confusion concerning the desirability of those stocks not listed on any exchange. Such stocks are commonly called "over-the-counter" stocks.

The reason for this confusion lies in basic changes that have come over common stock buying in the last quarter century—changes that make the markets of the 1950's very different even from those as recent as the never-to-be-forgotten 1920's. During most of the 1920's and in all of the period before that, the stock broker had as customers a relatively small number of rather rich men. Most buying was done in large blocks, frequently in multiples of thousands of shares. The motive was usually to sell out to someone else at a higher price. Gambling rather than investment was the order of the day. Buying on margin—that is, with borrowed funds—was then the accepted method of operation. Today a very large percentage of all buying is on a cash basis.

Many things have happened to change these colorful markets of the past. High income and inheritance tax rates are one. A more important influence is the tendency toward a levelling of incomes that continues year after year in every section of the United States. The very rich and the very poor each year grow smaller in number. Each year the middle groups grow larger. This has produced a steady shrinkage of big stock buyers, and an even greater growth of small stock buyers. Along with them has come a tremendous growth in another class of stock buyer, the institutional buyer. The investment trust, the pension and profit-sharing trusts, even to some degree the trust departments of the great banks do not represent a few big buyers. Rather they are a few professional managers entrusted with handling the collective savings of innumerable small buyers.

Partly as a result of all this, and partly as a cause helping to bring it about, basic changes have come in our laws and institutions as they affect the stock market. The Securities and Exchange Commission has been created to prevent the type of manipulation and pool operation that spurred on the rampant stock market gambling of the past. Rules are in force limiting margin buying to a fraction of what was formerly considered customary. But most important of all, as already discussed in an earlier chapter, the corporation of today is a very different thing from what it used to be. For the reasons already explained, today's corporation is designed to be far more suitable as an investment medium for those desiring long-range growth than as a vehicle for in-and-out trading.

All this has profoundly changed the market place. It undoubtedly represents tremendous improvement—improvement, however, at the expense of marketability. The liquidity of the average stock has decreased rather than increased. In spite of breathtaking economic growth and a seemingly endless procession of stock splits, the volume of trading on the New York Stock Exchange has declined. For the smaller exchanges it has almost vanished. The gambler, the in-and-out buyer, and even the "sucker" trying to outguess the pool manipulator were not conducive to a healthy economy. They did, however, help provide a ready market.

I do not want to get involved in semantics. Nevertheless, it must be realized that this has resulted in the gradual decline of the "stock broker" and the rise of what might be called the "stock salesman." So far as stocks are concerned, the broker works in an auction market. He takes an order from someone who has already decided on his investment course. He matches this order with an order he or some other broker has received to sell. This process is not overly time-consuming. If the orders received are for a large rather than small number of shares, the broker can operate on a very small commission for each share handled and still end the year with a handsome profit.

Contrast him with the salesman, who must go through the far more time-consuming routine of persuading the customer on the course of action to be taken. There are only a given number of hours in the day. Therefore, to make a profit commensurate with that of a broker, he must charge a higher commission for his services. This is particularly true if the salesman is serving a large number of small customers rather than a few big ones. Under today's economic conditions, small customers are the ones most salesmen must serve.

The stock exchanges are still primarily operating as a vehicle for stock brokers rather than stock salesmen. Their commission rates have gone up. They have only gone up, however, about in proportion to that of most other types of services. In contrast, the over-the-counter markets work on a quite different principle. Each day, designated members of the National Association of Security Dealers furnish the newspapers of that region with quotations on a long list of the more active unlisted securities of interest to stockholders in that locality. These are compiled by close contact with the over-the-counter houses most active in trading each of these securities. Unlike those furnished by the stock exchanges, these quotations are not the price ranges within which transactions took place. They cannot be, for there is no central clearing house to which transactions are reported. Instead these are bid-and-ask quotations. Such quotations supposedly give the highest price at which any of the interested financial houses will bid for each of these shares and the lowest offering price at which they will sell them.

Close checking will nearly always show that the reported quotations on the bid or buy side are closely in line with what could be obtained for shares at the moment the quotation was furnished. The sales or ask side is usually higher than the bid by an amount several times greater than the equivalent stock exchange commission for shares selling at the same price. This difference is calculated to enable the over-the-counter house to buy at the bid price, pay its salesmen an appropriate commission for the time spent in selling the security, and still leave a reasonable profit after allowing for general overhead. On the other hand, if a customer, particularly a large customer, approaches the same financial house with a bid to buy this stock so that no salesman's commission is involved, he can usually buy it at the bid price plus just about the equivalent of the stock exchange commission. As one over-the-counter dealer expressed it, "we have one market on the buy side. On the selling side we have two. We have a retail and a wholesale market, depending partly on the size of the purchase and partly on the amount of selling and servicing that is involved."

This system in the hands of an unscrupulous dealer is subject to obvious abuse. So is any other system. But if the investor picks the over-the-counter dealer with the same care he should employ in choosing any other specialist to serve him, it works surprisingly well. The average investor has neither the time nor the ability to select his own securities. Through the close supervision dealers give the securities they permit their salesmen to offer, he is receiving in effect something closely resembling investment counsel. As such it should be worth the cost involved.

From the standpoint of the more sophisticated investor, however, the real benefits of this system are not in regard to buying. They are in regard to the increased liquidity or marketability which it produces for those unlisted stocks he may desire to own. Because the profit margin available for dealers in such stocks is large enough to make it worthwhile, a great many over-the-counter dealers keep a regular inventory of the stocks they normally handle. They usually are not at all reluctant to take on additional 500- or 1000-share lots when they become available. When larger blocks appear in their favorite issues, they will frequently hold a sales meeting and put on a special drive to move the shares that may be available. Normally they will ask a special selling commission of a point or so for doing this. However, all this means that if an over-the-counter stock is regularly dealt in by two or more high-grade over-the-counter dealers, it usually has a sufficient degree of marketability to take care of the needs of most investors. Depending on the amount offered, a special selling commission may or may not be required to move a large block. However, for what is at most a relatively small percentage of the sales price, the stock which the investor desires to sell can actually be converted into cash without breaking the market.

How does this compare with the marketability of a stock listed on a stock exchange? The answer depends largely on what stock and on what stock exchange. For the larger and more active issues listed on the New York Stock Exchange, even under today's conditions a big enough auction market still exists so that in normal times all but the largest blocks can be moved at the low prevailing commission rates without depressing prices. For the less active stocks listed on the New York Stock Exchange, this marketability factor is still fair, but at times can sag rather badly if regular commissions are depended on when large selling orders appear. For common stocks listed on the small exchanges, it is my opinion that this marketability factor frequently becomes considerably worse.

The stock exchanges have recognized this situation and have taken steps to meet it. Nowadays, whenever a block of a listed stock appears which the exchange thinks is too big to market in the normal fashion, permission may be given for the use of devices such as "special offerings." This simply means that the offering is made known to all members, who are given a predetermined larger commission for selling these shares. In other words, when the block is too large for the brokers to handle it as brokers, they are given commissions large enough to reward them for selling as salesmen.

All this narrows the apparent gap between listed and unlisted markets in a period such as the present, when more and more purchases are being handled by salesmen rather than by brokers who just take orders. It does not mean that from the standpoint of marketability a well-known, actively-traded stock on the New York Stock Exchange has no advantage over the better over-the-counter stocks. It does mean that the better of these over-the-counter stocks are frequently more liquid than the shares of many of the companies listed on the American Stock Exchange and the various regional stock exchanges. I imagine those connected with the smaller stock exchanges would sincerely disagree with this statement. Nevertheless, I believe an unprejudiced study of the facts would show it to be true. It is why a number of the more progressive of smaller and medium-size companies have in recent years refused to list their stocks on the smaller exchanges. Instead they have chosen the over-the-counter markets until their companies reach a size that would warrant "big board,"—that is, New York Stock Exchange—listing.

In short, so far as over-the-counter securities are concerned, the rules for the investor are not too different from those for listed securities. First, be very sure that you have picked the right security. Then be sure you have selected an able and conscientious broker. If an investor is on sound ground in both these respects, he need have no fear of purchasing stock just because it is traded "over-the-counter" rather than on an exchange.

3. Don't buy a stock just because you like the "tone" of its annual report.

Investors are not always careful to analyze just what has caused them to buy one stock rather than another. If they did, they might be surprised how often they were influenced by the wording and format of the general comments in a company's annual report to stockholders. This tone of the annual report may reflect the management's philosophies, policies, or goals with as much accuracy as the audited financial statement should reflect the dollars and cents results for the period involved. The annual report may also, however, reflect little more than the skill of the company's public relations department in creating an impression about the company in the public mind. There is no way of telling whether the president has actually written the remarks in an annual report, or whether a public relations officer has written them for his signature. Attractive photographs and nicely colored charts do not necessarily reflect a close-knit and able management team working in harmony and with enthusiasm.

Allowing the general wording and tone of an annual report to influence a decision to purchase a common stock is much like buying a product because of an appealing advertisement on a billboard. The product may be just as attractive as the advertisement. It also may not be. For a low-priced product it may be quite sensible to buy in this way, to find out how attractive the purchase really is. With a common stock, however, few of us are rich enough to afford impulse buying. It is well to remember that annual reports nowadays are generally designed to build up stockholder good will. It is important to go beyond them to the underlying facts. Like any other sales tool they are prone to put a corporation's "best foot forward." They seldom present balanced and complete discussions of the real problems and difficulties of the business. Often they are too optimistic.

If, then, an investor should not let a favorable reaction to the tone of an annual report overly influence his subsequent action, how about the opposite? Should he let an unfavorable reaction influence him? Usually not, for again it is like trying to appraise the contents of a box by the wrapping paper on the outside. There is one important exception to this, however. This is when such reports fail to give proper information on matters of real significance to the investor. Companies which follow such policies are usually not the ones most likely to provide the background for successful investment.

4. Don't assume that the high price at which a stock may be selling in relation to earnings is necessarily an indication that further growth in those earnings has largely been already discounted in the price.

There is a costly error in investment reasoning that is common enough to make it worthy of special mention. To explain it, let us take a fictitious company. We might call it the XYZ Corporation. XYZ has qualified magnificently for years in regard to our fifteen points. For three decades there has been constant growth in both sales and profits, and also there have been enough new products under development to furnish strong indication of comparable growth in the period ahead. The excellence of the company is generally appreciated throughout the financial community. Consequently for years XYZ stock has sold for from twenty to thirty times current earnings. This is nearly twice as much for each dollar earned as the sales price of the average stock that has made up, say, the Dow Jones Industrial Averages.

Today this stock is selling at just twice the price-earnings ratio of the Dow Jones averages. This means that its market price is twice as high in relation to each dollar it is earning as is the average of the stocks comprising these Dow Jones averages in relation to each dollar they are earning. The XYZ management has just issued a forecast indicating they expect to double earnings in the next five years. On the basis of the evidence at hand, the forecast looks valid.

Whereupon a surprising number of investors jump to false conclusions. They say that since XYZ is selling twice as high as stocks in general, and since it will take five years for XYZ's earnings to double, the present price of XYZ stock is discounting future earnings ahead. They are sure the stock is overpriced.

No one can argue that a stock discounting its earnings five years ahead is likely to be overpriced. The fallacy in their reasoning lies in the assumption that five years from now XYZ will be selling on the same price-earnings ratio as will the average Dow Jones stock with which they compare it. For thirty years this stock, because of all those factors which make it an outstanding company, has been selling at twice the price-earnings ratio of these other stocks. Its record has been rewarding to those who have placed their faith in it. If the same policies are continued, five years from now its management will bring out still another group of new products that in the ensuing decade will swell earnings in the same way that new products are increasing earnings now, and others did five, ten, fifteen and twenty years ago. If this happens, why shouldn't this stock sell five years from now for twice the price-earnings ratio of these more ordinary stocks just as it is doing now and has done for many years past? If it does, and if the price-earnings ratio of all stocks remain about the same, XYZ's doubling of earnings five years from now will also cause its price to have doubled in the market over this five-year period. On this basis, this stock, selling at its normal price-earnings ratio, cannot be said to be discounting future earnings at all!

Obvious, isn't it? Well, look around you and see how many supposedly sophisticated investors get themselves crossed up on this matter of what price-earnings ratio to use in considering how far ahead a stock is actually discounting future growth. This is particularly true if a change has been taking place in the background of the company being studied.

Let us now consider the ABC Company instead of the XYZ Corporation. The two companies are almost exactly alike except that the ABC Company is much younger. Only in the last two years has its fundamental excellence been appreciated by the financial community to the point that its shares, too, are now selling at twice the price-earnings ratio of the average Dow Jones stock. It seems almost impossible for many investors to realize, in the case of a stock that in the past has not sold at a comparably high price-earnings ratio, that the price-earnings ratio at which it is now selling may be a reflection of its intrinsic quality and not an unreasonable discounting of further growth.

What is important here is thoroughly understanding the nature of the company, with particular reference to what it may be expected to do some years from now. If the earning spurt that lies ahead is a one-time matter, and the nature of the company is not such that comparable new sources of earning growth will be developed when the present one is fully exploited, that is quite a different situation. Then the high price-earnings ratio does discount future earnings. This is because, when the present spurt is over, the stock will settle back to the same selling price in relation to its earnings as run-of-the-mill shares. However, if the company is deliberately and consistently developing new sources of earning power, and if the industry is one promising to afford equal growth spurts in the future, the price-earnings ratio five or ten years in the future is rather sure to be as much above that of the average stock as it is today. Stocks of this type will frequently be found to be discounting the future much less than many investors believe. This is why some of the stocks that at first glance appear highest priced may, upon analysis, be the biggest bargains.

5. Don't quibble over eighths and quarters.

I have used fictitious examples in attempting to make clear various other matters. This time I will use an actual example. A little over twenty years ago, a gentleman who in most respects has demonstrated a high order of investment ability wanted to buy one hundred shares of a stock listed on the New York Stock Exchange. On the day he decided to buy, the stock closed at $35\frac{1}{2}$. On the following day it sold repeatedly at that price. But this gentleman would not pay $35\frac{1}{2}$. He decided he might as well save fifty dollars. He put his order in at 35. He refused to raise it.

The stock never again sold at 35. Today, almost twenty-five years later, the stock appears to have a particularly bright future. As a result of the stock dividends and splits that have occurred in the intervening years, it is now selling at over 500.

In other words, in an attempt to save fifty dollars, this investor failed to make at least $46,500. Furthermore, there is no question that this investor would have made the $46,500, because he still has other shares of this same company which he bought at even lower figures. Since $46,500 is about 930 times 50, this means that our investor would have had to save his fifty dollars 930 times just to break even. Obviously, following a course of action with this kind of odds against it borders on financial lunacy.

This particular example is by no means an extreme one. I purposely selected a stock which for a number of years was more of a market laggard than a market leader. If our investor had picked any one of perhaps fifty other growth stocks listed on the New York Stock Exchange, missing $3500 worth of such stock in order to save $50, would have cost a great deal more than the $46,500.

For the small investor wanting to buy only a few hundred shares of a stock, the rule is very simple. If the stock seems the right one and the price seems reasonably attractive at current levels, buy "at the market." The extra eighth, or quarter, or half point that may be paid is insignificant compared to the profit that will be missed if the stock is not obtained. Should the stock not have this sort of long-range potential, I believe the investor should not have decided to buy it in the first place.

For the larger investor, wanting perhaps many thousands of shares, the problem is not quite as simple. For all but a very small minority of stocks, the available supply is usually sufficiently limited that an attempt to buy at the market even half of this desired amount could well cause a sizable advance in quotations. This sudden price rise might, in turn, produce two further effects, both tending to make accumulating a block of this stock even more difficult. The price spurt by itself might be enough to arouse the interest and competition of other buyers. It might also cause some of those who have been planning to sell to hold their shares off the market with the hope that the rise might continue. What then should a large buyer do to meet this situation?

He should go to his broker or securities dealer. He should disclose to him exactly how much stock he desires to buy. He should tell the broker to pick up as much stock as possible but authorize him to pass up small offerings if buying them would arouse many competitive bids. Most important, he should give his broker a completely free hand on price up to a point somewhat above the most recent sale. How much above should be decided in consultation with the broker or dealer after taking into account such factors as the size of the block desired, the normal activity of the shares, how eager the investor may be for the holding, and any other special factors that might be involved.

The investor may feel he does not have a broker or dealer upon whom he may rely as having sufficient judgment or discretion to handle something of this sort. If so, he should proceed forthwith to find a broker or dealer in whom such confidence can be placed. After all, doing exactly this sort of thing is the primary function of a broker or the trading department of a security dealer.

9

FIVE MORE DON'TS
FOR INVESTORS

---

1. Don't overstress diversification.

No investment principle is more widely acclaimed than diversification. (Some cynics have hinted that this is because the concept is so simple that even stock brokers can understand it!) Be that as it may, there is very little chance of the average investor being influenced to practice insufficient diversification. The horrors of what can happen to those who "put all their eggs in one basket" are too constantly being expounded.

Too few people, however, give sufficient thought to the evils of the other extreme. This is the disadvantage of having eggs in so many baskets that a lot of the eggs do not end up in really attractive baskets, and it is impossible to keep watching all the baskets after the eggs get put into them. For example, among investors with common stock holdings having a market value of a quarter to a half million dollars, the percentage who own twenty-five or more different stocks is appalling. It is not this number of twenty-five or more which itself is appalling. Rather it is that in the great majority of instances only a small percentage of such holdings is in attractive stocks about which the investor or his advisor has a high degree of knowledge. Investors have been so oversold on diversification that fear of having too many eggs in one basket has caused them to put far too little into companies they thoroughly know and far too much in others about which they know nothing at all. It never seems to occur to them, much less to their advisors, that buying a company without having sufficient knowledge of it may be even more dangerous than having inadequate diversification.

How much diversification is really necessary and how much is dangerous? It is somewhat like infantrymen stacking rifles. A rifleman cannot get as firm a stack by balancing two rifles as he can by using five or six properly placed. However, he can get just as secure a stack with five as he could with fifty. In this matter of diversification, however, there is one big difference between stacking rifles and common stocks. With rifles, the number needed for a firm stack does not usually depend on the kind of rifle used. With stocks, the nature of the stock itself has a tremendous amount to do with the amount of diversification actually needed.

Some companies, such as most of the major chemical manufacturers, have a considerable degree of diversification within the company itself. While all of their products may be classified as chemicals, many of these chemicals may have most of the attributes found in products from completely different industries. Some may have completely different manufacturing problems. They may be sold against different competition to different types of customers. Furthermore at times when only one type of chemical is involved, the customer group may be such a broad section of industry that a considerable element of internal diversification may still be present.

The breadth and depth of a company's management personnel—that is, how far a company has progressed away from one-man management—are also important factors in deciding how much diversification protection is intrinsically needed. Finally, holdings in highly cyclical industries—that is, those that fluctuate sharply with changes in the state of the business cycle—also inherently require being balanced by somewhat greater diversification than do shares in lines less subject to this type of intermittent fluctuation.

This difference between the amount of internal diversification found in stocks makes it impossible to set down hard and fast rules as to the minimum amount of diversification the average investor requires for optimum results. The relationship between the industries involved will also be a factor. For example, an investor with ten stocks in equal amounts, but eight of them bank stocks, may have completely inadequate diversification. In contrast, the same investor with each of his ten stocks in a completely different industry may have far more diversification than he really needs.

Recognizing, therefore, that each case is different and that no precise rules can be laid down, the following is suggested as a rough guide to what might be considered as *minimum diversification* needs for all but the very smallest type of investor:

A. All investments might be confined solely to the large entrenched type of properly selected growth stock, of which Dow, Du Pont, and IBM have already been mentioned as typical examples. In this event, the investor might have a minimum goal of five such stocks in all. This means that he would not invest over 20 per cent of his total original commitment in any one of these stocks. It does *not* mean that should one grow more rapidly than the rest, so that ten years later he found 40 per cent of his total market value in one stock, he should in any sense disturb such a holding. This assumes, of course, that he has gotten to know his holding and the future continues to look at least as bright for these stocks as has the recent past.

An investor using this guide of 20 per cent of his original investment for each company should see that there is no more than a moderate amount of overlapping, if any, between the product lines of his five companies. Thus, for example, if Dow were one of his five companies there would seem to me to be no reason why Du Pont might not be another. There are relatively few places where the product lines of these two companies overlap or compete. If he were to have Dow and some other company closer to Dow in its fields of activity, his purchase might still be a wise one provided he had sufficient reason for making it. Having these two stocks in similar lines of activity might prove very profitable over the years. However, in such an instance the investor should keep in mind that his diversification is essentially inadequate, and therefore he should be alert for troubles which might affect the industry involved.

B. Some or all of his investments might fall into the category of stocks about midway between the young growth companies with their high degree of risk and the institutional type of investment described above. These would be companies with a good management team rather than one-man management. They would be companies doing a volume of business somewhere between fifteen and one hundred million dollars a year and rather well entrenched in their industries. At least two of such companies should be considered as necessary to balance each single company of the A type. In other words, if only companies in this B group were involved, an investor might start out with 10 per cent of his available funds in each. This would make a total of ten stocks in all. However, companies in this general classification can vary considerably among themselves as to their degree of risk. It might be prudent to consider those with the greater inherent risk as candidates for 8 per cent of original investment, rather than 10 per cent. In any event, looking to each stock of this class as a candidate for 8 to 10 per cent of total original investment—in contrast to 20 per cent for the A group—should again provide the framework for adequate minimum diversification.

Companies of this B group are usually somewhat harder for the investor to recognize than those of the A or institutional type. Therefore it might be worthwhile to furnish a brief description of one or two such companies which I have had the opportunity to observe rather closely and which could be considered typical examples.

Let us see what I said about such companies in the original edition and how they appear today. The first B company to which I referred was P. R. Mallory. I said:

"P. R. Mallory & Co., Inc. enjoys a surprising degree of internal diversification. Its principal products are components for the electronic and electrical industries, special metals, and batteries. For its more important product lines it is a major factor in the respective industries, and in a few of them it is the largest producer. Many of its product lines, such as electronic components and special metals, serve some of the most rapidly growing segments of American industry, giving indications that Mallory's growth should continue. In ten years sales have increased almost four-fold to a volume of about $80,000,000 in 1957, with about one-third of this increase resulting from carefully planned outside acquisitions and about two-thirds from internal growth.

"Profit margins over this period have been a bit lower than would normally be considered satisfactory for a company of this B group, but part of this is attributable to above-average expenditures on research. More significantly, steps have been taken which are beginning to show indications of important improvement in this factor. Management has demonstrated considerable ingenuity under a dynamic president, and in recent years has been increasing importantly in depth. Mallory shares enjoyed about a five-fold increase in value during the ten-year period of 1946 to 1956, frequently selling around fifteen times current earnings.

"Perhaps investment-wise one of the most important factors about Mallory lies not within the company itself but in its anticipated one-third interest in the Mallory-Sharon Metals Corporation. This company is being planned as a combination of the Mallory-Sharon Titanium Corporation—half of which is owned by P. R. Mallory & Co., and which has already proved to be an interesting venture for Mallory—and National Distillers' operations in the raw-material stages of the same industry. This new company gives indication of being one of the lowest-cost integrated titanium producers and as such should play a major role in the probable growth of this young industry. Meanwhile the corporation in 1958 is expected to start its first commercially significant zirconium product and has within its organization considerable know-how in other commercially new "wonder metals" such as tantalum and columbium. This partially owned company gives indications of becoming a world leader in not one but a series of metals that promise to play a growing part in the atomic, chemical, and guided-missile age of tomorrow. As such it could be an asset of tremendous dollar significance to increase the growth that appears inherent in Mallory itself."

If I were writing these words today, slightly over two years later, I would write them somewhat differently. I would tone down moderately my enthusiasm for the possible contributions of the one-third owned Mallory-Sharon Metals Corporation. I think everything I said two years ago could still occur. However, particularly so far as titanium is concerned, I believe it may take longer to find and develop sizable markets for this metal than had seemed to be the case two years ago.

On the other hand, I would be inclined to strengthen my words for the Mallory company itself by about the degree I would weaken them for its affiliate. The trend I mentioned of increasing management in depth has progressed importantly during this period. While Mallory, as a component supplier to the durable goods industry, is in a line of business that is bound to feel the ravages of any major general slide, the management showed unusual adroitness in adjusting to 1958 conditions and held earnings to $1.89 per share against the all-time peak of $2.06 the year before. Earnings came back fast in 1959 and promise to make new records for the full year somewhere around $2.75 per share. Furthermore these earnings are being established in the face of decreasing but still heavy costs for certain of the newer divisions. This showing gives promise that if general economic conditions remain reasonably prosperous significant further growth in profits will be seen in 1960.

Mallory stock is one of the few examples cited in this book that to date has done worse rather than better than the market as a whole. Although I suspect this company has been more successful than some of its competitors in meeting Japanese competition in the electronic components phases of its business, this threat may be a reason for the relatively poor market action. Another reason may be lack of interest by much of the financial community in a business that is not easily classified in one industry or another, but cuts across several. This may change in time, particularly as awareness grows that its miniature battery lines are not so far removed from some glamorous growth fields, for they should grow with the steady trend toward miniaturization in electronics. At any rate, this stock which was at 35 when the first edition was written, after allowing for two 2 per cent stock dividends since, is now selling at 37¼.

Now let us see what I said about the other *B* group example I discussed in the original edition:

"The Beryllium Corporation is another good example of a group *B* investment. The corporate title of this company has a young-company implication that causes uninformed people to assume that the stock carries with it a greater degree of risk than may actually exist. A low-cost producer, it is the only integrated company making master alloys of beryllium copper and beryllium aluminum and also operating a fabricating plant in which the master alloy is turned into rod, bar, strip, extrusions, etc. and, in the case of tools, into finished products. Sales have increased about six times during the ten-year period ending in 1957 to a total of approximately $16,000,000. A growing percentage of these sales is to electronic, computing machine, and other industries promising rapid growth in the years ahead. With important new uses such as beryllium copper dies just beginning to be of sales importance, it would seem that the good growth rate of the past ten years may be just an indication of what is to come. This would tend to justify the price-earnings ratio of around 20 at which this stock has frequently sold in the past five years.

"Indicating that this growth may continue for many years to come, the Rand Corporation, brilliant research arm of the Air Force owned by the government, has been quoted in the press as predicting an important future in the 1960's for the as yet almost non-existent field of beryllium metal as a structural material. The Rand Corporation among other things, correctly foretold, shortly after the war, the development in titanium.

"More immediate than any eventual market that may develop for beryllium as a structural material, 1958 should see this company bring into volume production another brand-new product. This is beryllium metal for atomic purposes. This product, being made in a completely separate plant from the older master-alloy lines, is under long-term contract to the Atomic Energy Commission. It gives indications of having a big future in the nuclear industry where demand will probably occur from both government and private industry sources. Management is alert. In fact, this company qualifies rather favorably under our fifteen points in regard to all aspects but one, where the deficiency is realized and steps have already been started to correct it."

As in the case of Mallory, the past two years have brought both pluses and minuses to the picture I portrayed at that time. However, the favorable developments seem to have by far outweighed the unfavorable, as should be the case if a company is to prove the right sort of investment. On the unfavorable side, the prospects for beryllium copper dies, mentioned two years before, appear to have lost much of their luster and the long-term growth curve of the entire alloy end of the business may be somewhat less brisk than indicated in that description. Meanwhile, nuclear demand for beryllium metal over the next few years appears to be somewhat less now than it did then. However, possibly far outbalancing this, there are steadily increasing signs that there may be a most dramatic growth in the demand for beryllium metal for many types of airborne purposes. The start of this demand is already here. It is appearing in so many places and for so many different kinds of products that no one is safe in predicting what its limitations may be. This may not prove quite as favorable as might otherwise be judged, for it may make the field so attractive as to bring threats of a major competitive technological breakthrough from some company not now in the field. However, fortunately, the company may have made major strides in strengthening itself in the only one of our fifteen points where it had been weak. This was in its research activities.

How has the stock responded to all this? When the first edition was written it was at 16.16, after allowing for the various stock dividends that have been paid since. Today it is at 26½, a gain of 64 per cent.

A few other companies, with which I am somewhat less familiar but which I believe have management, trade position, growth prospects, and other characteristics which easily qualify them as good examples of this *B* group are Foote Minerals Company, Friden Calculating Machine Co., Inc., and Sprague Electric Company. Each of these companies has proven a highly desirable investment for those who have held the shares for a period of years. Sprague Electric roughly quadrupled in value during the 1947–1957 period. Friden stock was first offered to the public in 1954, but in less than three years it had increased about two and a half times in market value. By 1957 it was selling at better than four times the price at which blocks of stock are believed to have changed hands privately about a year prior to this public offering. These price increases, satisfactory as they might appear to most investors, were relatively minor compared to what has happened to the shares of the Foote Minerals Company. This stock was listed on the New York Stock Exchange early in 1957. Prior to that time the stock was traded over the counter and was first available to the public in 1947. At that time the stock was selling at about $40 per share. Due to stock dividends and split-ups the investor who purchased 100 shares at the time of the original financing in 1947 and held on now has over 2400 shares. The stock recently sold at approximately $50.

C. Finally there are the small companies with staggering possibilities of gain for the successful, but complete or almost complete loss of investment for the unsuccessful. I have already pointed out elsewhere why I believe the amount, if any, of such securities in an investment list should vary according to the circumstances and goals of the particular investor. However, there are two good rules to follow in regard to investments of this type. One has already been mentioned. Never put any funds into them that you cannot afford to lose. The other is that larger investors should never at the time of the original investment put over 5 per cent of available funds into any one such company. As pointed out elsewhere, one of the risks of the small investor is that he may be too small to obtain the spectacular prospects of this type of investment and still get the benefits of proper diversification.

In the original edition, I referred to Ampex as it was in 1953 and Elox in 1956 as examples of the huge-potential but high-risk companies that fall into the *C* classification. How have these companies done since? Elox, which was at 10 when the first edition was completed, is at 7⅝ today. In contrast, Ampex's market performance continues brilliant and demonstrates why once an outstanding management has proven itself and fundamental conditions have not changed, shares should never be sold just because the stock has had a huge rise and may seem temporarily high priced. In the discussion on research in Chapter Three, I mentioned that in the first four years following the offering of this stock to the public in 1953, it had risen 700 per cent. When I finished the original edition, it was at 20.* Today with sales and earnings up dramatically year after year and with 80 per cent of today's sales in products that were not in existence only four years ago, it is at 107½. This is a gain of 437 per cent in just over two years. It is a gain of over 3500 per cent in six years. In other words, $10,000 placed in Ampex in 1953 would have a market value of over $350,000 today in a company with a proven ability to score one technical and business triumph after another.

Other situations with which I am less familiar but which might well fall in this category were Litton Industries, Inc. when its shares were first offered to the public, and Metal Hydrides. However, one characteristic of this type of company should be kept in mind from the standpoint of diversification. They entail so much risk and offer such promising prospects that, in time, one of two things usually happens. Either they fail, or else they grow in trade position, management depth, and competitive strength to a point where they can be classified in the *B* rather than the *C* group.

When this has happened, the shares held in them usually have advanced so spectacularly in market price that, depending on what has happened to the value of an investor's other holdings during the period, they may then represent a considerably greater per cent of the total portfolio than they formerly did. However, *B* stocks are so much safer than *C* stocks that they may be retained in greater volume without sacrificing proper diversification. Therefore, if the company has changed in this

---

*After allowing for the 2½-to-1 stock split that has since occurred.

way, there is seldom reason to sell stock—at least not on the ground that the market rise has resulted in this company representing too great a percentage of total holdings.

This change from a *C* to a *B* company is, for example, exactly what happened during the 1956–1957 period in the case of Ampex. As the company tripled in size and profits rose even faster, and as the market for its magnetic recorders and the components thereof broadened into more and more growth industries, this company grew in intrinsic strength to a point where it could be classified in the *B* group. It no longer carried with it the element of extreme investment risk. When this point had been reached, a considerably larger percentage of total investment might be held in Ampex without violating principles of prudent diversification.

All the above percentages represent merely a minimum or prudent standard of diversification. Going below this limit is a bit like driving an automobile above normal speeds. A driver doing this may get where he wants to go sooner than he otherwise would. However, he should keep in mind that he is driving at a rate requiring extra alertness and vigilance. Forgetting this, he may not only fail to arrive at his destination more quickly—he may never get there at all.

How about the other side of the coin? Is there any reason an investor should not have more diversification than something resembling the minimum amounts mentioned? There is no reason whatsoever, as long as the additional holdings are ones which appear equivalent in attractiveness to this minimum number of holdings in regard to two matters. These additional securities should be equivalent to the other holdings in regard to the degree of growth which appears attainable in relation to the risks involved. They should also be equivalent in regard to the investor's ability to keep in touch with and follow his investment, once he has made it. However, practical investors usually learn their problem is finding enough outstanding investments, rather than choosing among too many. The occasional investor who does find more such unusual companies than he really needs seldom has the time to keep in close enough touch with all additional corporations.

Usually a very long list of securities is not a sign of the brilliant investor, but of one who is unsure of himself. If the investor owns stock in so many companies that he cannot keep in touch with their managements directly or indirectly, he is rather sure to end up in worse shape than if he had owned stock in too few companies. An investor should always realize that some mistakes are going to be made and that he should have sufficient diversification so that an occasional mistake will not prove crippling. However, beyond this point he should take extreme care to own not the most, but the best. In the field of common stocks, a little bit of a great many can never be more than a poor substitute for a few of the outstanding.

2. Don't be afraid of buying on a war scare.

Common stocks are usually of greatest interest to people with imagination. Our imagination is staggered by the utter horror of modern war. The result is that every time the international stresses of our world produce either a war scare or an actual war, common stocks reflect it. This is a psychological phenomenon which makes little sense financially.

Any decent human being becomes appalled at the slaughter and suffering caused by the mass killings of war. In today's atomic age, there is added a deep personal fear for the safety of those closest to us and for ourselves. This worry, fear, and distaste for what lies ahead can often distort any appraisal of purely economic factors. The fears of mass destruction of property, almost confiscatory higher taxes, and government interference with business dominate what thinking we try to do on financial matters. People operating in such a mental climate are inclined to overlook some even more fundamental economic influences.

The results are always the same. Through the entire twentieth century, with a single exception, every time major war has broken out anywhere in the world or whenever American forces have become involved in any fighting whatever, the American stock market has always plunged sharply downward. This one exception was the outbreak of World War II in September 1939. At that time, after an abortive rally on thoughts of fat war contracts to a neutral nation, the market soon was following the typical downward course, a course which some months later resembled panic as news of German victories began piling up. Nevertheless, at the conclusion of all actual fighting—regardless of whether it was World War I, World War II, or Korea—most stocks were selling at levels vastly higher than prevailed before there was any thought of war at all. Furthermore, at least ten times in the last twenty-two years, news has come of other international crises which gave threat of major war. In every instance, stocks dipped sharply on the fear of war and rebounded sharply as the war scare subsided.

What do investors overlook that causes them to dump stocks both on the fear of war and on the arrival of war itself, even though by the end of the war stocks have always gone much higher than lower? They forget that stock prices are quotations expressed in money. Modern war always causes governments to spend far more than they can possibly collect from their taxpayers while the war is being waged. This causes a vast increase in the amount of money, so that each individual unit of money, such as a dollar, becomes worth less than it was before. It takes lots more dollars to buy the same number of shares of stock. This, of course, is the classic form of inflation.

In other words, war is always bearish on money. To sell stock at the threatened or actual outbreak of hostilities so as to get into cash is extreme financial lunacy. Actually just the opposite should be done. If an investor has about decided to buy a particular common stock and the arrival of a full-blown war scare starts knocking down the price, he should ignore the scare psychology of the moment and definitely begin buying. This is the time when having surplus cash for investment becomes least, not most, desirable. However, here a problem presents itself. How fast should he buy? How far down will the stock go? As long as the downward influence is a war scare and not war, there is no way of knowing. If actual hostilities break out, the price would undoubtedly go still lower, perhaps a lot lower. Therefore, the thing to do is to buy but buy slowly and at a scale-down on just a threat of war. If war occurs, then increase the tempo of buying significantly. Just be sure to buy into companies either with products or services the demand for which will continue in wartime, or which can convert their facilities to wartime operations. The great majority of companies can so qualify under today's conditions of total war and manufacturing flexibility.

Do stocks actually become more valuable in war time, or is it just money which declines in value? That depends on circumstances. By the grace of God, our country has never been defeated in any war in which it has engaged. In war, particularly modern war, the money of the defeated side is likely to become completely or almost worthless, and common stocks would lose most of their value. Certainly, if the United States were to be defeated by Communist Russia, both our money and our stocks would become valueless. It would then make little difference what investors might have done.

On the other hand, if a war is won or stalemated, what happens to the real value of stocks will vary with the individual war and the individual stock. In World War I, when the enormous prewar savings of England and France were pouring into this country, most stocks probably increased their real worth even more than might have been the case if the same years had been a period of peace. This, however, was a one-time condition that will not be repeated. Expressed in constant dollars—that is, in real value—American stocks in both World War II and the Korean period undoubtedly did fare less well than if the same period had been one of peace. Aside from the crushing taxes, there was too great a diversion of effort from the more profitable peace-time lines to abnormally narrow-margin defense work. If the magnificent research effort spent on these narrow-margin defense projects could have been channelled to normal peace-time lines, stockholders' profits would have been far greater—assuming, of course, that there would still have been a free America in which any profits could have been enjoyed at all. The reason for buying stocks on war or fear of war is not that war, in itself, is ever again likely to be profitable to American stockholders. It is just that money becomes even less desirable, so that stock prices, which are expressed in units of money, always go up.

3.   Don't forget your Gilbert and Sullivan.

Gilbert and Sullivan are hardly considered authorities on the stock market. Nevertheless, we might keep in mind their "flowers that bloom in the spring, tra-la" which, they tell us, have "nothing to do with the case." There are certain superficial financial statistics which are frequently given an undeserved degree of attention by many investors. Possibly it is an exaggeration to say that they completely parallel Gilbert and Sullivan's flowers that bloom in the spring. Instead of saying they have nothing to do with the case, we might say they have very little to do with it.

Foremost among such statistics are the price ranges at which a stock has sold in former years. For some reason, the first thing many investors want to see when they are considering buying a particular stock is a table giving the highest and lowest price at which that stock has sold in each of the past five or ten years. They go through a sort of mental mumbo-jumbo, and come up with a nice round figure which is the price they are willing to pay for the particular stock.

Is this illogical? Is it financially dangerous? The answer to both questions is emphatically yes. It is dangerous because it puts the emphasis on what does not particularly matter, and diverts attention from what does matter. This frequently causes investors to pass up a situation in which they would make big profits in order to go into one where the profits will be much smaller. To understand this we must see why the mental process is so illogical.

What makes the price at which a stock sells? It is the composite estimate *at that moment* of what all those interested think the corrective value of such shares may be. It is the composite appraisal of the outlook for this company by all potential buyers and sellers, weighted by the number of shares each buyer or seller is disposed to bid for or offer, in relation to a similar appraisal, at the same moment, of the outlook for other companies with their individual prospects. Occasionally, something like forced liquidation will produce a moderate deviation from this figure. This happens when a large holder presses stock on the market for reasons—such as liquidating an estate or paying off a loan—which may not be directly related to the seller's view of the real value of the shares. However, such pressures usually cause only moderate variation from the composite appraisal of the prevailing price of the shares, since bargain hunters normally step in to take advantage of the situation, which thereby adjusts itself.

The point which is of real significance is that the price is based on the *current* appraisal of the situation. As changes in the affairs of the company become known, these appraisals become correspondingly more or less favorable. In relation to other stocks, these particular shares then move up or down. If the factors appraised were judged correctly, the stock becomes permanently more or less valuable in relation to other stocks. The shares then stay up or down. If more of these same factors continue to develop, they in turn are recognized by the financial community. The stock then goes and stays either further up or down, as the case may be.

Therefore, the price at which the stock sold four years ago may have little or no real relationship to the price at which it sells today. The company may have developed a host of able new executives, a series of new and highly profitable products, or any number of similar desirable attributes that make the stock intrinsically worth four times as much in relation to the price of other stocks as it was worth four years ago. The company might have fallen into the hands of an inefficient management and slipped so badly in relation to competition that the only way recovery could occur would be through the raising of much new capital. This might force such a dilution of the shares that the stock today could not possibly be worth more than a quarter of the price of four years ago.

Against this background, it can be seen why investors so frequently pass up stocks which would have brought them huge future gains, for ones where the gain is very much smaller. By giving heavy emphasis to the "stock that hasn't gone up yet" they are unconsciously subscribing to the delusion that all stocks go up about the same amount and that the one that has already risen a lot will not climb further, while the one that has not yet gone up has something "due" it. Nothing could be further from the truth. The fact that a stock has or has not risen in the last several years is of no significance whatsoever in determining whether it should be bought now. What does matter is whether enough improvement has taken place or is likely to take place in the future to justify importantly higher prices than those now prevailing.

Similarly, many investors will give heavy weight to the per-share earnings of the past five years in trying to decide whether a stock should be bought. To look at the per-share earnings by themselves and give the earnings of four or five years ago any significance is like trying to get useful work from an engine which is unconnected to any device to which that engine's power is supposed to be applied. Just knowing, by itself, that four or five years ago a company's per-share earnings were either four times or a quarter of this year's earnings has almost no significance in indicating whether a particular stock should be bought or sold. Again, what counts is knowledge of background conditions. An understanding of what probably will happen over the next several years is of overriding importance.

The investor is constantly being fed a diet of reports and so-called analyses largely centered around these price figures for the past five years. He should keep in mind that it is the next five years' earnings, not those of the past five years, that now matter to him. One reason he is fed such a diet of back statistics is that if this type of material is put in a report it is not hard to be sure it is correct. If more important matters are gone into, subsequent events may make the report look quite silly. Therefore, there is a strong temptation to fill up as much space as possible with indisputable facts, whether or not the facts are significant. However, many people in the financial community place emphasis on this type of prior years' statistics for a different set of reasons. They seem to be unable to grasp how great can be the change in just a few years' time in the real value of certain types of modern corporations. Therefore they emphasize these past earnings records in a sincere belief that detailed accounting descriptions of what happened last year will give a true picture of what will happen next year. This may be true for certain classes of regulated companies such as public utilities. For the type of enterprise which I believe should interest an investor desiring the best results for his money, it can be completely false.

A striking example of this centers around events with which I had the good fortune to be quite familiar. In the summer of 1956, an opportunity arose to buy a fair-sized block of shares in Texas Instruments, Inc. from its principal officers who were also its largest stockholders. Careful study of this company revealed that it rated not just well but magnificently in regard to our fifteen-point test. Reason for the officers to sell appeared entirely legitimate; this occurs frequently in true growth companies. Their holdings had already advanced so much that several of them had become millionaires so far as their holdings in their own company were concerned. In contrast, their other assets were relatively negligible. Therefore, particularly since they were selling but a tiny part of the shares they owned, some diversification seemed entirely in order. The ever-present possibility of estate tax liability alone would be sufficient to make such a course prudent from the standpoint of these key executives, regardless of the future of their company.

At any rate, negotiations were completed to acquire these shares at a price of 14. This represented twenty times the anticipated 1956 per-share earnings of about 70 cents. To anyone who gave particular weight to past statistics, this seemed well beyond the bounds of prudence. Per-share earnings had been reported at 39¢, 40¢, 48¢, and 50¢ for the prior four years of 1952 to 1955 respectively—hardly an exciting growth record. Even more depressing to those who subordinate the more important factors of management and current business trends to superficial statistical comparisons, the company, through a corporate acquisition, had obtained the benefits of some loss carry-forward, which had made possible subnormal income tax charges during much of this period. This made any price calculated on the basis of past statistics seem even higher. Finally, even if 1956 earnings were included in an evaluation, a superficial study of this situation might still have produced grave forebodings. True, the company was currently doing remarkably well in the promising field of transistors. But regardless of the obviously glowing future for the semi-conductor industry as a whole, how long could a company of this size be expected to maintain its strong trade position against the larger and older companies, with much stronger balance sheets, which were sure to make a major competitive effort to participate in the great growth that lay ahead for transistors?

When the usual SEC channels reported this officer selling, a rash of heavy trading broke out in Texas Instruments shares with relatively little change in price. Much of this selling, I suspect, was induced by various brokerage comments that appeared. Most of these furnished the past statistical record and commented on the historically high price, the competition that lay ahead, and the inside selling. One such bulletin went so far as to express complete agreement with the management of Texas Instruments. It reported the officers were selling and stated: "We agree with them and recommend the same course!" Major buyer during this period, I have been told, was a large and well informed institution.

What happened in the next twelve months? Texas Instruments' geophysical and military electronic business, overlooked in the flurry of controversy, continued to grow. The semi-conductor (transistor) division grew even more rapidly. More important than the growth in transistor volume were the great strides taken by this able management in research, in plans for mechanization, and in building up the distribution organization in this key semi-conductor field. As evidence piled up that 1956 results were not a flash in the pan but that this relatively small company would continue as one of the largest and lowest cost producers in what promises to be one of the fastest growing segments of American industry, the financial community began revising upward the price-earnings ratio it would pay for a chance to participate in this well-run enterprise. As the summer of 1957 came around and the management publicly estimated that year's per-share earnings at around $1.10, the 54 per cent growth in earnings had produced in just twelve months an approximate 100 per cent increase in market value.

In the original edition I went on to say:

"I suspect that if the headquarters of the principal divisions of this company were not located in Dallas and Houston, but were situated along the northern half of the Atlantic seaboard or in the Los Angeles metropolitan area—where more financial analysts and other managers of important funds could more easily learn about the company—this price-earnings ratio might have gone even higher during this period. If, as appears probable, Texas Instruments' sales and earnings continue their sharp upward trend for some years to come, it will be interesting to see whether this continued growth, of itself, does not in time provide some further upward change in the price-earnings ratio. If this happens, the stock would again go up at an even faster rate than the earnings are advancing, the combination which always produces the sharpest increases in share prices."

Has this optimistic forecast been confirmed? A look at the record may jolt those who still insist that it is possible to appraise an investment by a superficial analysis of past earnings and little more. Profits rose from $1.11 per share in 1957 to $1.84 in 1958 and give promise of topping $3.50 in 1959. Since the first edition of this book was completed, the company attained honors that were bound to rivet the attention of the financial community upon it. In 1958, in the face of competition from some of the generally acclaimed giants of the electronics and electrical equipment industry, International Business Machines Corporation, overwhelmingly the largest electronic calculating machine manufacturer in the world, selected Texas Instruments to be its associate for joint research effort in the application of semi-conductors to this type of equipment. Again, in 1959 Texas Instruments announced a technological breakthrough whereby it was possible to use semi-conductor material of approximately the same size as existing transistors, not alone for a transistor but for a complete electronic circuit! What this may bring about in the way of miniaturization almost staggers the imagination. As the company has grown, its unusually able product research and development groups have increased proportionately. Today few informed people have much doubt that the company's long series of technical and business "firsts" will continue in the years ahead.

How has the market price of these shares responded to all this? Has the price-earnings ratio continued to advance as, twenty-two months ago, I indicated appeared probable? The record would appear to be in the affirmative. Per-share earnings have a little more than tripled since 1957. The stock is up over five times from the price of 26½ at which it was selling when the first edition was completed. The current price, incidentally, represents a gain of better than 1000 per cent from the price of 14, which was mentioned in the original edition as the price at which a fair-sized block of this stock had been bought less than three and one-half years before. In spite of this steep rise it will be interesting to see whether further gains in sales and earnings in the years ahead do not produce still more worthwhile appreciation.

This brings up another line of reasoning which causes some investors to pay undue attention to these unrelated statistics on past price ranges and per-share earnings. This is the belief that whatever has happened for a number of years is bound to continue indefinitely. In other words, some investors will find a stock the per-share earnings and market price of which have risen in each of the past five or ten years. They will conclude that this trend is almost certain to continue indefinitely. I will agree that this might happen. But in view of the uncertainty in timing the results of research and of the costliness of bringing out the new products that make this type of growth possible, it is quite common for even the most outstanding growth companies to have occasional one- to three-year dips in their rate of earnings. Such dips can produce sharp declines in their shares. Therefore, to give emphasis to this kind of past earning record, rather than to the background conditions that can control the future earning curve, may prove very costly.

Does all this mean that past earnings and price ranges should be completely ignored in deciding whether to buy a stock? No. It is only when given an importance they do not deserve that they become dangerous. They are helpful as long as it is realized they are only auxiliary tools to be used for specialized purposes and not major factors in deciding the attractiveness of a common stock. Thus, for example, a study of per-share earnings for various prior years will throw considerable light on how cyclical a stock may be, that is, on how much the company's profits will be affected by the varying stages of the business cycle. More important, comparing past per-share earnings with price ranges will furnish the price-earnings ratio at which the stock sold in the past. This serves as a base from which to start measuring what the price-earnings ratio may be in the future. Here again, however, it must be kept in mind that it is the future and not the past which governs. Perhaps the shares for years have steadily sold at only eight times earnings. Now, however, changes in management, establishment of an outstanding research department, etc. are putting the company into the class that is currently selling around fifteen times earnings instead of eight. Then anyone estimating future earnings and figuring the anticipated value of the shares at only eight instead of fifteen times earnings might again be leaning too heavily on past statistics.

I headed this subdivision of my comments "Don't forget your Gilbert and Sullivan." Perhaps I should have headed it "Don't be influenced by what doesn't matter." Statistics of former year earnings and particularly of per-share price ranges of these former years quite frequently "have nothing to do with the case."

4.   Don't fail to consider time as well as price in buying a true growth stock.

Let us consider an investment situation that occurs frequently. A company qualifies magnificently as to the standards set up under our fifteen points. Furthermore, very important gains in earning power are going to appear about a year from now, due to factors about which the financial community is, as yet, completely unaware. Even more important, there are strong indications that these new sources of earnings are going to grow importantly for at least several years after that.

Under normal circumstances this stock would obviously be a buy. However, there is a factor that gives us pause. Success of other ventures in prior years has given this stock so much glamour in the financial world that if it were not for these new and generally unknown influences, the stock might be considered to be reasonably priced around 20 and out of all reason at its present price of 32. Assuming that five years from now these new influences could easily cause it to be fully worth 75, should we, right now, pay 32—or 60 per cent more than we believe the stock is worth? There is always the chance that these new developments might not turn out to be as good as we think. There is also the possibility that this stock might sink back to what we consider its real value of 20.

Confronted with this situation, many conservative investors would watch quotations closely. If the stock got near 20 they would buy it eagerly. Otherwise they would leave the shares alone. This happens often enough to be worthy of somewhat closer analysis.

Is there anything sacred about our figure of 20? No, because it admittedly does not take into consideration an important element of future value—the factors we know and most others don't know which we believe will in a few years justify a price of 75. What is really important here is to find a way that we can buy the stock at a price close to the low point at which it will sell from here on in. Our concern is that if we buy at 32, the stock may subsequently go somewhere around 20. This would not alone cause us a temporary loss. More significant, it would mean that if the stock subsequently went to 75, we would have for our money only about 60 per cent of the shares that we could have gotten if we had waited and bought at 20. Assuming that in twenty years still other new ventures would have given these shares a value not of 75 but of 200, this factor of the total number of shares we could have obtained for our money would prove extremely important.

Fortunately, in a situation of this sort there is another guide-post which may be relied on, even if some of my friends in the insurance and banking worlds seem to regard it as about as safe as trying to walk over water. This is to buy the shares not at a certain price, but at a certain date. From a study of other successful ventures carried through in the past by this same company, we can learn that these ventures were reflected in the stock's price at a particular point in their development. Perhaps it averaged about one month before these ventures reached the pilot-plant stage. Assuming that our company's shares are still selling around 32, why not plan to buy these shares five months from today, which will be just one month before the pilot plant goes on stream? Of course, the shares can still go down after that. However, even if we had bought these shares at 20, there would have been no positive guarantee against a further drop. If we have a fair chance of buying at about as low a price as possible, aren't we accomplishing our objective, even if we feel that on the basis of the publicly known factors the stock should be lower? Under these circumstances, isn't it safer to decide to buy at a certain date rather than a certain price?

Fundamentally, this approach does not ignore the concept of value at all. It only appears to ignore it. Except for the probability that there would be a far greater increase in value coming in the future, it would be just as illogical as some of my financial friends claim it to be to decide to buy on a specific future date rather than at a specific price. However, when the indications are strong that such an increase is coming, deciding the time you will buy rather than the price at which you will buy may bring you a stock about to have extreme further growth at or near the lowest price at which that stock will sell from that time on. After all, this is exactly what you should be trying to do when you make any stock purchase.

5.   Don't follow the crowd.

There is an important investment concept which is frequently difficult to understand without considerable financial experience. This is because its explanation does not lend itself easily to precise wording. It does not lend itself at all to reduction to mathematical formulae.

Time and again throughout this book I have touched upon different influences that have resulted in a common stock going up or down in price. A change in net income, a change in a company's management, appearance of a new invention or a new discovery, a change in interest rates or tax laws—these are but a few random examples of conditions that will bring about a rise or fall in the quotations for a particular common stock. All these influences have one thing in common. They are real occurrences in the world about us. They are actions which have happened or are about to happen. Now we come to a very different type of price influence. This is a change which is purely psychological. Nothing has changed in the outside or economic world at all. The great majority of the financial community merely look upon the same circumstances from a different viewpoint than before. As a result of this changed way of appraising the same set of basic facts, they make a changed appraisal of the price or the price-earnings ratio they will pay for the same shares.

There are fads and styles in the stock market just as there are in women's clothes. These can, for as much as several years at a time, produce distortions in the relationship of existing prices to real values almost as great as those faced by the merchant who can hardly give away a rack full of the highest quality knee-length dresses in a year when fashion decrees that they be worn to the ankle. Let me give a specific example: In 1948 I was chatting with a gentleman whom I believe to be an able investment man. He has served as president of the New York Society of

Security Analysts, a position which is usually awarded only to the more able in the financial community. At any rate, I had just arrived in New York from a visit to the headquarters of the Dow Chemical Company at Midland, Michigan. I mentioned that earnings for the fiscal year just closing would be at new high levels and that I thought the stock was a real buy. He replied that he felt it was of historic and perhaps statistical interest that a company such as Dow could ever earn this much per share. He felt, however, that these earnings did not make the stock attractive, since it was obvious that the company was enjoying a temporary postwar boom that could not last. He further explained that he felt it was impossible to judge the real value of stocks of this sort until there had occurred the same type of postwar depression that within a few years followed the Civil War and World War I. His reasoning, unfortunately, completely ignored all the potential further increase in value to this stock promised by the many new and interesting products the company was then developing.

That in no future year did Dow's earnings fall anywhere near as low as this supposedly abnormal peak is not what should concern us here. Neither is the fact that from this supposedly high plateau at which it was then selling, the stock has since climbed many hundreds per cent. Our interest should be in why this normally able investment man would take this set of facts and derive from it a quite different conclusion as to the intrinsic value of the stock than he would have derived from the same facts in some other year.

The answer is that for these three years, from 1947 to 1949, almost the whole financial community was indulging in a mass delusion. With all the ease of hindsight we can now sit back and see that what appeared so frightening then was almost as little related to reality as the terror that gripped most of Christopher Columbus' crew in 1492. Night after night most of the common seamen on the Santa Maria were unable to sleep because of a paralyzing fear that at any moment their ship would fall off the ends of the earth and be lost forever. In 1948, the investment community gave little value to the earnings of any common stock because of the widespread conviction that nothing could prevent the near future bringing the same type of bitter depression and major stock market crash that happened about the same number of years after each of the two preceding major wars. In 1949, a slight depression did occur. When its modest nature was appraised and the financial community found that the subsequent trend was up, not down, a tremendous psychological change occurred in the way common stocks were regarded. Many common stocks more than doubled in price in the following few years, due to nothing more than this psychological change. Those common stocks which also had the benefit of more tangible outside occurrences improving their fundamental worth did a great deal better than just doubling.

These great shifts in the way the financial community appraises the same set of facts at different times are by no means confined to stocks as a whole. Particular industries and individual companies within those industries constantly change in financial favor, due as often to altered ways of looking at the same facts as to actual background occurrences themselves.

For example, in certain periods the armament industry has been considered unattractive by the investment community. One of its most outstanding characteristics has been considered to be domination by a single customer, the government. This customer in some years goes in for heavy military procurement, and in others cuts buying way down. Therefore the industry never knows from one year to the next when it may be subject to major contract cancellations and drying up of business.

To this must be added the abnormally low profit margin that customarily prevails in government work, and the tendency of the renegotiation laws to take most of what profit is made, but never correspondingly to allow for a mistake in calculations that causes a loss. Furthermore, the constant necessity to keep bidding on new models in a field where engineering changes come continuously means that risk and turmoil are the order of the day. It is impossible, no matter how good your engineering, to standardize anything that gives your company a long-term advantage over the aggressive competition. Finally, there is always the "danger" that peace might break out with an accompanying decline in business. When this view prevails, as it has many times in the past twenty years, the defense shares sell at a quite low price in relation to their earnings.

However, the financial community has at times in the recent past derived other conclusions from the same set of facts. The world situation is such that the need of heavy expenditures for airborne defense equipment will be with us for years. While the total value may vary from year to year, the pace of engineering change is causing more and more expensive equipment to be needed, so that the long-range trend will be upward. This means that the happy investor in these securities will be in one of the few industries which will in no sense feel the next business depression, which sooner or later will be felt by most other industries. While the profit margin is limited by law, so much business is available to the well-run company that this proves no ceiling upon total net profits. When this view prevails, a quite different appraisal is being given to exactly the same background facts. These stocks then sell on a quite different basis.

Examples could be given for industry after industry which in the past twenty years has been looked upon first one way, then another, by the financial community, with a resultant change in quoted values. In 1950, pharmaceutical stocks were generally regarded as having about the same set of desirable characteristics usually credited to industrial chemical companies. Endless growth due to the wonders of research and a steady rise in the standard of living seemed to warrant the best of these shares selling at the same ratio to earnings as the best of the chemicals. Then a single manufacturer got into trouble on a heretofore glamorous item. The realization swept the financial community that this was a field in which dominance today is no assurance of being even one of the top companies tomorrow. A reappraisal of the entire industry took place. Completely different price-earnings ratios prevailed, due, in all cases but one, not to a different set of facts but a different appraisal of the same facts.

In 1958, just the reverse took place. In the business slump of that year, one of the few industries that enjoyed increased rather than decreased demand for its products was the drug manufacturing industry. Profits of most companies in this group rose to new highs. At the same time earnings of the chemical producers fell rather sharply—largely because of excess capacity from major expansion moves that had just been completed. The volatile financial community again started sharply upgrading the price-earnings ratio of drug shares. Meanwhile sentiment started to grow that the chemical stocks were not as attractive as had previously been supposed. All this represented only changed financial appraisals. Nothing of fundamental or intrinsic consideration had happened.

A year later, some of this new sentiment had already been reversed.

As the better chemical companies proved among the first to recover lost earning power and as their growth trend caused profits soon to go to new all-time high levels, they rather quickly regained their temporarily lost prestige. With the long-range significance of an ever-growing number of important new drugs tending further to bolster the status of the pharmaceutical stocks as against governmental attacks on pricing and patent policies of this industry working in the opposite direction, it will be interesting to observe over the next several years whether the recently regained standing of the pharmaceutical stocks grows still further or starts to shrink.

In the original edition I went on to give one (then) current example of this same sort of changed financial appraisal, by saying:

"One more example is a change in outlook that is taking place right now. For years the shares of the machine tool manufacturers have sold at a very low ratio to earnings. It was almost unanimously felt that machine tools were the epitome of a feast or famine industry. No matter how good such earnings were, they did not mean much because they were just the product of a prevailing boom and could not last. Recently, however, a new school, while by no means predominating the thinking on this subject, has been gaining converts. This school believes that since World War II a fundamental change has taken place affecting these companies. All industry has been swinging from short- to long-range planning of capital expenditures. As a result, the cause of extreme fluctuation for the machine tool companies has disappeared. High and rising wage rates will prevent for many years, if not forever, a return to the feast or famine nature of this business. The steady pace of engineering advance has increased and will further increase the pace of obsolescence of this industry's products. Therefore, in place of the largely cyclical prewar trends, the growth trend of the recent past will continue further into the future. Automation may cause this growth trend to be spectacular.

"Under the influence of those who think this way, the better machine tool stocks are now appraised on a somewhat more favorable basis in relation to the market as a whole than they were only a few years ago. They still sell at a rather low ratio to earnings because the influence of the feast or famine idea is still strong, even if it is not as strong as it used to be. If the financial community comes more and more to accept this non-cyclical and growth outlook for machine tool stocks, their price-earnings ratio will improve more and more. They will then do much better than the market. If the old feast or famine concept regains its former hold, these shares will sell at a lower ratio to earnings than prevails today.

"This current machine tool example brings into clear relief what the common stock investor must do if he is to purchase shares to his greatest advantage. He must examine factually and analytically the prevailing financial sentiment about both the industry and the specific company of which he is considering buying shares. If he can find an industry or a company where the prevailing style or mode of financial thinking is considerably less favorable than the actual facts warrant, he may reap himself an extra harvest by not following the crowd. He should be extra careful when buying into companies and industries that are the current darlings of the financial community, to be sure that these purchases are actually warranted—as at times they well may be—and that he is not paying a fancy price for something which, because of too favorable interpretation of basic facts, is the investment fad of the moment."

Today, of course, we know the answer to the recent ideas of some that the machine tool industry is no longer feast or famine in its nature. The 1957 recession completely exploded the idea that long-range corporate planning now cushions these stocks from their normal extreme vulnerability to downward movements in the business cycle. However, for every problem of this sort which gets solved, the ever-increasing pace of today's technology opens up a dozen others from which the wise investor can profit if he can think independently of the crowd and reach the right answer when the majority of financial opinion is leaning the other way. Are the "exotic" fuel stocks and certain of the smaller electronics intrinsically worth the high appraisals being given them today? Is there such a future for manufacturers of ultrasonic equipment that ordinary price-earnings may be disregarded? Is a company better or worse for the American investor if an abnormally large part of its earning power is derived from foreign operations? These are all matters about which the ideas of the multitude may have swung too far or not far enough right now. If he is thinking of participating in the affected companies, the wise investor must determine which are fundamental trends that will go further, and which are fads of the moment.

These investment fads and misinterpretations of facts may run for several months or several years. In the long run, however, realities not only terminate them, but frequently, for a time, cause the affected stocks to go too far in the opposite direction. The ability to see through some majority opinions to find what facts are really there is a trait that can bring rich rewards in the field of common stocks. It is not easy to develop, however, for the composite opinion of those with whom we associate is a powerful influence upon the minds of all of us. There is one factor which all of us can recognize, however, and which can help powerfully in not just following the crowd. This is realization that the financial community is usually slow to recognize a fundamentally changed condition, unless a big name or a colorful single event is publicly associated with that change. The ABC Company's shares have been selling at a very low price, in spite of the attractiveness of its industry, because it has been badly managed. If a widely known man is put in as the new president, the shares will usually not only respond at once, but will probably over-respond. This is because the time it takes to bring about basic improvement will probably be overlooked in the first enthusiasm. However, if the change to a superb management comes from the brilliance of heretofore little-known executives, months or years may go by during which the company will still have poor financial repute and sell at a low ratio to earnings. Recognizing such situations—prior to the price spurt that will inevitably accompany the financial community's correction of its appraisal—is one of the first and simplest ways in which the fledgling investor can practice thinking for himself rather than following the crowd.

10

HOW I GO ABOUT
FINDING A GROWTH STOCK

A fter the publication of the original edition of *Common Stocks and Uncommon Profits*, I began receiving an amazing, to me, number of letters from readers all over the country. One of the most common requests made was for more detailed data about just what an investor (or his financial advisor) should do to find investments that will lead to spectacular gains in market price. Since there is so much interest in this matter, it may be beneficial to include some comments on this subject here.

Doing these things takes a great deal of time, as well as skill and alertness. The small investor may feel a disproportionate amount of work is involved for the sums he has at his disposal. It would be nice, not only for him but also for the large investor, if there were some easy, quick way of selecting bonanza stocks. I strongly doubt that such a way exists. How much time should be spent on these matters is, of course, something each investor must decide for himself in relation to the sums he has available for investment, his interests, and his capabilities.

I cannot say with any assurance that my method is the only possible system for finding bonanza investments. Nor can I even be completely sure that it is the best method although, obviously, if I thought some other available approach were better I would not be using this one. For some years, however, I have followed the steps I am about to outline in detail; doing this has worked and worked well for me. Particularly in the highly important earlier stages, someone else with greater background knowledge, better contacts, or more ability might make some important variations in these methods and attain further improvement in over-all results.

There are two stages in the following outline, at each of which the quality of the decisions made will have tremendous effect upon the financial results obtained. Everyone will recognize instantly the overwhelming importance of the decision at the second of these two critical points, which is, "Do I now buy this particular stock or do I not?" What may not be as easy to recognize is that right at the start of an organized method for selecting common stocks, decisions must also be made that can have just about as great impact on the chance of uncovering an investment that ten years later will have increased, say, twelve-fold in value rather than one that has not quite doubled.

This is the problem that confronts anyone about to start on a quest for a major growth security: there are literally thousands of stocks in dozens of industries that could conceivably qualify as worthy of the most intensive study. You cannot be sure about many of them until considerable work has been done. However, no one could possibly have the time to investigate more than a tiny percent of the available field. How do you select the one or the very few stocks to the investigation of which you will devote such time as you have to spare?

This is a far more complex problem than it seems. You must make decisions that can easily screen out from investigation situations that a few years later have produced fortunes. You may make decisions that limit your work to rather barren soil, in that as you gather more data the outlook appears more and more clear that you are approaching the answer you are bound to find in the overwhelming majority of all investigations. This is that the company is run of the mill or maybe a little better, but that it just is not the occasional bonanza that leads to spectacular profit. Yet this key decision determines whether, financially speaking, you are prospecting rich ore or poor on the basis of relatively little knowledge of the facts. This is because you must make decisions on what to or what not to spend your time before you have done enough work to have a proper basis for your conclusion. If you have done enough work to have adequate background for your decisions, you will have already spent so much time on each situation that, in effect, you will have made this vital first decision on a snap basis anyway. You just will not have realized that you have done so.

Some years ago I would sincerely but mistakenly have told you that I used what would have sounded like a neat method for solving this problem. As a result of companies which I had already investigated, and particularly as a result of familiarity with the companies in which the funds I manage were concentrated, I had become friendly with a sizable number of quite able business executives and scientists. I could talk to these people about companies other than their own. I believed that ideas and leads furnished by such unusually well-informed contacts would provide a magnificent supply of prospects for investigation that would contain an abnormally large per cent of companies that might prove to have the outstanding characteristics I am constantly seeking.

However, I attempt to use the same analytical and self-critical methods of improving the techniques of my own business that I expect the companies in which I invest to use to improve their operations. Therefore, some years ago I made a study to determine two things. How had I come to select the companies which I had chosen for investigation? With hindsight to help me, were there significant variations in the percentage of worthwhile results (in the way of outstanding investments subsequently acquired) between investigations made as a result of the original "spark plug" idea coming from one type of source and those coming from sources of a completely different nature?

What I found astonished me but is entirely logical on analysis. The business executive-scientist classification which I had believed was my main source of original ideas causing me to investigate one company rather than another, actually had furnished only about one-fifth of the leads that had excited me enough to engage in a further study. Of even greater significance, these leads had not proven an above average source of good investments. This one-fifth of total investigations had led to only about one-sixth of all worthwhile purchases.

In contrast, the first original idea for almost four-fifths of the investigations and almost five-sixths of the ultimate pay-out (as measured by worthwhile purchases) had come from a quite different group. Across the nation I had gradually come to know and respect a small number of men whom I had seen do outstanding work of their own in selecting common stocks for growth. A not necessarily complete list of these able investment men would include one or more living in such widely scattered places as New York, Boston, Philadelphia, Buffalo, Chicago, San Francisco, Los Angeles, and San Diego. In many instances I might not agree at all with the conclusions of any of these men as to a stock they particularly liked, even to the point of feeling it worthy of investigation. In one or two cases, I might even consider the thoroughness of their work as suspect. However, because in each case I knew their financial minds were keen and their records impressive, I would be disposed to listen eagerly to details they might furnish concerning any company within my range of interests that they considered unusually attractive for major appreciation.

Furthermore, since they were trained investment men, I could usually get rather quickly their opinion upon the key matters most important to me in my decision as to whether it might be a good gamble to investigate the company in question. What are these key matters? Essentially they cover how the company would measure up to our already discussed fifteen points, with special emphasis in this preliminary stage on two specific subjects. Is the company in, or being steered toward, lines of business affording opportunities of unusual growth in sales? Are these lines where, as the industry grows, it would be relatively simple for newcomers to start up and displace the leading units? If the nature of the business is such that there is little way of preventing newcomers from entering the field, the investment value of such growth as occurs may prove rather slight.

How about using investment men of fewer accomplishments or less ability as a source of original leads on what to investigate? If I did not feel that better men were available, I doubtless would use them somewhat more than I do. I always try to find the time at least to listen once to any investment man, if only to be on the alert for keen younger men coming up in the business and to be sure I am not overlooking one. However, the competition for time is terrific. As I downgrade either a financial man's investment judgment or his reliability as to facts presented, I find my tendency to spend time investigating the company he presents decreasing even more than proportionally.

How about selecting original leads for investigation from the ideas in printed material? Occasionally I have been influenced by the special reports issued by the most reliable brokerage houses when these reports are not for widespread distribution but solely to a few selected people. However, on the whole, I would feel the typical public printed brokerage bulletin available to everyone is not a fertile source. There is too much danger of inaccuracies in them. More important, most only repeat what is already common knowledge in the financial community. Similarly, I will occasionally get a worthwhile idea from the best of the trade and financial periodicals (which I find quite helpful for completely different purposes); but because I believe they have certain inherent limitations on what they can print about many of the matters of greatest interest to me, I do not find them a rich source of new ideas on the best companies to investigate.

There is another possible source of worthwhile original leads which others with better technical backgrounds or greater ability might be able to employ profitably, although I have not successfully done so. This source is the major consulting research laboratories such as Arthur D. Little, Stanford Research Institute, or Battelle. I have found that personnel of these organizations have great understanding of just the business and technical developments from which worthwhile original investment ideas should come. However, I have found the usefulness of this group largely blocked by their tendency (which is entirely praiseworthy) to be unwilling to discuss most of what they know because it might violate the confidence of the client companies for which they have worked. If someone smarter than I am could find a way, without injury to these client companies, of unlocking the mine of investment information I suspect these organizations possess, he might well have found a means of importantly improving on my methods regarding this particular step in the quest for growth stocks.

So much for step one. On the basis of a few hours' conversation, usually with an outstanding investment man, occasionally with a business executive or scientist, I have made a decision that a particular company might be exciting. I will start my investigation. What do I do next?

There are three things I emphatically do not do. I do not (for reasons that I think will soon become clear) approach anyone in the management at this stage. I do not spend hours and hours going over old annual reports and making minute studies of minor year-by-year changes in the balance sheet. I do not ask every stockbroker I know what he thinks of the stock. I will, however, glance over the balance sheet to determine the general nature of the capitalization and financial position. If there is an SEC prospectus I will read with care those parts covering breakdown of total sales by product lines, competition, degree of officer or other major ownership of common stock (this can also usually be obtained from the proxy statement) and all earning statement figures throwing light on depreciation (and depletion, if any), profit margins, extent of research activity, and abnormal or non-recurring costs in prior years' operations. Now I am ready really to go to work. I will use the "scuttlebutt" method I have already described just as much as I possibly can. Here, rather than as a source of original ideas for investment, is where the people I have come to know in the business executive-scientist group can be of inestimable value. I will try to see (or reach on the telephone) every key customer, supplier, competitor, ex-employee, or scientist in a related field that I know or whom I can approach through mutual friends. However, suppose I still do not know enough people or do not have a friend of a friend who knows enough of the people who can supply me with the required background? What do I do then?

Frankly, if I am not even close to getting much of the information I need, I will give up the investigation and go on to something else. To make big money on investments it is unnecessary to get some answer to every investment that might be considered. What is necessary is to get the right answer a large proportion of the very small number of times actual purchases are made. For this reason, if way too little background is forthcoming and the prospects for a great deal more is bleak, I believe the intelligent thing to do is to put the matter aside and go on to something else.

However, suppose quite a bit of background has become available. You have called on everyone you know or can readily approach, but have spotted one or two people who you believe could do much to complete your picture if they would talk freely to you. I would not just walk in on them off the street. Most people, interested as they may be in the industry in which they are engaged, are not inclined to tell to total strangers what they really think about the strong and weak points of a customer, a competitor, or a supplier. I would find out the commercial bank of the people I want to meet. If in matters of this sort you approach a commercial bank that knows you, tell them frankly whom you want to meet and exactly why, it is surprising how obliging most commercial bankers will be in trying to help you—provided you do not bother them too often. It is possibly even more surprising how helpful most business men will try to be if you are introduced to them by their regular bankers. Of course this help will only be forthcoming if the bankers in question have no doubt whatsoever that the information you are seeking is solely for background purposes in determining whether to make an investment, and that under no circumstance would you ever embarrass anyone by quoting the source of any derogatory information. If you follow these rules, banking help can, at times, help complete the stage of an investigation that otherwise might never be complete enough to be of any value.

It is only after "scuttlebutt" has obtained for you a large part of the data that in our chapter on the fifteen points I indicated can best be obtained from such sources, that you should be ready to take the next step and think about approaching the management. I think it rather important that investors thoroughly understand why this is so.

Good managements, those most suitable for outstanding investment, are nearly all quite frank in answering questions about the company's weak points as fully as about its strong points. However, no matter how punctilious a management may be in this respect, no corporate officer in his own self-interest can be expected, unasked, to volunteer some of the most significant matters for you, the investor, to know. How can a vice president to whom you say, "Is there anything else you think I, as a prospective investor, should know about your company?" give a reply to the effect that the other top members of the management team are doing splendidly but several years of poor work by the vice president for marketing is beginning to cause weakness in sales? Could he possibly volunteer further that this may not be too important, since young Williams, on the marketing staff, has outstanding ability and in another six months he will be in charge and the situation brought back under control? Of course he could not volunteer these things. However, I have found that if he learns you already know of the marketing weakness, his remark may be diplomatically worded, but with the right type of management and if they have confidence in your judgment, you will be furnished with a realistic answer as to whether anything is or is not being done to remedy weaknesses of this type.

In other words, only by having what "scuttlebutt" can give you before you approach management, can you know what you should attempt to learn when you visit a company. Without it you may be unable to determine that most basic of points—the competency of top management itself. In even a medium-sized company, there may be a key management team of as many as five men. You are not apt to meet all of them on your first or second visit. If you do, you will probably meet some for such a short time you will have no basis for determining their relative ability.

Frequently one or two men of the five will be far more able or far less able than the others. Without "scuttlebutt" to guide you, depending on whom you meet you may form far too high or far too low an estimate of the entire management. With "scuttlebutt" you may have formed a fairly accurate idea of who is particularly strong or particularly weak, and are in a better position to ask to meet the specific officers you may want to know better, thereby satisfying yourself as to whether this "scuttlebutt" impression is correct.

It is my opinion that in almost any field nothing is worth doing unless it is worth doing right. When it comes to selecting growth stocks, the rewards for proper action are so huge and the penalty for poor judgment is so great that it is hard to see why anyone would want to select a growth stock on the basis of superficial knowledge. If an investor or financial man wants to go about finding a growth stock properly, I believe one rule he should always follow is this: he should never visit the management of any company he is considering for investment until he has first gathered together at least 50 per cent of all the knowledge he would need to make the investment. If he contacts the management without having done this first, he is in the highly dangerous position of knowing so little of what he should seek that his chance of coming up with the right answer is largely a matter of luck.

There is another reason I believe it so important to get at least half the required knowledge about a company before visiting it. Prominent management and managements in companies in colorful industries get a tremendous number of requests for their time from people in the investment business. Because the price at which their stock sells can have so much significance to them in so many ways, they will usually devote the time of valuable people to such visitors. However, from company after company I have heard the same type of comment. To no one will they be rude, but the amount of time furnished by key men, rather than by those who receive financial visitors but make few executive decisions, depends far more on the company's estimate of the competence of the visitor than it does on the size of the financial interest he represents. More important, the degree of willingness to furnish information—that is, how far the company will go in answering specific questions and discussing vital matters—depends overwhelmingly on this estimate of each visitor. Those who just drop in on a company without real advance preparation, often have two strikes against them almost before the visit starts.

This matter of whom you see (that it be the men who make the real decisions, rather than a sort of financial public relations officer) is so important that it is wise to go to considerable trouble to be introduced to a management by the right people. An important customer or a major stockholding interest known to management can be an excellent source of introduction to pave the way for a first visit. So can the company's investment banking connections. In any event, those really wanting to get optimum results from their first visit should make sure that those introducing them have a high regard for the visitor and pass the reasons for this good opinion on to the management.

Just a few weeks prior to my writing these words an incident occurred which may illustrate how much preparation I feel should be made prior to a first call on management. I was lunching with two representatives of a major investment firm, one which is the investment banker for two of the handful of companies in which the funds I manage are invested. Knowing the small number of situations I go into and the long time I normally hold them, one of these gentlemen asked me the ratio between the new (to me) companies I visited and the ones of these into which I actually bought. I asked him to guess. He estimated I bought into one for every two hundred and fifty visited. The other gentleman ventured that it might be one for every twenty-five. Actually it runs somewhere between one to every two and one to every two and one-half! This is not because one out of every two and one-half companies I look at measures up to what I believe are my rather rigorous standards for purchase. If he had substituted "companies looked at" for "companies visited" perhaps one in forty or fifty might be about right. If he had substituted "companies considered as possibilities for investigation" (whether I actually investigated them or not) then the original estimate of one stock bought for every two hundred and fifty considered would be rather close to the mark. What he had overlooked was that I believe it so impossible to get much benefit from a plant visit until a great deal of pertinent "scuttlebutt" work has been done first, and that I have found that "scuttlebutt" so many times furnishes an accurate forecast of how well a company will measure up to my fifteen points, that usually by the time I am ready to visit the management there will be at least a fair chance that I will want to buy into the company. A great many of the less attractive situations will have been weeded out along the way.

This about sums up how I go about finding growth stocks. Possibly one-fifth of my first investigations start from ideas gleaned from friends in industry and four-fifths from culling what I believe are the more attractive selections of a small number of able investment men. These decisions are frankly a fast snap judgment on which companies I should spend my time investigating and which I should ignore. Then after a brief scrutiny of a few key points in an SEC prospectus, I will seek "scuttlebutt" aggressively, constantly working toward how close to our fifteen-point standard the company comes. I will discard one prospective investment after another along the way. Some because the evidence piles up that they are just run of the mill. Others because I cannot get enough evidence to be reasonably sure one way or the other. Only in the occasional case when I have a great amount of favorable data do I then go to the final step of contacting the management. Then if after meeting with management I find my prior hopes pretty well confirmed and some of my previous fears eased by answers that to me make sense, at last I am ready to feel I may be rewarded for all my efforts.

Because I have heard them so many times, I know the objections a few of you will make to this approach. How can anyone be expected to spend this amount of time finding just one investment? Why are not the answers already neatly worked out for me by the first person in the investment business to whom I ask what I should buy? I would ask those with this reaction to look at the world around them. In what other line of activity could you put $10,000 in one year and ten years later (with only occasional checking in the meantime to be sure management continues of high caliber) be able to have an asset worth from $40,000 to $150,000? This is the kind of reward gained from selecting growth stocks successfully. Is it either logical or reasonable that anyone could do this with an effort no harder than reading a few simply worded brokers' free circulars in the comfort of an armchair one evening a week? Does it make sense that anyone should be able to pick up this type of profit by paying the first investment man he sees a commission of $135, which is the New York Stock Exchange charge for buying 500 shares of stock at $20 per share? So far as I know, no other fields of endeavor offer these huge rewards this easily. Similarly, they cannot be made in the stock market unless you or your investment advisor utilize the same traits that will bring large rewards in any other field of activity. These are great effort combined with ability and enriched by both judgment and vision. If these attributes are employed and something fairly close to the rules laid down in this chapter are used to find companies measuring well on our fifteen-point standard but not yet enjoying as much status in the financial community as such an appraisal would warrant, the record is crystal clear that fortune-producing growth stocks can be found. However, they cannot be found without hard work and they cannot be found every day.

11

SUMMARY AND CONCLUSION

W e are starting the second decade of a half century that may well see the standard of living of the human race advance more than it has in the preceding five thousand years. Great have been the investment risks of the recent past. Even greater have been the financial rewards for the successful. However, in this field of investment, the risks and rewards of the past hundred years may be small beside those of the next fifty.

In these circumstances it may be well to take stock of our situation. We almost certainly have not conquered the business cycle. We may not even have tamed it. Nevertheless, we have added certain new factors that significantly affect the art of investment in common stocks. One of these is the emergence of modern corporate management, with all that this has done to strengthen the investment characteristics of common shares. Another is the economic harnessing of scientific research and developmental engineering.

The emergence of these factors has not changed the basic principles of successful common stock investment. It has made them more important than ever. This book has attempted to show what these basic principles are, what type of stock to buy, when to buy it, and most particularly, never to sell it—as long as the company behind the common stock maintains the characteristics of an unusually successful enterprise.

It is hoped that those sections dealing with the most common mistakes of many otherwise able investors will prove of some interest. It should be remembered, however, that knowing the rules and understanding these common mistakes will do nothing to help those who do not have some degree of patience and self-discipline. One of the ablest investment men I have ever known told me many years ago that in the stock market a good nervous system is even more important than a good head. Perhaps Shakespeare unintentionally summarized the process of successful common stock investment: "There is a tide in the affairs of men which, taken at the flood, leads on to fortune."

Part Two

CONSERVATIVE INVESTORS SLEEP WELL

All of my business life, I have believed that the success of my own business—or any business—depends on following the principles of two I's and an H. These principles are integrity, ingenuity, and hard work. I would like to dedicate this book to my three sons in the belief that Arthur and Ken are following the principles of the two I's and an H in businesses very similar to mine, as is Don in one that is quite different.

INTRODUCTION

W hile these things are hard to measure precisely, indications are
overwhelming that only once before in this century has the morale of the American investor been at anything like the low ebb that
exists as these words are being written. The well-known and much publicized Dow Jones industrial average is an excellent indicator of the day-
to-day change in stock-market levels. However, when a longer period is
under consideration, this average may mask rather than reveal the full
extent of the injuries suffered by many who have held common stocks
in the recent past. One index that purports to show what has happened
to all publicly traded common stocks but that does not weigh each stock
issue by the number of shares outstanding shows the average stock in
mid-1974 down 70 percent from its 1968 peak.

Faced with this kind of loss, large groups of investors have acted in
completely predictable ways. One group has pulled out of stocks completely. Yet many corporations are doing surprisingly well. In an environment where more and more inflation appears inevitable, properly
selected stocks may be far less risky than some other placements that
appear safer. There is an even larger group that is of particular interest:
people who have decided that "from now on we will act more conservatively." The usual rationale here is to confine purchases only to the
largest companies, the names of which at least are known to almost
everyone. There are probably few investors in the United States and
almost none in the Northeast who do not know the names Penn Central

and Consolidated Edison or the nature of these companies' services. By conventional standards, Penn Central some years ago and Consolidated Edison more recently were considered conservative investments. Unfortunately, often there is so much confusion between acting conservatively and acting conventionally that for those truly determined to conserve their assets, this whole subject needs considerable untangling—which should start with not one definition but two:

1. A conservative *investment* is one most likely to conserve (i.e., maintain) purchasing power at a minimum of risk.
2. Conservative *investing* is understanding of what a conservative investment consists and then, in regard to specific investments, following a procedural course of action needed properly to determine whether specific investment vehicles are, in fact, conservative investments.

Consequently, to be a conservative investor, not one but two things are required either of the investor or of those whose recommendations he is following. The qualities desired in a conservative investment must be understood. Then a course of inquiry must be made to see if a particular investment so qualifies. Without both conditions being present the buyer of common stocks may be fortunate or unfortunate, conventional in his approach or unconventional, but he is not being conservative.

It seems to me of overriding importance that confusion on matters such as these be swept aside for all time to come. Not only stockholders themselves but also the American economy as a whole cannot afford ever again to have those who *make a sincere effort to understand the rules* suffer the type of bloodbath recently experienced by this generation of investors—a bloodletting exceeded only by that which another generation experienced in the Great Depression some forty years earlier. America today has unparalleled opportunities for improving the way of life for all its people. It certainly has the technical knowledge and the know-how to do so. However, to do these things in the traditional American way will require some genuine re-education as to the basic fundamentals for a great many investors as well as for many of those in the investment industry itself. Only if many more investors come to feel financially secure because they truly are secure will there be a reopening of the markets for new stock issues that will enable companies legitimately requiring additional equity funds to be in a position to secure them on a basis conducive to going ahead with new projects. If this does not happen, all that is left is to try to go ahead with what needs to be done in the way that, both here and abroad, has always proven so costly, wasteful, and inefficient—by government financing, with management under the dead hand of bureaucratic officialdom.

For these reasons I believe that the investors' problems of today should be met head on and forthrightly. In an attempt to deal with these problems in this book, I have leaned heavily on the counsel of my son, Ken, who contributed the title as well as many other matters, including part of the basic conception of what lies herein. I cannot adequately acknowledge his assistance in this presentation.

This book is divided into four distinct sections. The first deals with the anatomy—if the word may be used—of a conservative stock investment as delineated in definition number one. The second analyzes the part played by the financial community—the mistakes, if you will—that helped produce the current bear market. This critique was not intended merely to throw rocks but to point out that similar errors can be avoided in the future and that certain basic investment principles become clear when the mistakes of the recent past are studied. The third section deals with the course of action that must be taken to qualify as conservative investing as delineated in definition number two. The final section deals with some of the influences rampant in today's world that have caused grave doubts in the minds of many as to whether any common stock is a suitable means for preserving assets—in other words, whether for anything other than as gambling vehicles common stocks should be considered at all. This book will, I hope, throw light on whether the problems that helped produce the recent bear market have created a condition where stock ownership is just a trap for the unwary or whether, as in every prior major bear market in U. S. history, they have created a magnificent opportunity for those with the ability and the self-discipline to think for themselves and to act independently of the popular emotions of the moment.

PHILIP A. FISHER
San Mateo, California

1

THE FIRST DIMENSION
OF A CONSERVATIVE
INVESTMENT

SUPERIORITY IN PRODUCTION,
MARKETING, RESEARCH, AND
FINANCIAL SKILLS

A corporation of the size and type to provide a conservative investment is necessarily a complex organization. To understand what must be present in such an investment we might start by portraying one dimension of the characteristics we must be sure exist. This dimension breaks down into four major subdivisions:

LOW-COST PRODUCTION

To be a truly conservative investment a company—for a majority if not for all of its product lines—must be the lowest-cost producer or about as low a cost producer as any competitor. It must also give promise of continuing to be so in the future. Only in this way will it give its owners a broad enough margin between costs and selling price to create two vital conditions. One is sufficient leeway below the break-even point of most competition. When a bad year hits the industry, prices are unlikely to stay for long under this break-even point. As long as they do, losses for much of the higher-cost competition will be so great that some of these competitors will be forced to cease production. This almost automatically increases the profits of the surviving low-cost companies because they benefit from the increased production that comes to them as they take over demand formerly supplied by the closed plants. The low-cost company will benefit even more when the decreased supply from

154

competitors enables it not only to do more business but also to increase prices as excess supplies stop pressing on the market.

The second condition is that the greater than average profit margin should enable a company to earn enough to generate internally a significant part or perhaps all of the funds required for financing growth. This avoids much or even all of the need for raising additional long-term capital that can (a) result in new shares being issued and diluting the value of already outstanding shares and/or (b) create an additional burden of debt, with fixed interest payments and fixed maturities (which must largely be met from future earnings) which greatly increase the risks of the common-stock owners.

However, it should be realized that, just as the degree to which a company is a low-cost producer increases the safety and conservatism of the investment, so in a boom period in a bullish market does it decrease its speculative appeal. The percentage that profits rise in such times will always be far greater for the high-cost, risky, marginal company. Simple arithmetic will explain why. Let us take an imaginary example of two companies of the same size that, when times were normal, were selling widgets at ten cents apiece. Company A has a profit of four cents per widget and Company B of one cent. Now let us suppose that costs remain the same but a temporary extra demand for widgets pushes up the price to twelve cents, with both companies remaining the same size. The strong company has increased profits from four cents per widget to six cents, a gain of 50 percent, but the high-cost company has made a 300 percent profit gain, or tripled its profits. This is why, short-range, the high-cost company sometimes goes up more in a boom and also why, a few years later, when hard times come and widgets fall back to eight cents, the strong company is still making a reduced but comfortable profit. If the high-cost company doesn't go bankrupt, it is likely to produce another crop of badly hurt investors (or perhaps speculators who thought they were investors) who are sure something is wrong with the system rather than with themselves.

All of the above has been written with manufacturing companies in mind; hence the term *production* has been used. Many companies, of course, are not manufacturers but are in service lines, such as wholesaling, retailing or one of the many subdivisions of the financial world such as banking or insurance. The same principles apply, but the word *operations* is substituted for *production* and a low- or high-cost operator for a low- or high-cost producer.

STRONG MARKETING ORGANIZATION

A strong marketer must be constantly alert to the changing desires of its customers so that the company is supplying what is desired today, not what used to be desired. At the turn of the century, for example, there was something wrong with the marketing efforts of a leading manufacturer of horse-drawn buggies if it persisted in trying to compete by making finer and finer buggies rather than turning to automobiles or going out of business altogether. To bring our example up to date, perhaps well before the Arab oil embargo made every home in America aware that large automobiles were big gas guzzlers, there was something wrong with the segment of the automobile industry that failed to recognize the ever-increasing popularity of small imported compacts as a sign that public demand was swinging toward a product that cost less, was cheaper to operate, and was easier to park than the larger, flashier models that for so many years had been favorites.

But recognizing changes in public taste and then reacting promptly to these changes is not enough. As has been said before, in the business world customers simply do not beat a path to the door of the man with the better mousetrap. In the competitive world of commerce it is vital to make the potential customer aware of the advantages of a product or service. This awareness can be created only by understanding what the potential buyer really wants (sometimes when the customer himself doesn't clearly recognize why these advantages appeal to him) and explaining it to him not in the seller's terms but in *his* terms.

Whether this is best done by advertising, by salesmen making calls, by specialized independent marketing organizations, or by any combination of these depends on the nature of the business. But what is required in every instance is close control and constant managerial measurement of the cost effectiveness of whatever means are used. Lack of outstanding management in these areas can result (a) in losing a significant volume of business that would otherwise be available; (b) in having much higher costs and therefore obtaining smaller profit on what business is obtained; and (c), because of companies' having variations in the profitability of various elements of their product line, in failing to attain the maximum possible profit mix within the line. An efficient producer or operator with weak marketing and selling may be compared to a powerful engine that, because of a loose pulley belt or badly adjusted differential, is producing only a fraction of the results it otherwise would have attained.

OUTSTANDING RESEARCH AND TECHNICAL EFFORT

Not so very long ago it seemed that outstanding technical ability was vital only to a few highly scientifically oriented industries such as electronics, aerospace, pharmaceutical and chemical manufacturing. As these have grown, their ever-widening technologies have so penetrated virtually all lines of manufacturing and nearly all the service industries that today to have outstanding research and technical talent is nearly, if not quite, as important for a shoe manufacturer, a bank, a retailer or an insurance company as it is for what were once considered the exotic scientific industries that maintained large research staffs. Technological efforts are now channeled in two directions: to produce new and better products (in this connection, research scientists may, of course, do somewhat more for a chemical company than for a grocery chain) and to perform services in a better way or at a lower cost than in the past. With regard to the latter objective, outstanding technical talent can be equally valuable for either group. Actually, in some of the service businesses, technological groups are opening up new product lines as well as paving the way for performing old services better. Banks are an example. Low-cost electronic input devices and minicomputers are enabling them to offer accounting and bookkeeping services to customers, thus creating a new product line for these institutions.

In research and technology, there is as much variation between the efficiency of one company and another as there is in marketing. In new product development, the complexity of the task almost guarantees this. Important as it is, the degree of technical competence or ingenuity of one company's research staff as compared to that of another is only one of the factors affecting the benefits that the company derives from its research efforts. Developing new products usually calls for the pooling of the efforts of a number of researchers, each skilled in a different technological specialty. How well these individuals work together (or can be induced by a leader to work together and stimulate each other) is often as important as the individual competence of the people involved. Furthermore, to maximize profits, it is vital not to develop just any product but one for which there will be significant customer demand, one that (nearly always) can be sold by the company's existing marketing organization, and one that can be made at a price that will yield a worthwhile profit. All of this requires efficient liaison between research and both marketing and production. The best corporate research team in the world can become nothing but a liability if it develops only products that cannot be readily sold. For true investment superiority a company must have above-average ability to control all these complex relationships yet at the same time not so overcontrol them as to cause its researchers to lose the drive and the ingenuity that made them outstanding in the first place.

FINANCIAL SKILL

Again and again in this discussion of production, marketing and research, the terms *profit* and *profit margin* have been used. In a large company with a diverse product line, it is not a simple matter to be sure of the cost of each product in relation to the rest, as most costs other than materials and direct labor are spread over a number of such products, maybe over all of them. Companies with above-average financial talent have several significant advantages. Knowing accurately how much they make on each product, they can make their greatest efforts where these will produce maximum gains. Intimate knowledge of the extent of each element of costs, not just in manufacturing but in selling and research as well, spotlights in even minor phases of company activity the places where it is logical to make special efforts to reduce costs, either through technological innovations or by improving people's specific assignments. Most important of all, through skillful budgeting and accounting, the truly outstanding company can create an early-warning system whereby unfavorable influences that threaten the profit plan can be quickly detected. Remedial action can then be taken to avoid the painful surprises that have jolted investors in many companies. Nor do the "goodies" that accrue to investors from superior financial skills stop at this point. They usually lead to a better choice of capital investments that bring the highest return on the company's investment capital. They also can lead to better control of receivables and inventory, a matter of increasing importance in periods of high interest rates.

To summarize: The company that qualifies well in this first dimension of a conservative investment is a very low-cost producer or operator in its field, has outstanding marketing and financial ability and a demonstrated above-average skill on the complex managerial problem of attaining worthwhile results from its research or technological organization. In a world where change is occurring at an ever-increasing pace, it is (1) a company capable of developing a flow of new and profitable products or product lines that will more than balance older lines that may become obsolete by the technological innovations of others; (2) a company able now and in the future to make these lines at costs sufficiently low so as to generate a profit stream that will grow at least as fast as sales and that even in the worst years of general business will not diminish to a point that threatens the safety of an investment in the business; and (3) a company able to sell its newer products and those which it may develop in the future at least as profitably as those with which it is involved today.

This is a one-dimensional picture of a prudent investment—one which, if not spoiled by the view from other dimensions, represents an investment with which the investor is unlikely to become disillusioned. But before going on to examine these other dimensions, there is one additional point that should be fully understood. If the objective is conserving one's funds, if the goal is safety, why have we been talking about growth and the development of new and additional product lines? Why isn't it enough to maintain a business at its existing size and level of profits without running all the risks that occur when new endeavors are started? When we come to a discussion of the influence of inflation on investments, other reasons for the importance of growth will present themselves. But fundamentally it should never be forgotten that, in a world where change is occurring at a faster and faster pace, nothing long remains the same. It is impossible to stand still. A company will either grow or shrink. A strong offense is the best defense. Only by growing better can a company be sure of not growing worse. Companies that have failed to go uphill have invariably gone downhill—and, if that has been true in the past, it will be even more true in the future. This is because, in addition to an ever-increasing pace of technological innovation, changing social customs and buying habits and new demands of government are altering at an ever-increasing pace the rate at which even the stodgiest industries are changing.

2

THE SECOND DIMENSION

THE PEOPLE FACTOR

B riefly summarized, the first dimension of a conservative investment consists of outstanding managerial competence in the basic areas of production, marketing, research, and financial controls. This first dimension describes a business as it is today, being essentially a matter of results. The second dimension deals with what produced these results and, more importantly, will continue to produce them in the future. The force that causes such things to happen, that creates one company in an industry that is an outstanding investment vehicle and another that is average, mediocre, or worse, is essentially *people*.

Edward H. Heller, a pioneer venture capitalist whose comments during his business life greatly influenced some of the ideas expressed in this book, used the term "vivid spirit" to describe the type of individual to whom he was ready to give significant financial backing. He said that behind every unusually successful corporation was this kind of determined entrepreneurial personality with the drive, the original ideas, and the skill to make such a company a truly worthwhile investment.

Within the area of very small companies that grew into considerably larger and quite prosperous ones (the field of his greatest interest and where he scored his most spectacular successes), Ed Heller was undoubtedly right. But as these smaller companies grow larger on the way to becoming suitable for conservative investment, Ed Heller's view might be tempered by that of another brilliant businessman who expressed

161

serious doubts about the wisdom of investing in a company whose president was his close personal friend. This man's reason for lack of enthusiasm: "My friend is one of the most brilliant men I've ever known. He always has to be right. In a small company this may be fine. But as you grow, your men have to be right sometimes, too."

Here is an indication of the heart of the second dimension of a truly conservative investment: a corporate chief executive dedicated to long-range growth who has surrounded himself with and delegated considerable authority to an extremely competent team in charge of the various divisions and functions of the company. These people must be engaged not in an endless internal struggle for power but instead should be working together toward clearly outlined corporate goals. One of these goals, which is absolutely essential if an investment is to be a truly successful one, is that top management take the time to identify and train qualified and motivated juniors to succeed senior management whenever a replacement is necessary. In turn, at each level down through the chain of command, detailed attention should be paid to whether those at this level are doing the same thing for those one level below them.

Does this mean that a company that qualifies for truly conservative investing should promote only from within and should never recruit from the outside except at the lowest levels or for those just starting their careers? A company growing at a very rapid rate may have such need for additional people that there just isn't time to train from within for all positions. Furthermore, even the best-run company will at times need an individual with a highly specialized skill so far removed from the general activities of the company that such a specialty simply cannot be found internally. Someone with expertise in a particular subdivision of the law, insurance, or a scientific discipline well removed from the company's main line of activity would be a case in point. In addition, occasional hiring from the outside has one advantage: It can bring a new viewpoint into corporate councils, an injection of fresh ideas to challenge the accepted way as the best way.

In general, however, the company with real investment merit is the company that usually promotes from within. This is because all companies of the highest investment order (these do not necessarily have to be the biggest and best-known companies) have developed a set of policies and ways of doing things peculiar to their own needs. If these special ways are truly worthwhile, it is always difficult and frequently impossible to retrain those long accustomed to them to different ways of getting things done. The higher up in an organization the newcomer may be, the more costly the indoctrination can be. While I can quote no statistics to prove the point, it is my observation that in better-run companies a surprising number of executives brought in close to the top tend to disappear after a few years.

Of one thing the investor can be certain: A large company's need to bring in a new chief executive from the outside is a damning sign of something basically wrong with the existing management—no matter how good the surface signs may have been as indicated by the most recent earnings statement. It may well be that the new president will do a magnificent job and in time will build a genuine management team around him so that such a jolt to the existing organization will never again become necessary. Consequently, in time such a stock may become one worthy of a wise investor. But such rebuilding can be so long and risky a process that, if an investor finds this sort of thing happening in one of his holdings, he will do well to review all his investment activities to determine whether his past actions have really been proceeding from a sound base.

A worthwhile clue is available to all investors as to whether a management is predominantly one man or a smoothly working team (this clue throws no light, however, on how good that team may be). The annual salaries of top management of all publicly owned companies are made public in the proxy statements. If the salary of the number-one man is very much larger than that of the next two or three, a warning flag is flying. If the compensation scale goes down rather gradually, it isn't.

For optimum results for the investor it is not enough that management personnel work together as a team and be capable of filling vacancies above them. There should also be present the greatest possible number of those "vivid spirits" of Ed Heller's—people with the ingenuity and determination not to leave things just at their present, possibly quite satisfactory, state but to build significant further improvements upon them. Such people are not easy to find. Motorola, Inc. has for some time been conducting an activity that the financial community has paid little or no attention to that indicates it is possible to accomplish dramatically more in this area than is generally considered possible.

In 1967 Motorola management recognized that the rapid rate of growth anticipated in the years ahead would inevitably require steady expansion in the upper layers of management. It was decided to meet the problem head on. In that year Motorola opened its Executive Institute at Oracle, Arizona. It was designed so that, in an atmosphere remote from the daily details of the company's offices and plants, two things would happen: Motorola personnel of apparent unusual promise would be trained in matters beyond the scope of their immediate activities in order to be able to take on more important jobs; top management would be furnished significant further evidence as to the degree of promotability of these same people.

At the time of the Executive Institute's founding, skeptics within the management questioned whether the effort would be worth the cost. This was largely because of their belief that fewer than a hundred people would be found in the whole Motorola organization with sufficient talent to make it worthwhile from the company's standpoint to provide them with this special training. Events have proven these skeptics spectacularly wrong. The Institute handles five to six classes a year, with fourteen in each class. By mid-1974 about 400 Motorola people had gone through the school; and a significant number, including some present vice-presidents, were found to have capabilities vastly greater than anything contemplated at the time they were approved for admission. Furthermore, those involved in this work feel that, from the company's standpoint, results in the more recent classes are even more favorable than in the earlier ones. It now appears that, as total employment at Motorola continues to expand with the company's growth, enough promising Motorola people can be found to maintain this activity indefinitely. All of this shows, from the investor's standpoint, that if enough ingenuity is used, even the companies with well-above-average growth rates can also "grow" the needed unusual people from within so as to maintain competitive superiority without running the high risk of friction and failure that so often occurs when a rapidly growing company must go to the outside for more than a very small part of its outstanding talent.

Everyone has a personality—a combination of character traits that sets him or her apart from every other individual. Similarly, every corporation has its own ways of doing things—some formalized into well-articulated policies, others not—that are at least slightly different from those of other corporations. The more successful the corporation, the more likely it is to be unique in some of its policies. This is particularly true of companies that have been successful for a considerable period of time. In contrast to individuals, whose fundamental character traits change but little once they reach maturity, the ways of companies are influenced not only by outside events but by the reactions to those events of a whole series of different personalities who, as time goes on, follow one another in the top posts within the organization.

However much policies may differ among companies, there are three elements that must always be present if a company's shares are to be worthy of holding for conservative, long-range investment.

1. The company must recognize that the world in which it is operating is changing at an ever-increasing rate.

All corporate thinking and planning must be attuned to challenge what is now being done—to challenge it not occasionally but again and again. Every accepted way of doing things must be examined and re-examined to be as sure as is permitted by human fallibility that this way is really the best way. Some risks must be accepted in substituting new methods to meet changing conditions. No matter how comfortable it may seem to do so, ways of doing things cannot be maintained just because they worked well in the past and are hallowed by tradition. The company that is rigid in its actions and is not constantly challenging itself has only one way to go, and that way is down. In contrast, certain managements of large companies that have deliberately endeavored to structure themselves so as to be able to change have been those producing some of the most striking rewards for their shareholders. An example of this is the Dow Chemical Company, with a record of achievements over the last ten years that is frequently considered to surpass that of any other major chemical company in this country, if not in the entire world. Possibly Dow's most significant departure from past ways was to break its management into five separate managements on geographical lines (Dow USA, Dow Europe, Dow Canada, etc.). It was believed that only in this way could local problems be handled quickly as best suited local conditions and without suffering from the bureaucratic inefficiencies that so often accompany bigness. The net effect of this as told by the president of Dow Europe: "The results that today challenge us are being made by our sister [Dow] companies throughout the world. They, not our direct competitors, are turning in the gains that push us to be first." From the investor's standpoint perhaps the most important feature of this change was not that it was made but that it was made when Dow still had a total sales volume much smaller than many other multinational companies that were operating successfully in the established way. In other words, change and improvement arose from innovative thinking to make a workable system better—not from a forced reaction to a crisis.

This is but one of the many ways this pioneering company has broken with the past to attain its striking competitive record. Another was the unprecedented step for an industrial company of starting from scratch to make a success of a wholly owned bank in Switzerland so as to help finance the needs of its customers in the export market. Here again the management did not hesitate to break with the past in ways that engendered some risk in the early stages but that ended up by enhancing the intrinsic strength of the company.

Many other examples could be cited from the record of this company. However, just one more will be mentioned merely to show the extreme variety of areas such actions may cover. Far earlier than most other companies, Dow not only recognized the need to spend sizable sums to avoid pollution but concluded that, if major results were to be attained, something more was needed than just exhortations from top management. It was necessary to obtain the consistent cooperation of middle-level managers. It was decided that the surest way of doing this was to appeal to the profit motives of those most directly involved. They were encouraged to find profitable methods of converting the polluting materials to salable products. The rest is now business history. With the full power of top management, plant management, and highly skilled chemical engineers behind these projects, Dow has achieved a series of firsts in eliminating pollution that has won them the praise of many environmental groups that are usually quite antibusiness in their viewpoints. Possibly more important, they have avoided hostility in most, although not all, of the communities where their plants are located. They have done this at very little over-all dollar cost and in some cases at an operating profit.

2. There must always be a conscious and continuous effort, based on fact, not propaganda, to have employees at every level, from the most newly hired blue-collar or white-collar worker to the highest levels of management, feel that their company is a good place to work.

This is a world that requires most of us to put in a substantial number of hours each week doing what is asked of us by others in order to receive a paycheck even though we might prefer to spend those hours on our own amusement or recreation. Most people recognize the necessity for this. When a management can instill a belief, not just among a few top people but generally among the employees, that it is doing everything reasonably to be expected to create a good working environment and take care of its employees' interests, the rewards the company receives in greater productivity and lower costs can vastly outweigh the costs of such a policy.

The first step in this policy is seeing (not just talking about it but actually assuring) that every employee is treated with reasonable dignity and consideration. A year or so ago I read in the press that a union official claimed that one of the nation's largest companies was compelling its production-line employees to eat lunch with grease-stained hands because there was not sufficient time, with the number of washroom facilities available, for most of them to be able to wash before lunch. The stock of this company was of no investment interest to me for quite different reasons. Therefore, I have no knowledge of whether the charge was based on fact or was made in the heat of an emotional battle over wage negotiations. However, if true, this condition alone would, in my opinion, make the shares of this company unsuitable for holding by careful investors.

Besides treating employees with dignity and decency, the routes to obtaining genuine employee loyalty are many and varied. Pension and profit-sharing plans can play a significant part. So can good communication to and from all levels of employees. Concerning matters of general interest, letting everyone know not only exactly what is being done but why frequently eliminates friction that might otherwise occur. Actually knowing what people in various levels of the company are thinking, particularly when that view is adverse, can be even more important. A feeling throughout the company that people can express their grievances to superiors without fear of reprisal can be beneficial, although this open-door policy is not always simple to maintain because of the time wasted by cranks and nuts. When grievances occur, decisions on what to do about them should be made quickly. It is the long-smoldering grievance that usually proves the most costly.

A striking example of the benefits that may be attained through creating a unity of purpose with employees is the "people-effectiveness" program of Texas Instruments. The history of this program is an excellent example of how brilliant management perseveres with and perfects policies of this sort even when new outside influences force some redirection of these policies. From the early days of this company, top management held a deep conviction that everyone would gain if a system could be set up whereby all employees participated in managerial-type decisions to improve performance but that, to sustain interest on the part of employees, all participants must genuinely benefit from the results of their contributions. In the 1950s semiconductor production was largely a matter of hand assembly, offering many opportunities for employees to make brilliant individual suggestions for improving performance. Meetings, even formal classes, were held in which production workers were shown how they could as individuals or groups show the way to improving operations. At the same time, through both profit-sharing plans and awards and honors, those participating benefited both financially and by feeling they were part of the picture. Then mechanization of these former manual operations started to appear. As this trend grew, there was somewhat less opportunity for certain types of individual contributions, as in certain ways the machines controlled what would be done. A few foremen within the organization began feeling that there was no longer a place for lower-level contributions to management-type participation. Top management took quite the opposite viewpoint: People-participation would play a greater role than ever before. Now, however, it would be a group or team effort with the workers as a group estimating what could be done and setting their own goals for performance.

Because workers started feeling that they (1) were genuinely participating in decisions, not just being told what to do, and (2) were being rewarded both financially and in honors and recognition, the results have been spectacular. In instance after instance, teams of workers have set for themselves goals quite considerably higher than anything management would have considered suggesting. At times when it appeared that targeted goals might not be met or when inter-team competition was producing rivalry, the workers proposed and voluntarily voted such unheard-of things (for this day and age) as cutting down on coffee breaks or shortening lunch periods to get the work out. The pressure of peer groups on the tardy or lazy worker who threatens the goals the group has set for itself dwarfs any amount of discipline that might be exerted from above through conventional management methods. Nor are these results confined to U.S. workers with their lifelong background in political democracy. They appear to be equally effective and mutually beneficial to people, regardless of the color of their skin and their origins from countries of quite different economic backgrounds. Though the performance-goal plan was first initiated in the United States, equally striking results have appeared not just in Texas Instruments plants in the so-called developed industrial nations such as France and Japan but also in Singapore, with its native Asian employees, and in Curaçao, where those on the payroll are overwhelmingly black. In all countries the morale effects appear striking when worker teams not only report directly to top management levels but also know their reports will be heeded and their accomplishments recognized and acknowledged.

What all this has meant to investors was spelled out when company president Mark Shepherd, Jr., addressed stockholders at the 1974 annual meeting. He stated that a people-effectiveness index had been established consisting of the net sales billed divided by the total payroll. Since semiconductors, the company's largest product line, are one of the very few products in today's inflationary world that consistently decline in unit price and since wages have been rising at the company's plants at rates from 7 percent a year in the United States to 20 percent in Italy and Japan, it would be logical to expect, in spite of improvements in people-effectiveness, this index to decline. Instead it rose from about 2.25 percent in 1969 to 2.5 percent by the end of 1973. Furthermore, with definite plans for additional improvement and with further increases in profit-sharing funds tied into such improvement, it was announced that it was the company's goal to bring the index up to 3.1 percent by 1980—a goal that, if attained, would make the company a dramatically profitable place to work. Over the years Texas Instruments has frequently publicized some rather ambitious long-range goals and to date has rather consistently accomplished them.

From the investment standpoint, there are some extremely important similarities in the three examples of people-oriented programs that were chosen to illustrate aspects of the second dimension of a conservative investment. It is a relatively simple matter to mention and give a general description of Motorola's institute for selecting and training unusual talent to handle the growing needs of the company. It is an equally simple affair to mention that Dow found a means to stimulate people to work together to master environmental problems and to make them profitable for the company, or to state a few facts about the remarkable people-effectiveness program at Texas Instruments. However, if another company decided to start programs like these from scratch, the problems that could arise might be infinitely more complicated than merely persuading a board of directors to approve the necessary appropriation. Programs of this kind are easy to formulate, but their implementation is a quite different matter. Mistakes can be very costly. It is not hard to imagine what might happen if a training school such as Motorola's selected the wrong people for promotion, with the result that the best junior talent quit the company in disgust. Similarly, suppose a company tried to follow, in general, a people-effectiveness plan but either failed to create an atmosphere where workers genuinely felt themselves involved or failed to compensate their employees adequately, with the result that they became disillusioned. The misapplication of such a program could literally wreck a company. Meanwhile, companies that do perfect advantageous people-oriented policies and techniques usually find more and more ways to benefit from them. For these companies, such policies and techniques— these special ways of approaching problems and of solving them—are in a sense *proprietary*. For this reason they are of great importance to long-range investors.

3. **Management must be willing to submit itself to the disciplines required for sound growth.**

It has already been pointed out that in this rapidly changing world companies cannot stand still. They must either get better or worse, improve or go downhill. The true investment objective of growth is not just to make gains but to avoid loss. There are very few companies whose managements will not make claims to being growth companies. However, a management that talks about being growth-oriented is not necessarily actually so oriented. Many companies seem to have an irresistible urge to show the greatest possible profits at the end of each accounting period—to bring every possible cent down to the bottom line. This a true growth-oriented company can never do. Its focus must be on earning sufficient current profits to finance the costs of expanding the business. When adjustment for earning the required additional financial strength has been made, the company worthy of farsighted investment will give priority to curtailing maximum immediate profits when there are genuine worthwhile opportunities for developing new products or processes or for starting new product lines or for any one of the hundred and one more mundane actions whereby a dollar spent today may mean many dollars earned in the future. Such actions can vary all the way from hiring and training new personnel that will be needed as the business grows to forgoing the greatest possible profit on a customer's order to build up his permanent loyalty by rushing something to him when he needs it badly. For the conservative investor, the test of all such actions is whether management is truly building up the long-range profits of the business rather than just seeming to. No matter how well known, the company with a policy that only gives lip service to these disciplines is not likely to prove a happy vehicle for investment funds. Neither is one that tries to follow these disciplines but falls down in executing them, as, for example, a company that makes large research expenditures but so mishandles its efforts as to gain little from them.

3

THE THIRD DIMENSION

INVESTMENT CHARACTERISTICS OF SOME BUSINESSES

The first dimension of a conservative stock investment is the degree of excellence in the company's activities that are most important to present and future profitability. The second dimension is the quality of the people controlling these activities and the policies they create. The third dimension deals with something quite different: the degree to which there does or does not exist *within the nature of the business itself* certain inherent characteristics that make possible an above-average profitability for as long as can be foreseen into the future.

Before examining these characteristics it may be well to point out why above-average profitability is so important to the investor, not only as a source of further gain but as a protection for what he already has. The vital role of growth in this connection has already been discussed. Growth costs money in many ways. Part of what otherwise would be the profit stream has to be diverted to experimenting, inventing, test-marketing, new-product marketing, and all the other operating costs of expansion, including the complete loss of the inevitable percentage of such expansion attempts that are bound to fail. Even more costly may be the additions to factories or stores or equipment that must be made. Meanwhile, as the business grows, more inventory will inevitably be needed to fill the pipelines. Finally, except for the very few businesses that sell only for cash, there will be a corresponding drain on corporate resources to take care of the growing volume of receivables. To accomplish all these things, profitability is vital.

In inflationary periods the matter of profitability becomes even more important. Usually when prices and, therefore, costs are rising on a broad front, a business can, in time, pass these costs along through higher prices of its own. However, this often cannot be done immediately. During the interim, obviously a much smaller bite is taken out of the profits of the broad-profit-margin company than occurs for its higher-cost competition, since the higher-cost company is probably facing comparably increased costs of doing business.

Profitability can be expressed in two ways. The fundamental way, which is the yardstick used by most managements, is the return on invested assets. This is the factor that will cause a company to decide whether to go ahead with a new product or process. What percent return can the company expect on the part of its capital invested in this particular way in comparison to what the return might be if the same amount of its assets were employed in some other way? It is considerably more difficult for the investor to use this yardstick than it is for the corporate executive. What the investor usually sees is not the return on a specific amount of present-day dollars utilized in a specific subdivision of the business but the total earnings of the business as a percentage of its total assets. When the cost of capital equipment has risen as much as it has in the last forty years, comparisons of the return on total invested capital between one company and another may be so distorted by variations in the price levels at which different companies made major expenditures that the figures are highly misleading. For this reason, comparing the profit margins per dollar of sales may be more helpful as long as one other point is kept in mind. This is that a company that has a high rate of sales in relation to assets may be a more profitable company than one with a higher profit margin to sales but a slower rate of sales turnover. For example, a company that has annual sales three times its assets can have a lower profit margin but make a lot more money than one that needs to employ a dollar of assets in order to obtain each dollar of annual sales. However, while from the standpoint of *profitability* return on investment must be considered as well as profit margin on sales, from the standpoint of *safety of investment* all the emphasis is on profit margin on sales. Thus if two companies were each to experience a 2 percent increase in operating costs and were unable to raise prices, the one with a 1 percent margin of profit would be running at a loss and might be wiped out, while, if the other had a 10 percent margin, the increased costs would wipe out only one fifth of its profits.

There is one final matter to be kept in mind in order to place this dimension of conservative investing in proper perspective: In today's highly fluid and competitive business world, obtaining well-above-average profit margins or a high return on assets is so desirable that, whenever a company accomplishes this goal for any significant period of time, it is bound to be faced with a host of potential competitors. If the potential competitors actually enter the field, they will cut into markets the established company now has. Normally, when potential competition becomes actual competition the ensuing struggle for sales results in anything from a minor to a major reduction in the high profit margin that had theretofore existed. High profit margins may be compared to an open jar of honey owned by the prospering company. The honey will inevitably attract a swarm of hungry insects bent on devouring it. In the business world there are but two ways a company can protect the contents of its honey jar from being consumed by the insects of competition. One is by monopoly, which is usually illegal, although, if the monopoly is due to patent protection, it may not be. In any event, monopolies are likely to end quite suddenly and do not commend themselves as vehicles for the safest type of investing. The other way for the honey-jar company to keep the insects out is to operate so much more efficiently than others that there is no incentive for present or potential competition to take action that will upset the existing situation.

Now let us turn from this background discussion of relative profitability to the heart of the third dimension of conservative investing— namely, the specific characteristics that enable certain well-managed companies to maintain above-average profit margins more or less indefinitely. Possibly the most common characteristic is what businessmen call the "economies of scale." A simple example of economy of scale: A well-run company making one million units a month will often have a lower production cost for each unit than a company producing only 100,000 units in the same period. The difference between the cost per unit of these two companies, one ten times larger than the other, can vary considerably from one line of business to another. In some there may be almost no difference at all. Furthermore, it should never be forgotten that in any industry the larger company will have a maximum advantage only if it is exceedingly well run. The bigger a company is, the harder it is to manage efficiently. Quite often the inherent advantages of scale are fully balanced or even more than balanced by the inefficiencies produced by too many bureaucratic layers of middle management, consequent delays in making decisions, and, at times, the seeming inability of top executives in the largest companies to know quickly just what needs corrective attention in various subdivisions of their far-flung complexes.

On the other hand, when a company clearly becomes the leader in its field, not just in dollar volume but in profitability, it seldom gets displaced from this position as long as its management remains highly competent. As discussed in examining the second dimension of a conservative investment, such a management must retain the ability to change corporate ways to match the ever-changing external environment. There is a school of investment thinking that advocates acquiring shares in the number-two or -three company in a field because "these can go up to number one, whereas the leader is already there and might slip." There are some industries where the largest company does not have a clear leadership position; but, where it does, we emphatically do not agree with this viewpoint. It has been our observation that, in many years of trying, Westinghouse has not surpassed General Electric, Montgomery Ward has not overtaken Sears, and—once IBM established early dominance in its areas of the computer market—even the extreme efforts of some of the largest companies in the country, including General Electric, did not succeed in displacing IBM from its overwhelming share of that market. Neither have scores of smaller price-cutting suppliers of peripheral equipment been able to displace IBM as the main and most profitable operator in that phase of the computer industry.

What enables a company to obtain this advantage of scale in the first place? Usually getting there first with a new product or service that meets worthwhile demand and backing this up with good enough marketing, servicing, product improvement, and, at times, advertising to keep existing customers happy and coming back for more. This frequently establishes an atmosphere in which new customers will turn to the leader largely because that leader has established such a reputation for performance (or sound value) that no one is likely to criticize the buyer adversely for making this particular selection. In the heyday of the attempts of others to cut into IBM's computer business, no one will ever know how many employees of corporations planning to use a computer for the first time recommended IBM rather than a smaller competitor whose equipment they privately thought was better or cheaper. In such instances the primary motive was probably a feeling that if, later on, the equipment should fail to perform, those making the recommendation would not be blamed if they had chosen the industry leader but could very well find their necks out a mile if a failure occurred and they had chosen a smaller company without an established reputation.

There is a saying in the pharmaceutical industry that, when a truly worthwhile new drug is created, the company that gets in first takes and holds 60 percent of the market, thereby making by far the bulk of the profits. The next company to introduce a competitive version of the same product gets perhaps 25 percent of the market and makes moderate profits. The next three companies to arrive divide perhaps 10 percent to 15 percent of the market and earn meager profits. Any further entrants usually find themselves in a quite unhappy position. A trend toward the substitution of generic for trade names may or may not upset these ratios, and in any case there cannot be said to be an exact formula applicable to other industries; nevertheless, the concept behind them should be kept in mind when an investor attempts to appraise which companies have a natural advantage in regard to profitability and which do not.

Lower production costs and greater ability to attract new customers because of a well-recognized trade name are not the only ways that scale can consistently give a company competitive strength. Examining some of the factors behind the investment strength of the soup division of the Campbell Soup Company is illuminating. In the first place, as by far the largest soup canners in the nation, this company can reduce total costs through backward integration as smaller companies cannot. Making many of their own cans exactly to meet their own needs is a case in point. More important, Campbell has enough business so that it can scatter canning plants at strategic spots across the nation, which makes for a sizable double advantage: It is both a shorter haul for the grower delivering his produce to the cannery and a shorter average haul from cannery to supermarket. Since canned soup is heavy in relation to its value, freight costs are significant. This puts the smaller canner with only one or two plants at a big disadvantage in trying to compete in a nationwide market. Next, and probably most important of all, because Campbell's is a recognized product that the customer knows and wants when he enters the supermarket, the retailer automatically awards to it a prominent and fairly sizable area of his always sought-after shelf space. In contrast, he is usually quite reluctant to do as much for a less-known or unknown competitor. This prominent shelf space helps to sell the soup and is still another factor tending to keep the number-one company on top, a factor extremely discouraging for potential competitors. Also discouraging for them is Campbell's normal advertising budget, which adds very much less to the cost per can sold than such a budget would for a competitor with a very much smaller output. For reasons such as these, this particular company has strong inherent forces tending to protect profit margins. However, to present a complete picture, we must note some influences working in the opposite direction. When Campbell's own costs rise, as they can do sharply in an inflationary period, prices to the consumer cannot be raised more than the average of other foods or there could be a shift in demand away from soups to other staples. Far more important, Campbell has a major competitor that most companies do not have to contend with and that, as rising production costs cause higher prices to the consumer, can cut significantly into Campbell's market. This is the American housewife fighting her battle of the budget by making soup in her own kitchen. This point is mentioned merely to show that even when scale affords huge competitive advantages and a company is well run, these characteristics, important as they are, do not, of themselves, assure extreme profitability.

Scale is by no means the only investment factor tending to perpetuate the much greater profitability and investment appeal of some companies over others. Another which we believe is of particular interest is the difficulty of competing with a highly successful, established producer in a technological area where the technology depends on not one scientific discipline but the interplay of two or preferably several quite different disciplines. To explain what I mean, let us suppose that someone develops an electronic product that promises to open up sizable new markets in either the computer or instrument field. There are enough highly capable companies in both areas that have in-house experts able to duplicate both the electronic hardware and the software programming that such products require so that if the new market appears large enough, sufficient competition may soon develop to make the profits of the smaller innovator rather tenuous. In areas such as these, the successful large company has a further built-in advantage. Many such lines cannot be sold unless a network of service people is available to make rapid repair at the customers' locations. The large established company usually has such an organization in being. It is extremely difficult and expensive for a small new company introducing a worthwhile new product to establish such a network. It may be even harder for the new company to convince a potential buyer that it has the financial staying power not only to have the service network in place when the sale is made but to keep it there in the future. Furthermore, while all these influences have made it difficult in the past for the newcomer with an exciting product to establish real leadership in most subdivisions of the electronics industry, although a few companies have done so, it is likely to be still more difficult in the future. This is because the semiconductor is becoming a larger and larger percentage of both the total content and the total technical know-how of more and more products. The leading companies making these devices also now have at least as much in-house knowledge as the top old-line computer and instrument companies if they elect to compete in many new product areas that are largely electronic. A case in point is the dramatic success of Texas Instruments in the sensationally growing area of hand-held calculators and the difficulties of some of the early pioneers in this field.

However, notice how the balance changes if, instead of just a technology based on electronic hardware and software, producing the product calls for these skills to be combined with some quite different ones such as nucleonics or some highly specialized area of chemistry. The large electronic companies simply do not have the in-house skills to enter these interdisciplinary technologies. This affords the best-run innovators a far better opportunity to build themselves into the type of leadership position in their particular product line that carries with it the broad profit margin that tends to continue as long as managerial competence does not weaken. I believe that some of these multidisciplinary technological companies, in not all of which is electronics a significant factor, have recently proven some of the finest opportunities for truly farsighted investing. I am inclined to think that more such opportunities will occur in the future. Thus, for example, I suspect that sometime in the future new leading companies will arise through products or processes that utilize some of these other disciplines combined with biology, although so far I have not seen any company in this area that so qualifies. This is not to say that none exists.

Technological development and scale are not the only aspects of a

company's activities in which unusual circumstances may raise opportunities for sustained high profit margins. In certain circumstances these
can also occur in the area of marketing or sales. An example is a company
that has created in its customers the habit of almost automatically spec-
ifying its products for reorder in a way that makes it rather uneconomical
for a competitor to attempt to displace them. Two sets of conditions are
necessary for this to happen. First, the company must build up a reputation for quality and reliability in a product (a) that the customer rec-
ognizes is very important for the proper conduct of his activities,
(b) where an inferior or malfunctioning product would cause serious
problems, (c) where no competitor is serving more than a minor segment
of the market so that the dominant company is nearly synonymous in
the public mind with the source of supply, and yet (d) the cost of the
product is only a quite small part of the customer's total cost of operations. Consequently, moderate price reductions yield only very small savings in relation to the risk of taking a chance on an unknown supplier.
However, even this is not enough to ensure that a company fortunate
enough to get itself in this position will be able to enjoy above-average
profit margins year after year. Second, it must have a product sold to
many small customers rather than a few large ones. These customers
must be sufficiently specialized in their nature that it would be unlikely
for a potential competitor to feel they could be reached through advertising media such as magazines or television. They constitute a market
in which, as long as the dominant company maintains the quality of its
product and the adequacy of its service, it can be displaced only by
informed salesmen making individual calls. Yet the size of each customer's orders make such a selling effort totally uneconomical! A company
possessing all these advantages can, through marketing, maintain an
above-average profit margin almost indefinitely unless a major shift in
technology (or, as already mentioned, a slippage in its own efficiency)
should displace it. Companies of this type can most often be found in
the moderately high technology supply area. One of their characteristics
is to maintain their image of leadership by holding frequent technical
seminars on the use of their product, a marketing tool that proves highly
effective once a company attains this type of position.

It should be noted that the "above-average" profit margin or "greater
than normal" return on investment need not be—in fact, should not be—
many times that earned by industry in general to give a company's shares

great investment appeal. Actually, if the profit or return on investment is too spectacular, it can be a source of danger, as the inducement then becomes almost irresistible for all sorts of companies to try to compete so as to get a share of the unusual honey pot. In contrast, a profit margin consistently just 2 or 3 percent of sales greater than that of the next best competitor is sufficient to ensure a quite outstanding investment.

To summarize the matter of the third dimension of a truly conservative investment: It is necessary not just to have the quality of personnel discussed in the second dimension but to have had that personnel (or their predecessors) steer the company into areas of activity where there are inherent reasons within the economics of the particular business so that above-average profitability is not a short-term matter. Put simply, the question to ask in regard to this third dimension is: "What can the particular company do that others would not be able to do about as well?" If the answer is almost nothing, so that, as the business gets more prosperous, others can rush in to share in the company's prosperity on about equal terms, the evidence is conclusive that while the company's stock may be cheap, the investment fails to qualify as to this third dimension.

4

THE FOURTH DIMENSION

PRICE OF A CONSERVATIVE INVESTMENT

T he fourth dimension of any stock investment involves the price-earnings ratio—that is, the current price divided by the earnings per share. In the attempt to appraise whether the price-earnings ratio is in line with a proper valuation for that specific stock, trouble begins to arise. Most investors, including many professionals who should know better, become confused on this point because they don't have a clear understanding of what makes the price of the particular stock go up or down by a significant amount. This misunderstanding has resulted in losses in billions of dollars by investors who find out later that they own stocks bought at prices that they never should have paid. Even more billions have been lost as investors have sold out, at the wrong time and for the wrong reasons, shares they had every reason to hold and which, if held, would have become extremely profitable as long-range investments. Still another result is one that, if it happens repeatedly, will seriously impair the ability of deserving corporations to obtain adequate financing, with all that this could mean in a lower standard of living for everyone: Every time individual stocks take sickening plunges, another group of badly burned investors places the blame on the system rather than on their own mistakes or those of their advisors. They conclude that common stocks of any type are not suitable for their savings.

The other side of the coin is that many other investors can be found who over the years have prospered mightily from holding the right stocks for considerable periods of time. Their success may be due to understanding basic investment rules. Or it may be due to just plain good luck.

However, the common denominator in this success has been the refusal to sell certain unusual high-quality stocks simply because each has had such a sharp fast rise that its price-earnings ratio suddenly looks high in relation to that to which the investment community had become accustomed.

In view of the importance of all this, it is truly remarkable that so few have looked beneath the surface to understand exactly what causes these sharp price changes. Yet the law that governs them can be stated reasonably simply: *Every significant price move of any individual common stock in relation to stocks as a whole occurs because of a changed appraisal of that stock by the financial community.*

Let us see how this works in practice. Two years ago company G was considered quite ordinary. It had earned $1 per share and was selling at ten times earnings, or $10. During these last two years most companies in its industry have been showing a downward profit trend. In contrast, a series of brilliant new products, combined with better profit margins on old products, enabled G company to report $1.40 per share last year and $1.82 this year and to give promise of further gains over the next several years. Obviously the actions within the company that produced the sharp contrast between G's recent results and those of others in the industry could not have started just two years ago but must have been going on for some time; otherwise the operating economies and the brilliant new products would not have occurred. However, belated recognition (i.e., appraisal) of how well G is qualifying in regard to matters covered in our discussions of the first three dimensions has now caused the price-earnings ratio to rise to 22. When compared with other stocks showing similar above-average business characteristics and comparable growth prospects, this ratio of 22 does not appear at all high. Since 22 times $1.82 is $40, here is a stock that has legitimately gone up 400 percent in two years. Equally important, a record such as G's is frequently an indication that there is now functioning a management team capable of continued growth for many years ahead. Such a growth, even at a more modest rate averaging, say, 15 percent in the next decade or two could easily result in profits by that time running into the thousands rather than the hundreds of percent.

The matter of "appraisal" is the heart of understanding the seeming vagaries of price-earnings ratios. It should never be forgotten that an appraisal is a subjective matter. It has nothing necessarily to do with what is going on in the real world about us. Rather, it results from what the person doing the appraising believes is going on, no matter how far from the actual facts such a judgment may be. In other words, any individual stock does not rise or fall at any particular moment in time because of what is actually happening or will happen to that company. It rises or falls according to the current consensus of the financial community as to what is happening and will happen regardless of how far off this consensus may be from what is really occurring or will occur.

At this point many pragmatic individuals simply throw up their hands in disbelief. If the huge price changes that occur in individual stocks are made solely because of changed appraisals by the financial community, with these appraisals sometimes completely at variance with what is going on in the real world of a company's affairs, what significance have the other three dimensions? Why bother with the expertise of business management, scientific technology, or accounting at all? Why not just depend on psychologists?

The answer involves timing. Because of a financial-community appraisal that is at variance with the facts, a stock may sell for a considerable period for much more or much less than it is intrinsically worth. Furthermore, many segments of the financial community have the habit of playing "follow the leader," particularly when that leader is one of the larger New York City banks. This sometimes means that when an unrealistic appraisal of a stock is already causing it to sell well above what a proper recognition of the facts would justify, the stock may stay at this too high level for a long period of time. Actually, from this already too high a price it may go even higher.

These wide variations between the financial community's appraisal of a stock and the true set of conditions affecting it may last for several years. Always, however—sometimes within months, sometimes only after a much longer period of time—the bubble bursts. When a stock has been selling too high because of unrealistic expectations, sooner or later a growing number of stockholders grow tired of waiting. Their selling soon more than exhausts the buying power of the small number of additional buyers who still have faith in the old appraisal. The stock then comes tumbling down. Sometimes the new appraisal that follows is quite realistic. Frequently, however, as this re-examination evolves under the emotional pressure of falling prices, the negative is overemphasized, resulting in a new financial-community appraisal that is significantly less favorable than the facts warrant and that may then prevail for some time. However, when this happens, much the same thing occurs as when the appraisal is too favorable. The only difference is that the process is reversed. It may take months or years for a more favorable image to supplant the existing one. Nevertheless, as pleasing earnings mount upward, sooner or later this happens.

Fortunate holders—those who don't sell out as such a stock starts to rise—then benefit from the phenomenon that provides the greatest reward in relation to the risk involved the stock market can produce. This is the dramatic improvement in price that results from the combined effect of both a steady improvement in per-share earnings and a sharp, simultaneous increase in the price-earnings ratio. As the financial community quite correctly discovers that the fundamentals of the company (now its new image) have much more investment worth than had been recognized when the old image was in effect, the resulting increase in the price-earnings ratio is frequently an even more important factor in the increased price of the stock than the actual increase in per-share earnings that accompanies it. This is precisely what happened in our G-company example.

We are now in a position to begin to get a true perspective on the degree of conservatism—that is, of basic risk in any investment. On the lowest end of the risk scale and most suitable for wise investment is the company that measures quite high in regard to the first three dimensions but currently is appraised by the financial community as less worthy, and therefore has a lower price-earnings ratio, than these fundamental facts warrant. Next least risky and usually quite suitable for intelligent investment is the company rating quite high in regard to the first three dimensions and having an image and therefore a price-earnings ratio reasonably in line with these fundamentals. This is because such a company will continue to grow if it truly has these attributes. Next least risky and, in my opinion, usually suitable for retention by conservative investors who own them but not for fresh purchase with new funds are companies that are equally strong in regard to the first three dimensions but, because these qualities have become almost legendary in the financial community, have an appraisal or price-earnings ratio higher than is warranted by even the strong fundamentals.

In my opinion there are important reasons such stocks should usually be retained, even though their prices seem too high: If the fundamentals are genuinely strong, these companies will in time increase earnings not only enough to justify present prices but to justify considerably higher prices. Meanwhile, the number of truly attractive companies in regard to the first three dimensions is fairly small. Undervalued ones are not easy to find. The risk of making a mistake and switching into one that seems to meet all of the first three dimensions but actually does not is probably considerably greater for the average investor than the temporary risk of staying with a thoroughly sound but currently overvalued situation until genuine value catches up with current prices. Investors who agree with me on this particular point must be prepared for occasional sharp contractions in the market value of these temporarily overvalued stocks. On the other hand, it is my observation that those who sell such stocks to wait for a more suitable time to buy back these same shares seldom attain their objective. They usually wait for a decline to be bigger than it actually turns out to be. The result is that some years later when this fundamentally strong stock has reached peaks of value considerably higher than the point at which they sold, they have missed all of this later move and may have gone into a situation of considerably inferior intrinsic quality.

Continuing up our scale of ascending risks, we come next to the stocks that are average or relatively low in quality in regard to the first three dimensions but have an appraisal in the financial community either lower than, or about in line with, these not very attractive fundamentals. Those with a poorer appraisal than basic conditions warrant may be good speculations but are not suitable for the prudent investor. In the fast-moving world of today there is just too much danger of adverse developments severely affecting such shares.

Finally we come to what is by far the most dangerous group of all: companies with a present financial-community appraisal or image far above what is currently justified by the immediate situation. Purchase of such shares can cause the sickening losses that tend to drive investors away from stock ownership in droves and threaten to shake the investment industry to its foundations. If anyone wants to make a case-by-case study of the contrast between the financial-community appraisals that prevailed at one time about some quite colorful companies and the fundamental conditions that subsequently came to light, he will find plenty of material in a business library or the files of the larger Wall

Street houses. It is alarming to read some of the reasons given in brokerage reports recommending purchase of these shares and then to compare the outlook described in such documents with what actually was to happen. A fragmentary list of such companies might include: Memorex high $173^7/8$, Ampex high $49^7/8$, Levitz Furniture high $60^1/2$, Mohawk Data Sciences high 111, Litton Industries high $101^3/4$, Kalvar high $176^1/2$.

The list could go on and on and on. However, more examples would serve only to make the same point over and over. Since it should already be quite apparent how important is the habit of evaluating any difference that may exist between a contemporary financial-community appraisal of a company and the fundamental aspects of that company, it should be more productive for us to spend our time examining further the characteristics of these financial-community appraisals. First, however, to avoid risk of misunderstanding, it seems advisable to avoid semantic confusion by defining two of the words in our original statement of the rule governing all major changes in the price of common stocks: *Every significant price move of any individual common stock in relation to stocks as a whole occurs because of a changed appraisal of that stock by the financial community.*

The phrase "*significant* price changes" is used rather than merely "price changes." This is to exclude the kind of minor price variation that occurs if, say, an estate has twenty thousand shares of a stock that a clumsy broker rapidly dumps on the market with the result that the stock drops a point or two and then usually recovers as the liquidation ends. Similarly, at times an institution will determine that on going into a new situation it must buy a minimum number of shares. The result is frequently a small onetime bulge that subsides on completion of this sort of buying. Such moves, in the absence of a genuinely changed appraisal of the company by the financial community as a whole, have no important or long-term effect on the price of the shares. Usually such small price changes disappear once the special buying or selling is over.

The term "financial community" has been used to include all those able and enough interested to be potentially ready to buy or sell a particular stock at some price, keeping in mind that, with regard to impact on price, the importance of each of these potential buyers and sellers is weighted by the amount of buying or selling power each is in a position to exercise.

5

MORE ABOUT
THE FOURTH DIMENSION

U p to this point our discussion of the financial community's appraisal of a stock may have given the impression that this appraisal is nothing more than an evaluation of that particular equity, considered by itself. This is oversimplification. Actually it always results from the blending of three separate appraisals: the current financial-community appraisal of the attractiveness of common stocks as a whole, of the industry of which the particular company is a part, and, finally, of the company itself.

Let us first examine the matter of industry appraisals. Everyone knows that, over long periods of time, there can be a sizable decline in the price-earnings ratio the financial community will pay to participate in an industry as it passes from an early stage when huge markets appear ahead to a much later period where it, in turn, may be threatened by new technologies. Thus, in the early years of the electronics industry, companies making electronic tubes, in that period the fundamental building block of all electronics, sold at very high price-earnings ratios. Then price-earnings ratios shrank drastically as the development of semiconductors steadily narrowed the tube market. Makers of magnetic memory devices have more recently suffered the same fate for the same reason. All this is obvious and thoroughly understood. What is not so obvious or comparably understood is how the image of an industry can rise or fall in financial-community status, not because of such overpowering influences as these but because at a given time the financial community is stressing one particular set of industry background influences rather than another. Yet both sets of background conditions may have been quite valid for some time, and both may give every indication of continuing to be for the reasonable future.

The chemical industry may be cited as an example. From the depths of the Great Depression until the middle 1950s, the shares of the largest U. S. chemical companies sold at quite high price-earnings ratios compared to most other stocks. The financial community's idea of these companies might have been depicted in a cartoon as an endless conveyor belt. At one end were scientists making breathtaking new compounds in test tubes. After passing through mysterious and hard-to-imitate factories, these materials came out at the other end as fabulous new products such as nylon, DDT, synthetic rubber, quick-drying paint, and endless other new materials that seemed sure to be an ever-increasing source of wealth for their fortunate producers. Then, as the 1960s arrived, the image changed. The chemical industry, to the investment community, came to resemble steel or cement or paper in that it was selling bulk commodities on a basis of technical specification so that Jones's chemicals were more or less identical with Smith's. Capital-intensive industries usually are under major pressure to operate at high rates of capacity in order to amortize their large fixed investments. The result is frequently intense price competition and narrowing profit margins. This changed image caused the shares of the major chemical companies to sell at significantly lower price-earnings ratios in relation to stocks as a whole in the, say, ten-year period that ended in 1972 than they had in the past. While still considerably higher than in many industries, chemical price-earnings ratios started more closely to resemble those of industries like steel, paper, and cement.

Now the remarkable thing about all this is that with one important exception there was little or nothing different in the fundamental background of this industry in the 1960s than there was in the prior thirty years. It is true that in the latter half of the 1960s there was a serious glut of capacity in certain areas such as the manufacture of most synthetic textile products. This was a major temporary depressant of the earnings of certain of the leading chemical companies, particularly DuPont. But the basic characteristics of the industry had in no way changed sufficiently to account for this rather drastic change in the industry's status in the financial community. Chemical manufacture always had been capital-intensive. Most products had always been sold on a technical specification basis so that Jones could seldom raise his price above Smith's. On the other hand, as a host of new and greatly improved pesticides, packaging materials, textiles, drugs, and countless other products have shown, the 1960s and the 1970s have afforded this industry an ever-expanding market. Opportunities seem almost limitless for human brains to rearrange molecules so as to create products not found in nature that will have special properties to cater to the needs of man better or more cheaply than the previously used natural materials.

Finally, in both the previous period of higher and the more recent period of lower esteem for chemical stocks, still another factor had remained almost constant. The older and larger-volume chemical products, representing in a sense the "first step" processing of tailored materials from such basic sources of molecules as salt or hydrocarbons, were inevitably products sold mainly by specification and on a price-competitive basis. Nevertheless, for the alert company there always was and continued to be the opportunity to process these first-step products into much more complicated and higher-priced ones. These, at least for a while, could be sold on a much more proprietary and therefore less competitive basis. As these products in turn become price competitive, the alert companies have consistently found still newer ones to add to the higher-profit-margin end of their lines.

In other words, all the favorable factors, so much in the financial community's mind when chemical stocks were darlings of the market, continued to be there after they had lost considerable status. But the unfavorable factors so much in the forefront in the 1960s were also there in the earlier period when they were largely ignored. What had shifted was the emphasis, not the facts.

But the facts, too, can change. Starting about the middle of 1973, chemical stocks began regaining favor in the financial community. This was because a new view of the industry was starting to prevail. In the scarcity-plagued economy the major industrial nations have been experiencing for the first time (except during major wars) in modern times, manufacturing capacity can be increased only gradually; hence, it may be years before cutthroat price competition will occur again. This image opens up a whole new ballgame for the investor in chemical stocks. The problem for investors now becomes one of determining whether the background facts warrant the new image and, if they do, whether chemical stocks, in relation to the market as a whole, have risen more than or not as much as may be warranted by the new situation.

Recent financial history offers countless other examples of much larger changes in price-earnings ratios that occurred because the financial community's appraisal of the industry's background changed radically while the industry itself remained almost exactly the same. In 1969 the computer peripheral stocks were great market favorites. These were the companies making all the special equipment that could be added to the central computing unit or main frame of a computer to increase the user's benefits from that central unit. High-speed printers, extra memory units, and keyboard devices to eliminate the need for keypunch operators in getting data into a computer were some of the major products in this group. The prevailing image then was that these companies had an almost limitless future. While the central computer itself was largely developed and its market would be dominated by a few strong, established companies, the small independent would be able to undercut the big companies in these peripheral areas. Today there is a new awareness of the financial strain on small companies with products that are usually leased rather than sold and of the determination of the major computer main-frame manufacturers to fight for the market of the products "hung on" their equipment. Have the fundamentals changed or is it the appraisal of the fundamentals that has changed?

An extreme case of a changed appraisal is the way in which the financial community looked on the fundamentals of the franchising business and franchise stocks in 1969 in contrast to 1972. Here again, as with computer peripheral stocks, all the problems of the industry were inherently there when these stocks were being bought at such high price-earnings ratios but were being overlooked when the prevailing image was one of uninterrupted growth for the company momentarily doing well.

In this whole matter of industry image, the investor's problem is always the same. Is the current prevailing appraisal one more favorable, less favorable, or about the same as that warranted by the basic economic facts? At times this can present an acute problem to even the most sophisticated investors. One example occurred in December 1958 when Smith, Barney & Co., traditionally conservative investment bankers, took a pioneering step that seems purely routine today but appeared quite the contrary at that time: They made a public offering of the equity shares of the A. C. Nielsen Co. This company had no factories, no tangible product, and therefore no inventories. Instead it was in the "service business," receiving fees for supplying market-research information to its customers. It was true that in 1958 banks and insurance companies had long been well regarded in the marketplace as industries worthy of conservative investment. However, such industries were hardly comparable. Since the book value of a bank or insurance company is in cash, liquid investments or accounts receivable, the investor buying a bank or insurance stock seemed to have a hard core of value to fall back on that did not exist for this new kind of service company being introduced to the financial public. However, investigation of the A. C. Nielsen situation revealed unusually good fundamentals. There was an honest and capable management, a uniquely strong competitive position and good prospects for many years of further growth. Nevertheless, until experience showed how the financial community would react to its first exposure to this kind of an industry, there did appear to be some reason for hesitation in buying. Would it take years for a realistic appraisal of the investment worth of such a company to displace the fear that might be engendered by the lack of some of the familiar yardsticks of value? It may seem ridiculous today, when for many years a company like A. C. Nielsen has enjoyed a price-earnings ratio signifying a very high investment appraisal, but some of us who decided to take a chance on the fundamentals being recognized and bought these shares at that time experienced a sensation almost like stepping off a cliff and seeing if the air would support us, so new was the concept of a service company in contrast to concepts to which we were accustomed. Actually within a few years the pendulum swung quite the other way. As A. C. Nielsen's profits grew and grew, a new concept arose in Wall Street. A large number of companies, many quite different in economic fundamentals but all dealing in services rather than products, were lumped together in a financial-community image as parts of a highly attractive service industry. Some began selling at higher price-earnings ratios than they might have deserved. As always, in time, fundamentals dominated, and this false image formed by lumping quite different companies into one group faded away.

This point cannot be overstressed: *The conservative investor must be aware of the nature of the current financial-community appraisal of any industry in which he is interested.* He should constantly be probing to see whether that appraisal is significantly more or less favorable than the fundamentals warrant. Only by judging properly on this point can he be reasonably sure about one of the three variables that will govern the long-term trend of market price of stocks of that industry.

6

STILL MORE ABOUT
THE FOURTH DIMENSION

The financial community's appraisal of a company's own characteristics is an even more important factor in the price-earnings ratio
than is the appraisal of the industry in which the company is engaged.
The most desirable investment traits of individual companies have been
defined in our discussion of the first three dimensions of a conservative
investment. In general, the more closely the financial community's appraisal of a particular stock approaches these characteristics, the higher
will be its price-earnings ratio. To the degree by which it falls below
these standards, the price-earnings ratio will tend to decline. The investor can best determine which stocks are importantly undervalued or overvalued by a shrewd determination of the degree to which the real facts
concerning any particular company present an investment situation significantly better or significantly worse than that painted by the current
financial image of that company.

In making a determination as to the relative attractiveness of two or
more stocks, investors often confuse themselves by attempting too simple
a mathematical approach to such a problem. Let us suppose, for example,
they compare two companies, the profits of each of which, after careful
study, appear to afford prospects of growing at a rate of 10 percent a
year. If one is selling at ten times earnings and the other at twenty times,
the stock selling at ten times earnings appears cheaper. It may be. It also
may not be. There can be a number of reasons for this. The seemingly
cheaper company may have such a leveraged capitalization (interest

charges and preferred dividends that must be earned before anything accrues to the common-stock-holder) that the danger of interruption of the expected growth rate may be much greater in the lower price-earnings-ratio stock. Similarly, for purely business reasons, while the growth rate would seem a most probable estimate for both stocks, nevertheless the chance of the unexpected upsetting these estimates may be considerably more for the one stock than for the other.

Another far more important and far less understood way to reach wrong conclusions is to rely too much on simple comparisons of the price-earnings ratios of stocks that seem to be offering comparable opportunities for growth. To illustrate this, let us assume that there are two stocks with an equally strong prospect of doubling earnings over the next four years and that both are selling at twenty times earnings, while in the same market companies which are sound otherwise but have no growth prospects are selling at ten times earnings. Let us suppose that four years later the price-earnings ratios of stocks as a whole are unchanged so that generally sound stocks, but ones with no growth prospects, are still selling at ten times earnings. Let us also suppose that at this same time, four years later, one of our two stocks has much the same growth prospects for the time ahead as it had four years before so that the financial community's appraisal is that this stock should again double its earnings over the next four years. This means it would still be selling at twenty times the doubled earnings of the past four years, or, in other words, that it had also doubled in price in that period. In contrast, at this same time, four years after our example had started, the second stock had also doubled its earnings, just as had been expected, but at this point the financial community's appraisal is for flat earnings in an otherwise sound company over the next four years. This would mean that owners of this second stock were in for a market disappointment even though the four-year doubling of earnings had come through exactly as forecast. With an image of "no growth in earnings for the next four years," they would now be seeing a price-earnings ratio of only ten in this second stock. Therefore, while the earnings had doubled, the price of the stock had remained the same. All this can be summarized in a basic investment rule: The further into the future profits will continue to grow, the higher the price-earnings ratio an investor can afford to pay.

This rule, however, should be applied with great caution. It should never be forgotten that the actual variations in price-earnings ratio will result not from what will actually happen but from what the financial community currently believes will happen. In a period of general market optimism a stock may sell at an extremely high price-earnings ratio because the financial community quite correctly envisages many years of great growth ahead. But many years will have to elapse before this growth is fully realized. The great growth that had been correctly discounted in the price-earnings ratio is likely to become "undiscounted" for a while, particularly if the company experiences the type of temporary setback that is not uncommon for even the best of companies. In times of general market pessimism, this kind of "undiscounting" of some of the very finest investments can reach rather extreme levels. When it does, it affords the patient investor, with the ability to distinguish between current market image and true facts, some of the most attractive opportunities common stocks can offer for handsome long-term profits at relatively small risk.

A rather colorful example of how sophisticated investors attempt to anticipate a changed investment-community appraisal of a company occurred on March 13, 1974. The previous day the New York Stock Exchange closing price of Motorola was 48⅝. On March 13 the closing quotation was 60, a gain of almost 25 percent! What had happened was that after the close of the exchange on the 12th, an announcement was made that Motorola was getting out of the television business and was selling its U.S. television plants and inventory to Matsushita, a large Japanese manufacturer, for approximate book value.

Now it had been known generally that Motorola's television business was operating at a small loss and to that extent was draining the profits of the rest of the company's business. This of itself would warrant the news to cause some increase in the price of the shares, although hardly the degree of rise that actually occurred. Considerably more complex reasoning was the main motivation behind the buying. For some time a considerable body of investors had believed that Motorola's profitable divisions, particularly its Communications Division, made this company one of the very few American electronics companies qualified as being of truly high-grade investment status. For example, Spencer Trask and Co. had issued a report by security analyst Otis Bradley that discussed the investment merits of Motorola's Communications Division in considerable detail. This report took the unusual approach of calculating the current and estimated future price-earnings ratio, not for Motorola's earnings as a whole but merely for this one division alone. The report compared the estimated sales volume and price-earnings ratio of just this one division with those of Hewlett Packard and Perkin-Elmer, generally considered to be among the very finest of electronics companies from an investment standpoint. From the report the inference could easily be drawn (this was not specifically stated) that the investment quality of Motorola's Communications Division was such that it was worth, by itself, the then current price of Motorola shares so that, in effect, a buyer of the stock was getting all the other divisions for nothing.

With this opinion about Motorola existing in some highly sophisticated places, what may be judged to have induced such eager buying on the Matsushita news? These Motorola enthusiasts had long known that many elements of the financial community were inclined to look with disfavor on the stock because of its television-manufacturing image. Most of the financial community, upon hearing "Motorola," first thought of television and secondly of semiconductors. At the time of the Matsushita announcement, Standard & Poor's stock guide, in the small amount of space available for listing the principal business of each company, described Motorola as "Radio & T.V.: semiconductors," all of which, though not inaccurate, was misleading in that it suggested a different sort of company from what, in fact, Motorola really was and completely overlooked the very important Communications Division, which at the time comprised almost half of the company.

Some of those buying Motorola on the Matsushita news undoubtedly rushed in merely because the news was good and therefore could be expected to send the stock up. But there is reason to ascribe considerable buying to the belief that the financial community's appraisal of the company had been considerably less favorable than the facts warranted. The historical record was such that in the television business Motorola was regarded more as an "also ran" than as an industry leader such as Zenith. With the television operations no longer blurring investors' vision of what else was there, a new image with a very much higher price-earnings ratio would arise.

Were those who rushed in to pay these higher prices for Motorola wise in so doing? Not entirely. In subsequent weeks the shares lost the immediate gain so that a degree of patience would have paid. In downward markets, a change for the worse in the financial community's image of a company gets accepted far more quickly than a change for the better. Just the opposite is true in rising markets. Unfortunately for those who rushed in to buy Motorola on this news, the immediately ensuing weeks saw a sharp upturn in short-term interest rates which produced a downward trend in the general market and accentuated the widespread bear-market psychology then prevailing.

Perhaps another influence was also at work against those who snapped up Motorola shares overnight. This influence is one of the most subtle and dangerous in the entire field of investment and one against which even the most sophisticated investors must constantly be on guard. When for a long period of time a particular stock has been selling in a certain price range, say from a low of 38 to a high of 43, there is an almost irresistible tendency to attribute true value to this price level. Consequently, when, after the financial community has become thoroughly accustomed to this being the "value" of the stock, the appraisal changes and the stock, say, sinks to 24, all sorts of buyers who should know better rush in to buy. They jump to the conclusion that the stock must now be cheap. Yet if the fundamentals are bad enough, it may still be very high at 24. Conversely, as such a stock rises to, say, 50 or 60 or 70, the urge to sell and take a profit now that the stock is "high" becomes irresistible to many people. Giving in to this urge can be very costly. This is because the genuinely worthwhile profits in stock investing have come from holding the surprisingly large number of stocks that have gone up many times from their original cost. The only true test of whether a stock is "cheap" or "high" is not its current price in relation to some former price, no matter how accustomed we may have become to that former price, but whether the company's fundamentals are significantly more or less favorable than the current financial-community appraisal of that stock.

As previously mentioned, there is a third element of investment-community appraisal that also must be considered, along with its appraisal of the industry and of the particular company. Only after all three are blended together can a worthwhile judgment be reached as to whether a stock is cheap or high at any given time. This third appraisal is that of the outlook for stocks in general. To see the rather extreme effect such general market appraisals can have in certain periods and how far these views can vary from the facts, it may be well to review the two most extreme such appraisals of this century. Ridiculous as it may seem to us today, in the period from 1927 to 1929, the majority of the financial community actually believed we were in a "new era." For years earnings of most U.S. companies had been growing with monotonous regularity. Not only had serious business depressions become a thing of the past but a great engineer and businessman, Herbert Hoover, had been elected President. His competence was expected to assure even greater prosperity from then on. In such circumstances it seemed to many that it had become virtually impossible to lose by owning stocks. And many who wanted to cash in as much as possible on this sure thing bought on margin to obtain more shares than they could otherwise afford. We all know what happened when reality shattered this particular appraisal. The agony of the Great Depression and the bear market of 1929 to 1932 will be long remembered.

Contrary in outlook, but similar in being spectacularly wrong, was the investment community's appraisal of common stocks as an investment vehicle in the three years from mid-1946 to mid-1949. Most companies' earnings were extremely pleasing. However, pursuant to the then current appraisal, stocks were selling at the lowest price-earnings ratios in many years. The financial community was saying that "these earnings don't mean anything," that they were "just temporary and would shrink sharply or disappear in the depression that must come." The financial community remembered that the Civil War had been followed by the panic of 1873, which marked the onset of a very severe depression that lasted until 1879. Following World War I had come the even worse crash of 1929 and another six years of major depression. Since World War II had involved a vastly greater effort and therefore a greater distortion of the economy than World War I, it was assumed that an even bigger bear market and an even worse depression were on the horizon. As long as this appraisal lasted, most stocks were so much on the bargain counter that when it began to dawn on the investment community that this image was false and that no severe depression lay in wait, the foundations had been laid for one of the longest periods of rising stock prices in U.S. history.

Since the bear market of 1972–1974 brought with it the only other time in this century when most price-earnings ratios were about as low as they were in the 1946–1949 period, the question obviously arises as to the soundness of the financial community's appraisal that brought this about. Are the fears engendering these historically low price-earnings ratios valid? Could this be another 1946–1949 all over again? An attempt will be made to throw some light on these matters in a later section of this book.

There is a basic difference between the factors that affect changes in the general level of all stock prices and those that affect the relative price-earnings ratio of one stock compared to another within that general level. For reasons already discussed, the factors at any given moment that affect this relative price-earnings ratio of one stock to another are solely matters of the current image in the investment community of the particular company and the particular industry to which that company belongs. However, the level of stocks as a whole is not solely a matter of image but results partly from the financial community's current appraisal of the degree of attractiveness of common stocks and partly from a certain purely financial factor from the real world.

This real-world factor is mainly involved with interest rates. When interest rates are high in either the long- or short-term money markets, and even more so when they are high in both, there is a tendency for a larger part of the pool of investment capital to flow toward those markets, so the demand for stocks is less. Stocks may be sold to transfer funds to these markets. Conversely, when rates are low, funds flow out of those markets and into stocks. Therefore, higher interest rates tend to lower the level of all stocks and lower interest rates to raise that level. Similarly, when the public is in a mood to save a larger percentage of its income, more funds flow into the total capital pool and there is a more bullish pull on stock prices than when the pool of capital funds is rising more slowly. However, this is a much smaller influence than is the level of interest rates. An even smaller influence is the degree of fluctuation in new stock issues, which are a drain on the capital pool available to the stock market. The reason the new-issue supply is not a bigger factor on the general level of stock prices is that when other influences cause stocks to be in favor, the new-issue volume rises to take advantage of this situation. When common-stock prices reach low levels, supply of new issues tends to diminish drastically. As a result, fluctuations in new-issue volume are much more a result of other influences than an influencing factor themselves.

This fourth dimension to stock investing might be summarized in this way: The price of any particular stock at any particular moment is determined by the current financial-community appraisal of the particular company, of the industry it is in, and to some degree of the general level of stock prices. Determining whether at that moment the price of a stock is attractive, unattractive or somewhere in between depends for the most part on the degree these appraisals vary from reality. However, to the extent that the general level of stock prices affects the total picture, it also depends somewhat on correctly estimating coming changes in certain purely financial factors, of which interest rates are by far the most important.

Part Three

DEVELOPING AN
INVESTMENT
PHILOSOPHY

Dedication to Frank E. Block

This book was first published at the request of the Institute of Chartered Financial Analysts made under the C. Stewart Shepard Award. This award was conferred on Frank E. Block C.F.A. in recognition of his outstanding contribution through dedicated effort and inspiring leadership in advancing the Institute of Chartered Financial Analysts as a vital force in fostering the education of financial analysts. In establishing high ethical standards of conduct, and in developing programs and publications to encourage the continuing education of financial analysts.

1
ORIGINS OF A PHILOSOPHY

To understand any disciplined approach to investment, it is first necessary to understand the objective for which the methodology is designed. For any part of the funds supervised by Fisher & Co., except for funds temporarily in cash or cash equivalents awaiting more suitable opportunities, it is the objective that they be invested in a very small number of companies that, because of the characteristics of their management, should both grow in sales and more importantly in profits at a rate significantly greater than industry as a whole. They should also do so at relatively small risk in relation to the growth involved. To meet Fisher & Co. standards, a management must have a viable policy for attaining these ends with all the willingness to subordinate immediate profits for the greater long-range gains that this concept requires. In addition, two characteristics are necessary. One is the ability to implement long-range policy with superior day-to-day performance in all the routine tasks of business operation. The other is that when significant mistakes occur, as is bound at times to happen when management strives for unique benefits through innovative concepts, new products, etc., or because management becomes too complacent through success, these mistakes are recognized clearly and remedial action is taken.

Because I believe I best understand the characteristics of manufacturing companies, I have confined Fisher & Co. activities largely to manufacturing enterprises that use a combination of leading edge technology and superior business judgment to accomplish these goals. In recent years, I have confined Fisher & Co. investments solely to this group, because on the few occasions when I have invested outside it, I have not been satisfied with the results. However, I see no reason why the same principles should not be equally profitable when applied by those with the necessary expertise in such fields as retailing, transportation, finance, etc.

No investment philosophy, unless it is just a carbon copy of someone else's approach, develops in its complete form in any one day or year. In my own case, it grew over a considerable period of time, partly as a result of what perhaps may be called logical reasoning, and partly from observing the successes and failures of others, but much of it through the more painful method of learning from my own mistakes. Possibly the best way of trying to explain my investment approach to others is to use the historical route. For this reason I will go back into the early, formative years, attempting to show block by block how this investment philosophy developed.

THE BIRTH OF INTEREST

My first awareness of the stock market and the opportunities which changing stock quotations might make possible occurred at a fairly early age. With my father the youngest of five and my mother the youngest of eight, at my birth I had only one surviving grandparent. This may have been one of the reasons why I felt particularly close to my grandmother. At any rate, I went to see her one afternoon when I was barely out of grammar school. An uncle dropped in to discuss with her his views of business conditions in the year ahead, and how this might affect the stocks she owned. A whole new world opened up to me. By saving some money, I had the right to buy a share in the future profits of any one I might choose among hundreds of the most important business enterprises of the country. If I chose correctly, these profits could be truly exciting. I thought the whole subject of judging what makes a business grow an intriguing one, and here was a game that if I learned to play it properly would by comparison make any other with which I was familiar seem drab, meaningless and unexciting. When my uncle left, my grandmother turned to me and said how sorry she was that he happened to come in when I was there, forcing her to spend time on matters which could not possibly interest me. I told her that, to the contrary, the hour he spent with her had seemed like ten minutes, and that I had just heard something that interested me tremendously. Years later I was to realize how very few were the shares she owned and how extremely superficial were the comments I heard that day, but the interest that was kindled by that conversation has continued all during my life.

With this degree of interest and in a period when most businesses were far less concerned with the legal hazards of dealing with minors than is the case today, I was able to make a few dollars for myself during the roaring bull market of the middle 1920's. I was strongly discouraged from this, however, by my physician father, who felt that it would simply teach me gambling habits. This was unlikely, as I am not by nature inclined to take chances merely for the sake of taking chances, which is the nature of gambling. On the other hand, as I look back upon it, my tiny scale stock activities of that period taught me almost nothing of any great value so far as investment policies were concerned.

FORMATIVE EXPERIENCES

Before the Great Bull Market of the 1920's was to come to its crashing end, I did have an experience, however, that was to teach me much of real importance for use in the years ahead. In the 1927–28 academic year I was enrolled as a first-year student in Stanford University's then fledgling Graduate School of Business. Twenty per cent of that year's course, that is one day a week, was devoted to visiting some of the largest business enterprises in the San Francisco Bay area. Professor Boris Emmett, who conducted this activity, had not been given this responsibility because of the usual academic background. In those days, the large mail order companies obtained a significant part of their merchandise through contracts with suppliers whose sole customer was one or the other of these firms. These contracts frequently were so hard on the manufacturer and afforded him so little profit margin that from time to time a manufacturer would find himself in severe financial difficulty. It was not in the interest of the mail order houses to see their vendors fail. Professor Emmett had for some years been the expert employed by one such mail order firm with the job of salvaging these faltering companies when they had been squeezed too tightly. As a result, he knew a great deal about management. One of the rules under which this course was conducted was that we would visit no company that would just take us through the plant. After "seeing the wheels go around," the management had to be willing to sit down with us so that, under the very shrewd questioning of our professor, we could learn something of what the strengths and weaknesses of the business really were. I recognized that this was a learning opportunity of just the type that I was seeking. I was able to jockey myself into a position to take particular advantage of it. In that day, over a half century ago, when the ratio of automobiles to people was tremendously lower than it is today, Professor Emmett did not have a car. I did. I offered to drive him to these various plants. I did not learn much from him on the way over. However, each week on the way back to Stanford, I would hear comments of what he really thought of that particular company. This provided me with one of the most valuable learning experiences I have ever been privileged to enjoy.

Also on one of these trips I formed a specific conviction that was to prove of tremendous dollar value to me a few years in the future. It was actually to lay the foundation for my business. One week we visited not one but two manufacturing plants that were located next door to each other in San Jose. One was the John Bean Spray Pump Company, the world leaders in the manufacture of the type of pumps that were used to spray insecticides on orchards to combat natural pests. The other was the Anderson-Barngrover Manufacturing Company, also world leaders, but in the field of equipment used by fruit canneries. In the 1920's the concept of a "growth company" had not yet been verbalized by the financial community. However, as I somewhat awkwardly worded it to Professor Emmett, "I thought that those two companies had probabilities of growing very much beyond their present size to a degree that I had seen in no other company we had visited." He agreed with me.

Also, through spending part of the time on these automobile trips by asking Professor Emmett about his previous business experiences, I learned something else that was to stand me in good stead in the years ahead. This was the extreme importance of selling in order to have a healthy business. A company might be an extremely efficient manufacturer or an inventor might have a product with breathtaking possibilities, but this was never enough for a healthy business. Unless that business contained people capable of convincing others as to the worth of their product, such a business would never really control its own destiny. It was later that I was to build on this base to conclude that even a strong sales arm is not enough. For a company to be a truly worthwhile investment, it must not only be able to sell its products, but also be able to appraise changing needs and desires of its customers; in other words, to master all that is implied in a true concept of marketing.

FIRST LESSONS IN THE SCHOOL OF EXPERIENCE

As the summer of 1928 approached and my first year in the business school came to an end, an opportunity arose which seemed to me too good to pass up. In contrast to the hundreds of students that are enrolled each year in this school today, my class, being only the third in the graduate school's history, contained nineteen students. The graduating class one year ahead of me contained only nine. Just two of these nine were trained in finance. In that day of great stock market ferment, both were snapped up by New York-based investment trusts. At the last minute, an independent San Francisco bank, which years later was acquired by the Crocker National Bank of that city, sent down to the school a request for a graduate trained in investments. The school was anxious not to pass up this opportunity because if their representative merited the approval of the bank, it could be the forerunner of many opportunities for placing future graduates in the years to come. However, they had no graduate to send. It was not easy to do, but when I heard of this opportunity, I finally persuaded the school to send me with the thought that if I were to make good, I would stay there. If I could not fill the job, I would come back and take second-year courses, with the bank realizing that the school had made no pretense of sending them a completely trained student.

Security analysts in those pre-crash days were called statisticians. It was three successive years of sensationally falling stock prices that were to occur just a short time ahead that caused the work of Wall Street's statisticians to fall into such disrepute that the name was changed to security analysts.

I found that I was to be the statistician for the investment banking end of the bank. In those days, there was no legal barrier to banks being in the brokerage or investment banking business. The work I was assigned to do was extremely simple. In my opinion, it was also intellectually dishonest. The investment arm of the bank was chiefly engaged in selling high interest rate, new issues of bonds on which they made quite sizable commissions as part of underwriting syndicates. No attempt was made to evaluate the quality of these bonds or any stocks they sold, but rather in that day of a seller's market they gratefully accepted any part of a syndicate offered them by their New York associates or by the large investment banking houses. Then the security salesmen for the bank would portray to their customers that they had a statistical department capable of surveying those customers' holdings and issuing to them a report on each security handled. What was actually done in those "security analyses" was to look up the data on a particular company in one of the established manuals of the day, such as *Moody's* or *Standard Statistics*. Then someone like myself, with no further knowledge than what was reported in that manual, would simply paraphrase the wording of the manual to write his own report. Any company that was doing a large volume of sales was invariably reported as "well managed," just because it was big. I was under no direct orders to recommend that customers switch some of the securities I "analyzed" into whatever security the bank was attempting to sell at the moment, but the whole atmosphere was one of encouraging this type of analysis.

BUILDING THE BASICS

It was not very long before the superficiality of the whole procedure caused me to feel that there must be a better way to do this. I was extremely fortunate in having an immediate boss who completely understood why I was concerned and granted me the time to make an experiment which I proposed to him. At that time, in the fall of 1928, there was a great deal of speculative interest in radio stocks. I introduced myself as a representative of the investment arm of the bank to the buyers of the radio department of several retail establishments in San Francisco. I asked them their opinions of the three major competitors in this industry. I was given surprisingly similar opinions from each of them. In particular, I learned a great deal from one man who was himself an engineer and who had worked for one of these companies. One company, Philco, which from my standpoint unfortunately was privately owned so that it represented no stock market opportunity, had developed models which had especial market appeal. As a result, they were getting market share at a beautiful profit to themselves because they were highly efficient manufacturers. RCA was just about holding its own market share, whereas another company, which was a stock market favorite of the day, was slipping drastically and showing signs of getting into trouble. None of this was the direct business of the bank, for it was not handling radio stocks. Nevertheless, an evaluative report seemed likely to help me considerably within the bank because many key bank officers who would see it were personally involved in speculation in these issues. Nowhere in material from Wall Street firms who were talking about these "hot" radio issues could I find a single word about the troubles that were obviously developing for this speculative favorite.

In the ensuing twelve months, as the stock market continued on its reckless but merry way with most stocks climbing to new highs, I noticed with increasing interest how the stock I had singled out for trouble was sagging further and further in that rising market. It was my first lesson in what later was to become part of my basic investment philosophy: reading the printed financial records about a company is never enough to justify an investment. One of the major steps in prudent investment must be to find out about a company's affairs from those who have some direct familiarity with them.

At this early point, however, I had not achieved the next logical step in this type of reasoning: it is also necessary to learn as much as possible about the people who are running a company under investment considerations, either by getting to know those people yourself or by finding someone in whom you have confidence who knows them well.

As 1929 started to unfold, I became more and more convinced of the unsoundness of the wild boom that seemed to be continuing. Stocks continued climbing to ever higher prices on the amazing theory that we were in a "new era." Therefore, in the future, year after year of advancing per share earnings could be taken as a matter of course. Yet as I tried to appraise the outlook for America's basic industries, I saw a number of them with supply-demand problems that seemed to me to indicate their outlook was getting rather wobbly.

In August of 1929 I issued another special report to the officers of the bank. I predicted that the next six months would see the beginning of the greatest bear market in a quarter of a century. It would be very satisfying to my ego, if at this point, I could alter drastically the tale of just what happened and leave the impression that, having been exactly right in my forecasting, I then profited greatly from all this wisdom. The facts were quite to the contrary.

Even though I felt strongly that the whole stock market was too high in those dangerous days of 1929, I was nevertheless entrapped by the lure of the market. This caused me to look around to find a few stocks that "were still cheap" and were worthwhile investments because "they had not gone up yet." As a result of the small profits from the tiny amount of stock transactions a few years back and the saving of a good part of my salary, plus some money I had earned in college, I managed to scrape together several thousand dollars as 1929 went along. I divided this almost equally among three stocks which, in my ignorance, I thought were still undervalued in that overpriced market. One was a leading locomotive company with a still quite low price earnings ratio. With railroad equipment being one of the most cyclical of all industries, it takes very little imagination to see what was to happen to that company's sales and profits in the business depression that was about to engulf us. The other two were a local billboard company and a local taxicab company, also selling at very low price earnings ratios. In spite of my success in ferreting out what was going to happen to the radio stocks, I just did not have the sense to start making similar inquiries from people who knew about these two local enterprises, even though obtaining such information or even getting to meet the people who ran these businesses would have been relatively simple, since they were close at hand. As the depression increased, I learned rather vividly why these companies had been selling at such low price earnings ratios. By 1932, only a tiny percentage of my original investment was represented by the market value of the shares in these companies.

THE GREAT BEAR MARKET

Fortunately for my future well-being, I have an intense dislike for losing money. I have always believed that the chief difference between a fool and a wise man is that the wise man learns from his mistakes, while the fool never does. The corollary of this is that it behooved me to go over my mistakes pretty carefully and not to repeat them again.

My approach to investing expanded as I learned from my 1929 mistakes. I learned that, while a stock could be attractive when it had a low price earnings ratio, a low price earnings ratio by itself guaranteed nothing and was apt to be a warning indicator of a degree of weakness in the company. I began realizing that, all the then current Wall Street opinion to the contrary, what really counts in determining whether a stock is cheap or overpriced is not its ratio to the current year's earnings, but its ratio to the earnings a few years ahead. If I could build up in myself the ability to determine within fairly broad limits what those earnings might be a few years from now, I would have unlocked the key both to avoiding losses and to making magnificent profits!

In addition to learning that a low price earnings ratio was just as apt to be a sign that a stock was an investment trap as that it was a bargain, acute awareness of my miserable investment performances during the Great Bear Market made me vividly aware of something of possibly even greater importance. I had been spectacularly right in my timing of when the bull market bubble was about to burst, and almost right in judging the full force of what was to happen. Yet except for a possible small boost in my reputation among a very small circle of people, this had done me no good whatsoever. From then on, I was to realize that all the correct reasoning about an investment policy or about the desirability or purchase or sale of any particular stock did not have the least bit of value until it was translated into action through the completion of specific transactions.

A CHANCE TO DO MY THING

In the spring of 1930 I made a change of employers, I only mention this because it triggered the events that were to cause the emergence of the investment philosophy that has guided me since that time. A regional brokerage firm came to me and made me a salary offer which, at age 22 and for that time and place, I found quite difficult to refuse. Furthermore, they offered me a vastly more appealing work assignment than the dissatisfying experience as a "statistician" in the investment banking arm of the bank. With no assigned duties whatsoever, I was to be free to devote my time to finding individual stocks which I thought were particularly suitable candidates for either purchase or sale because of their characteristics. I was then to write reports on my conclusions to circulate among the brokers employed by this firm to help them stimulate business that would be profitable for their clients.

This offer came to me just after Herbert Hoover had made his famous "Prosperity is just around the corner" statement. Several partners of the firm involved implicitly believed this. As a result of the 1929 crash, their total payroll had dropped from 125 employees to 75. They told me that if I accepted their offer, I would be number 76. I was just as bearish at the time as they were bullish. I felt sure the bear market was a long way from over. I told them that I would come on one condition. While they were free to fire me at any time if they did not like the quality of my work, lack of seniority must be no influence whatsoever if adverse financial markets forced them to make further reduction in payroll. They agreed to this provision.

FROM DISASTER, OPPORTUNITY SPRINGS

As employers, I could not have asked for nicer people. In the ensuing eight months, I had one of the most valuable business educational experiences of my life. I saw at first hand example after example of how the investment business should not be conducted. As 1930 unfolded and stocks once again continued on what seemed like an almost endless decline, my employers' position got more and more precarious. Then, just before Christmas of 1930, we, who had so far survived the economic holocaust, witnessed the grim picture of the whole firm being suspended from the San Francisco Stock Exchange for insolvency.

This grim news for my associates was to prove one of the most fortunate business developments, if not the most fortunate, of my life. For some time I had had vague plans that when prosperity returned I would start my own business by charging clients a fee for managing their investments. I am purposely using this roundabout way to describe the activities of an investment counselor or an investment advisor because in those days neither of these terms had yet been used. However, with almost everyone in the financial business retrenching during that gloomy January of 1931, the only security industry job I could find was a purely clerical and, to me, a quite unattractive one. If I had properly analyzed the situation, I would have realized that this was exactly the right time to start a new business of the kind I had in mind. I was to find that there were two reasons for this. One was that, after almost two years of the most severe bear market this nation had ever seen, nearly everyone was so dissatisfied with their existing brokerage connections that they were in the mood to listen even to someone both young and advocating a radically different approach to the handling of their investments as was

I. Also, as the economy reached its depths in 1932, many key business-men had so little to do in pursuing their own affairs that they had the time to see someone who was calling on them. In more normal times, I would never have gotten by their secretaries. One of the most worthwhile clients of my entire business career and a man whose family's investments I still handle was a typical example of this. Some years afterwards he told me that on the day I called he had had almost nothing to do and had already finished reading the sports section of the newspaper. So when my name and purpose were told him by his secretary, he thought, "Listening to this guy will at least occupy my time." He confessed, "If you had come to see me a year or so later, you never would have gotten into my office."

A FOUNDATION IS FORMED

All this was to result in several years of very hard work in a tiny office with low overhead. With no windows and merely glass partitions to serve as two of the walls, my total floor space was little larger than that needed to jam together a desk, my chair, and one other chair. For this, together with free local telephone service and a reasonable amount of secretarial help from the secretary-receptionist of the gentleman from whom I leased this space, I paid the princely sum of $25 per month. My only other expenses were stationery, postage and a very occasional long distance call. The account book still in my possession provides an indication of how difficult it really was to start a new business in 1932. After very long hours of work over and above this overhead, I made a net profit averaging $2.99 per month for that year. In the still difficult year of 1933, I did a trifle better, showing an improvement of just under 1000%, an average monthly earnings of just over $29. This possibly was about what I would have made as a newsboy selling papers on the street. Yet in what those years were to bring me in the future, they were two of the most profitable years of my life. They provided me with the foundation for an extremely profitable business and with a group of highly loyal clients by 1935. It would be nice if I could claim that it was brilliant thinking on my part that caused me to start my business when I did rather than waiting until better times were to arrive. Actually, it was the unattractiveness of the only job that seemed open to me that pushed me into it.

2

LEARNING FROM EXPERIENCE

W hile I had been working at the bank, I had noticed with considerable interest a news item about the two neighboring San Jose companies that had intrigued me so much during my student days at the Stanford Business School. In 1928 the John Bean Manufacturing Co. and the Anderson-Barngrover Manufacturing Co. had merged with a leading vegetable canning manufacturer, Sprague Sells Corporation of Hoopeston, Illinois, to form a brand new entity called the Food Machinery Corporation.

As in other periods of rampant speculation the nation was in the throes of such a stock buying mania, that the supply of Food Machinery Corporation stock offered for sale rose in price in an attempt to meet the demand. In that same year of 1928, at least twenty other new issues, and perhaps twice that many, were sold by members of the San Francisco Stock Exchange to eager buyers in the Bay area. The lack of soundness of some of these issues was little short of appalling. An officer of one stock exchange firm, that sold shares in a company that was to sell bottled water from across the Pacific, told me that these shares were sold without a complete set of financial statements in the hands of the underwriters, who had little more than a photograph of the spring from which the water was supposed to come and a minor amount of personal contact with the selling shareholders! In the public mind, the stock of the Food Machinery Corporation was just another of the exciting new offerings of that year, neither significantly better nor worse than the rest. It was offered at a price of $21½.

214

In those days, pools for the manipulation of shares were entirely legal. A local group with little expertise in running a pool but headed by a man with great enthusiasm for Food Machinery Corporation decided to "run an operation" in the company's shares. The methods of all these pools were fundamentally similar. The members would sell stock back and forth among themselves at gradually rising prices. All this activity on the stock tape would attract the attention of others, who would then start to buy and take the pool's shares off its hands at still higher prices. Some highly skilled manipulators, some of whom had made many millions of dollars and one of whom, a year or so later, was to offer me a junior partnership, were quite experienced and able practitioners of this rather questionable art. Manipulation was not the objective of the operators of this Food Machinery pool, however. As the autumn of 1929 was to arrive and stocks were to face the precipice that lay ahead, the pool managed to buy for itself most of the shares that had been offered to the public. Although the quoted price of the Food Machinery shares at the peak was in the high 50's, there was very little stock in the hands of the public as a result.

As in each of the succeeding years the general level of business activities worsened relative to the year before, it was obvious what was to happen to the flotsam and jetsam of small companies that went public in the 1928 excitement. One after another of these companies passed into bankruptcy, with many of the remainder reporting losses rather than profits. The market for the shares of these firms largely dried up.

There were one or two companies in this group other than Food Machinery that were fundamentally both sound and attractive. However, the general public showed no discrimination whatsoever, considering all of them little more than speculative junk. By the time the market was to reach its final low in 1932, and again equal that low at the time of closing of the entire banking system of the country coincidental with the inauguration of Franklin D. Roosevelt on March 4, 1933, Food Machinery shares were down to a price of between $4 and $5, with the all-time low being 100 shares at $3¾.

FOOD MACHINERY AS AN INVESTMENT OPPORTUNITY

As 1931 unfolded and I cast about seeking an opportunity for my infant business, I looked upon Food Machinery's situation with increasing excitement. Recognizing the costliness of my not having taken the trouble to meet with and judge the managements of the two local companies in which I had lost such a large percentage of my investment a few years before, I determined never to make this mistake again. The more I got to know the Food Machinery people, the greater my respect for them grew. Because in many ways this company, as it existed in the depths of the Great Depression, was a microcosm of the type of opportunity I was to seek in the years ahead. It may be helpful to explain just what it was that caused me nearly a half century ago to see such a future in this particular corporation.

Parenthetically and unfortunately, I did not carry my policy of in-depth field analysis through to its logical conclusion in the immediate years. I was less diligent in getting to know and to judge managements that were located in more distant areas.

In the first place, even though Food Machinery was relatively small, it was a world leader in size and, I believe, in quality of the product line in each of the three activities in which it was engaged. This gave the firm the advantage of scale; that is, as a large and efficient manufacturer the firm could also be a low cost producer.

Next, its marketing position was, from a competitive standpoint, extremely strong. Its products were highly regarded by its customers. It controlled its own sales organization. Furthermore, its canning machinery lines, with a large number of installations already in the field, had a "locked up" market of some proportions. This consisted of spare and replacement parts for the equipment already in the field.

Added to this sound base was the most exciting part of the business. For a company of its size, the firm enjoyed a superbly creative engineering or research department. The company was perfecting equipment in promising new product areas. Among these were the first mechanical pear peeler ever to be offered to the industry, the first mechanical peach pitter, and a process for synthetically coloring oranges. Oranges from areas which produced fruit with the most juice were at a competitive disadvantage because the product looked less attractive to the housewife than other types in which intrinsic quality were no better. At only one other time in my business life have I seen a company which, in my judgment, had on the horizon as big a dollar volume of potentially successful new products in relation to the then existing size of business as was the case with the Food Machinery Corporation in the period from 1932 through 1934.

By this time, I had learned enough to know that, no matter how attractive, such matters by themselves were not sufficient to assure great success. The quality of the people involved in the company was just as critical. I use the word quality to encompass two quite different characteristics. One of these is business ability. Business ability can be further broken down into two very different types of skills. One of these is handling the day to day tasks of business with above average efficiency. In the day to day tasks, I include a hundred and one matters, varying all the way from constantly seeking and finding better ways to produce more efficiently to watching receivables with sufficient closeness. In other words, operating skill implies above average handling of the many things that have to do with the near-term operation of the business.

However, in the business world, top-notch managerial ability also calls for another skill that is quite different. This is the ability to look ahead and make long-range plans that will produce significant future growth for the business without at the same time running financial risks that may invite disaster. Many companies contain managements that are very good at one or the other of these skills. However, for real success, both are necessary.

Business ability is only one of the two "people" traits that I believe is absolutely essential for a truly worthwhile investment. The other falls under the general term of integrity and encompasses both the honesty and the personal decency of those who are running a company. Anyone receiving his first indoctrination into the investment world in the period that preceded the 1929 crash would have seen rather vivid examples of the extreme importance of integrity. The owners and managers of a business are always closer to that business's affairs than are the stockholders. If the managers do not have a genuine sense of trusteeship for the stockholders, sooner or later the stockholders may fail to receive a significant part of what is justly due them. Managers preoccupied by their own personal interests are not likely to develop an enthusiastic team of loyal people around them—something that is an absolute must if a business is to grow to a size that one or two people can no longer control.

As I saw the situation in those dark days of the deep depression, and as I see it now after all these years, this infant Food Machinery Corporation was unusually attractive from the "people" standpoint. John D. Crummey, the president and son-in-law of the original founder of the

John Bean Manufacturing Co., was not only an extremely efficient operating head and highly regarded by his customers and his employees, but also he was a deeply religious man who scrupulously lived up to a high moral code. The chief engineer of the company was a brilliant conceptual designer. Also of considerable importance, he was a man who designed along lines that would give his products worthwhile patent protection. Finally, to round out the strength of this relatively small organization, John Crummey persuaded his son-in-law, Paul L. Davies, who was reluctant to abandon what appeared to be a most promising career in banking, to join the company to give it financial strength and conservatism. Actually, Paul Davies at first made this move so reluctantly that he only agreed to take a one-year leave of absence from the bank to help his family business over the first rough year of merger. During that year, he became so interested in the exciting prospects that lay ahead that he decided to stay permanently with the company. Later, as its president, he was to lead it to a size and degree of prosperity that was to dwarf the pleasing accomplishments of the next few years.

This then was a company that inherently had desirable characteristics that are only occasionally found among available investments. The people were outstanding. Yet, small as the company was, it was not just one man who was making key contributions. In relation to competitors, the company was unusually strong, it was handling its business well, and it had in the offing enough new product lines with potentials that were large in relation to the then size of the company. Even if some of these products did not materialize, the future should be very bright with others.

ZIGGING AND ZAGGING

However, to all this should be added something of equal importance if an investment is to prove a genuine bonanza. The largest profits in the investment field go to those who are capable of correctly zigging when the financial community is zagging. If the future of the Food Machinery Corporation had been properly appraised at that time, the profits that were to accrue to those who bought the shares in the 1932–1934 period would have been very much smaller. It was only because the true worth of this company was not generally recognized and Food Machinery was thought to be just another of the many "flaky" companies which were sold to the public at the height of a speculative orgy that it was possible to buy these shares in quantity at the ridiculous price to which they had sunk. This matter of training oneself not to go with the crowd but to be able to zig when the crowd zags, in my opinion, is one of the most important fundamentals of investment success.

I wish I had the command of English to be able to describe adequately the degree of my internal, emotional and intellectual excitement as I contemplated what this as yet financially unrecognized Food Machinery Corporation might do for both my tiny personal finances and for the infant business I was attempting to get started. My timing seemed right. Like a spring that had been compressed too far and was starting to recoil, the years from 1933 to 1937 were to see stocks as a whole advancing slowly at first, and then bursting into a full bloom bull market, followed by a sizable break in 1938 and a full recovery the following year. With a deep conviction that Food Machinery would vastly outperform the market as a whole, I bought my clients every share that I was able to convince them to hold. I made the possibilities of this business the spearhead of my approach in talking to any potential clients I could reach. I felt that here was just the type of unique, almost once in a lifetime, opportunity that as Shakespeare so well described when he said, "There is a tide in the affairs of men which, taken at the flood, leads on to fortune." In those exciting years when my hopes were high and both my purse and reputation in the financial community were almost non-existent, I quoted those exciting words to myself time and time again to stiffen my determination.

CONTRARY, BUT CORRECT

Much has been written in the literature of investments on the importance of contrary opinion. Contrary opinion, however, is not enough. I have seen investment people so imbued with the need to go contrary to the general trend of thought that they completely overlook the corollary of all this which is: when you do go contrary to the general trend of investment thinking, you must be very, very sure that you are right. For example, as it became obvious that the automobile was largely to displace the streetcar and the shares of the once favored urban railways began to sell at ever lower price earnings ratio, it would have been a rather costly thing just to be contrary and buy streetcar securities only on the grounds that because everyone thought they were in a declining stage, they must be attractive. Huge profits are frequently available to those who zig when most of the financial community is zagging, providing they have strong indications that they are right in their zigging.

If a quotation from Shakespeare was a vital force in formulating my policies on the matter, so also, strangely enough, was a popular song from World War I. As one of the very thinning ranks of those who can still remember how the home front reacted in the stirring days of 1918, I might point out that in its excitement and enthusiasm for that war the American public had a naivete then quite different from its grimness about such matters in World War II, when the horrors of war were more clearly understood. Firsthand news of the casualties and the filth and the terror of those in the front lines had not yet permeated the continental United States in 1918. As a result, the popular music of the day was filled with cheerful and humorous war songs in a way that happened on a much smaller scale in World War II, and not at all during the Viet Nam fiasco. Most of these songs came out in the form of sheet music for pianos. One of these songs, published with a picture of a proud mama looking down on parading soldiers, had the title, "They're All Out of Step But Jim."

I recognized from the very first that I was running a distinct risk of being "out of step." My very early purchases of Food Machinery and a number of other companies were bought "out of phase," when their intrinsic merit was completely unrecognized by the financial community. I might be completely wrong in my thinking and the financial community could be right. If so, nothing would be worse for my clients or myself than letting my firm convictions about a particular situation lock up a sizable amount of funds unprofitably for an endless period of years because I zigged when the financial community had zagged, and I had been wrong in doing so.

However, while I realized thoroughly that if I were to make the kinds of profits that are made possible by the process that I have described as zigging when the rest zags, it was vital that I have some sort of quantitative check to be sure that I was right in zigging.

PATIENCE AND PERFORMANCE

With this in mind, I established what I called my three-year rule. I have repeated again and again to my clients that when I purchase something for them, not to judge the results in a matter of a month or a year, but to allow me a three-year period. If I have not produced worthwhile results for them in that time, they should fire me. Whether I have been successful in the first year or unsuccessful can be as much a matter of luck as anything else. In my management of individual stocks over all these years I have followed the same rule, only once having made an exception. If I have a deep conviction about a stock that has not performed by the end of three years, I will sell it. If this same stock has performed worse rather than better than the market for a year or two, I won't like it. However, assuming that nothing has happened to change my original view of the company, I will continue to hold it for three years.

In the second half of 1955, I bought a substantial number of shares in two companies in which I had never previously invested. They proved to be almost a classic example of the advantages and problems of investing contrary to the currently accepted view of the financial community. Looking back, 1955 could be considered the beginning of a period of almost fifteen years that might be termed the "first Golden Age of electronic stocks." I am using the adjective "first" so that there can be no confusion in anyone's mind with what I believe will be considered the Golden Age for semiconductor stocks, something which I suspect lies ahead of us and will be associated with the 1980's. At any rate, in 1955 and immediately thereafter, the financial community was about to be dazzled by a whole series of electronic companies which were to show gains that by 1969 had reached truly spectacular proportions. IBM, Texas Instruments, Varian, Litton Industries and Ampex are a few that come to mind. However, in 1955, all of that lay ahead. At that time, with the exception of IBM, all these stocks were considered highly speculative and beneath the notice of conservative investors or big institutions. However, sensing part of what might lie ahead, I acquired what for me were rather sizable positions in both Texas Instruments and Motorola during the latter parts of 1955.

Today Texas Instruments is the largest world-wide producer of semiconductors, with Motorola running a close second. At that time, Motorola's position in the semiconductor industry was insignificant. It was no factor at all in causing me to buy the shares. Rather, I became impressed both with the people and with Motorola's dominant position in the mobile communications business, where an enormous potential seemed to lie; whereas the financial community was valuing it as just another television and radio producer. Motorola's subsequent rise in the semiconductor area, resulting at least in part from their acquiring the services of Dr. Daniel Noble, was all to come later and was additional icing on the cake not anticipated by me at the time of purchase. In the case of Texas Instruments, aside from an equally great liking and respect for the people, I was influenced by a quite different set of beliefs. I saw, as did others, a tremendous future that could be built out of their transistor business as the complexities of semiconductors were yielding to human ingenuity. I felt that those were people who could compete on at least even terms, and probably better than even terms, with General Electric, RCA, Westinghouse, and other giant companies despite the opinion of much of Wall Street. A number of people criticized me for risking funds in a small "speculative company" which they felt was bound to suffer from the competition of the corporate giants.

After buying these shares, the near-term results in the stock market were quite different. Within a year, Texas Instruments had increased in value quite handsomely. Motorola fluctuated in a range from 5% to 10% below my cost of purchase. It performed sufficiently poorly that one of my major clients became so irritated by its market action that he refused to call Motorola by name. He only referred to it as "that turkey which you bought me." These unsatisfactory quotations were to continue for moderately over a year. Yet as awareness of the investment significance of the communications arm of Motorola was to seep into the consciousness of the financial community, together with the first signs of a turnabout in the semiconductor area, the stock then became a rather spectacular performer.

While I was buying Motorola, I was doing so in conjunction with a large insurance company that had let the Motorola management know that they were also interested in the conclusions of my first visit. Shortly after the insurance company too had bought a significant amount of Motorola stock, they submitted their entire portfolio to a New York bank for appraisal. With the exception of Motorola, the bank divided their portfolio into three groups: most attractive, less attractive, and least attractive. They refused to place Motorola in any category, however, saying this was not the type of company on which they spent time; therefore they had no opinion about it. Yet one of the officials of the insurance company told me over three years later that in the face of this rather negative Wall Street view, Motorola had by that time outperformed every other stock in their portfolio! If I had not had my "three-year rule," I might have been less firm in holding my own Motorola intact through a period of poor market action and of some client criticism.

TO EVERY RULE, THERE ARE EXCEPTIONS . . . BUT NOT MANY

Have I ever sold stock because of this three-year rule and then later wished I had not made this sale because of a subsequent major rise in the stock? Actually, there have only been a relatively small number of times when I have made a sale triggered by this three-year rule and nothing else. This is not because there have been so few times that purchases made by me have failed to provide the major rise which was my purpose in initiating them. In the majority of such cases, further insights about the company opened up as I continued to investigate additional aspects of the situation and these insights caused me to change my views about it. However, in those relatively few cases where it was the three-year rule and only that which caused me to sell, I cannot recall a single case where subsequent market action caused me to wish I had held on to the shares.

Have I ever violated my own three-year rule? The answer is yes, exactly once, and this was many years later, toward the middle of the 1970's. Three years before, I had acquired a moderately substantial block of shares in the Rogers Corporation. Rogers had expertise in certain areas of polymer chemistry and I believed they were on the way to developing various semiproprietary families of products which would show quite dramatic increase in sales and not just for a year or two, but for many years. Yet, at the end of three years the stock was down, and so were the earnings of the company. Several influences were at work, however, which made me feel this was one time to ignore my own standards and to make this "the exception that proves the rule." One of these influences was my strong feeling about Norman Greenman, the company's president. I was convinced he had unusual ability, the determination to see these matters through, as well as something else which I consider of great value to an intelligent investor: the kind of honesty that caused him not to conceal repeated bad news that could not fail but be embarrassing for him to tell. He saw to it that those interested in his company understood all the unfavorable aspects of what was happening, as well as the favorable potentials.

There was another element which influenced me greatly: a major reason the company's profits were so poor was that Rogers was spending a quite disproportionate amount of money on a single new product development seeming to offer prospects of great results. This was diverting both money and people from other potentially exciting new products which were getting less corporate effort. New products of this type do have magnificent potential. When the painful decision was made to abandon all the effort on this one particular product, it was not long before it became quite apparent that several other innovations of great promise were starting to flower. All this, however, took time. In the meanwhile, the company's failure to live up to the hopes of many of those who had bought the shares caused the stock to drop to levels that were absurd in relation to its sales, its assets, or any type of normal earning power. Here seemed a classic example of zigging when the financial community was zagging. Therefore, three-year rule or no, I sizably further increased my holdings and those of my clients, even though a few of those clients, influenced by the years of waiting and the negative performance, looked at this with a degree of apprehension. As so often happens in situations of this sort, when the turn came, it came fast. As it became apparent that the betterment of earnings was not a one or two-year matter, but gave strong indications of being but the basis for years of genuine growth, the stock continued to rise proportionately.

AN EXPERIMENT WITH MARKET TIMING

All this, however, gets me years ahead of my story, because back in the 1930's there were other things I also had to learn through trial and error as my investment philosophy was gradually taking shape. In my casting around for ways to make money through common stocks, I began realizing that I might have a worthwhile by-product from my study of the Food Machinery Corporation. Enough of their business was dependent on the fruit and vegetable canning industry so that in order to be reasonably sure I was right about my Food Machinery purchases, I had inadvertently learned a good deal about what influenced the fortunes of the fruit and vegetable canning companies themselves. This industry was highly cyclical because of both fluctuating general business conditions and erratic weather influences as they affected specific crops.

As long as I was becoming somewhat familiar with the characteristics of the packing industry anyway, I decided I might as well try and take advantage of this knowledge, not through long-term investments, as I was doing with Food Machinery, but through in and out transactions in the shares of the California Packing Corporation, then an independent company and the largest fruit and vegetable canner. Three different times, from the depths of the Big Depression to the end of that decade, I bought shares of this company. Each time, I sold them at a profit.

Superficially, this might sound like I was doing something quite worthwhile. Nevertheless when, for reasons I will explain shortly, I endeavored a few years later to analyze the wise and unwise moves I made in my business, it became increasingly apparent to me how silly these activities were. They took a great deal of time and effort that could well have been devoted to other things. Yet the total rewards in dollars in relation to the sums at risk were insignificant in comparison to the profits I had made for my people in Food Machinery and in other situations where I had bought for long-range gains and held over a considerable period of years. Furthermore, I had seen enough of in and out trading, including some done by extremely brilliant people, that I knew that being successful three times in a row only made it that much more likely that the fourth time I would end in disaster. The risks were considerably more than those involved in purchasing equal amounts of shares in companies I considered promising enough to want to hold them for many years of growth. Therefore, at the end of World War II, by which time much of my present investment philosophy was largely formulated, I had made what I believe was one of the more valuable decisions of my business life. This was to confine all efforts solely to making major gains over the long run.

REACHING FOR PRICE, FOREGOING OPPORTUNITY

During the 1930's I learned, or at least partially learned, something else which I consider truly important. I have already mentioned my complete failure to benefit from my correct forecasts of the Great Bear Market which started in 1929. All the correct reasoning in the world is of no benefit in stock investment unless it is turned into specific action. My first experience in operating my own business occurred during the depth of the Great Depression, when very small amounts of money became of abnormal significance. Possibly because of this, or possibly because of my personal characteristics, as I started my business I found myself constantly battling for "eighths and quarters." Brokers who knew much more than I did kept telling me if I believed that a stock would rise in a few years to several times its current price, it really made very little difference whether I acquired its shares at $10 or $10¼. Yet I continually placed limit orders with no better reason for a limit than a purely arbitrary decision on my part that I would pay, say, $10⅛ and no more. Logically, this is ridiculous. I have observed it to be a bad investment habit that is deeply ingrained in many people besides myself, but not ingrained at all in others.

The potential dangers of arbitrary limits was made clear to me as the result of a mistake of someone else. I remember as though it were yesterday running into one of my more important clients by chance on the sidewalk in front of a San Francisco bank. I told him that I had just come back from visiting the Food Machinery Corporation, the outlook was never so exciting, and that I thought he should buy some additional shares. He completely agreed with me and asked where the stock had closed that particular afternoon. I told him $34½. He gave me a significant order and said he would pay $33¾ but no more. Over the next day or two the stock fluctuated in a range just fractionally above his bid. It never got down to it. I phoned him twice, urging him to go up a quarter of a point so that I could buy stock. Unfortunately he replied, "No, that is my price." Within a few weeks the stock had risen over 50% and, after allowing for stock split-ups, never again in the company's history was it to come down to anywhere near where he could have bought it.

This gentleman's actions made an impression on me that my own stupidity had not. Gradually, I was to overcome much of this weakness of mine. I am thoroughly aware that if a buyer desires to acquire a very large block of stock, he cannot completely ignore this matter of an eighth or a quarter, because by buying a very few shares he can significantly put the price up on himself for the balance. However, for the great majority of transactions, being stubborn about a tiny fractional difference in the price can prove extremely costly. In my own case, I have completely conquered it in regard to buying, but only partially in regard to selling. Within the past year, my placing a small sell order with a limit rather than at the market caused me to miss a transaction by exactly a quarter of a point, with the result that, as I write this, the shares are now down 35% from where I placed my order. At levels only half way between that limit order and current prices, I sold only part of this not very large holding.

3

THE PHILOSOPHY MATURES

O ur entry into World War II was not entirely without some significance in the development of my investment philosophy. Early in 1942 I found myself in an unaccustomed role as a ground officer doing various business related jobs for the Army Air Corps. For three and a half years, I simply "beached" my business as I performed my not very valuable services on behalf of Uncle Sam. In recent years, I have frequently said that I did quite a job for my country. Neither Hitler nor Emperor Hirohito ever succeeded in getting a man into the territories I defended. These were Arkansas, Texas, Kansas, and Nebraska! At any rate, during this time of various desk type jobs wearing Uncle Sam's uniform, I found that almost without warning I would alternate between two different types of periods. For a while, I would have so much to do that the last thing I would be able to think about was my peacetime business. At other times, I would sit at my desk with very little to do. When things were slow, I found it less unpleasant to analyze in great detail just how I would build up my business when the happy day that I would no longer be wearing a uniform might arise than it was to think of the personal living and Army type problems with which, from a short-range point of view, I was confronted. It was during such periods that my present investment philosophy took steadily more definite shape. It was then I decided there was not enough future in the type of in and out trading that I have described in the stock of California Packing.

During this period, I reached two other conclusions that were to be of some significance to my future business. Before the war I had served all types of clients, large and small, with varying types of objectives. Most, but not all, of my business had been focused on finding unusual companies that would enjoy significant, above-average growth in future years. After the war, I would limit my clientele to a small group of large investors with the objective of concentrating solely on this single class of growth investment. For tax reasons, growth was more likely to benefit these clients.

My other major conclusion was that the chemical industry would enjoy a period of major growth in the postwar years. Therefore, a high priority project on returning to civilian life was to endeavor to find the most attractive of the larger chemical companies and make this a major holding for the funds I was handling. I by no means spent 100 percent of my time doing this, but in the first year after restarting my business I did spend a rather considerable amount of time in talking to anyone I could find who had real knowledge of this complex industry. Such people as distributors who handled the lines of one or more large companies, professors in the chemical departments of the universities who had intimate knowledge of chemical business people, and even some of those in the major construction companies that had put up plants for various of the chemical producers all proved extremely worthwhile sources of background information. By combining these inputs with analyses of the usual financial data, it only took about three months to narrow the choices down to one of three companies. From there on, the going was slower and the decisions more difficult. However, by the spring of 1947 I decided that the Dow Chemical Company would be my choice.

E PLURIBUS UNUM

There were many reasons for the choice of Dow Chemical from the many promising chemical firms. I believe it might be worthwhile to enumerate some of them because they are clear examples of the type of things I seek in the relatively small number of companies in which I desire to place funds. As I began to know various people in the Dow organization, I found that the growth that had already occurred was in turn creating a very real sense of excitement at many levels of management. The belief that even greater growth lay ahead permeated the organization. One of my favorite questions in talking to any top business executive for the first time is what he considers to be the most important long-range problem facing his company. When I asked this of the president of Dow, I was tremendously impressed with his answer: "It is to resist the strong pressures to become a more military-like organization as we grow very much larger, and to maintain the informal relationship whereby people at quite different levels and in various departments continue to communicate with each other in a completely unstructured way and, at the same time, not create administrative chaos."

I found myself in complete agreement with certain other basic company policies. Dow limited its involvement to those chemical product lines where it either was or had a reasonable chance of becoming the most efficient producer in the field as the result of greater volume, better chemical engineering and deeper understanding of the product or for some other reason. Dow was deeply aware of the need for creative research not just to be in front, but also to stay in front. There was also a strong appreciation of the "people factor" at Dow. There was in particular a sense of need to identify people of unusual ability early, to indoctrinate them into policies and procedures unique to Dow, and to make real efforts to see if seemingly bright people were not doing well at one job, they be given a reasonable chance to try something else that might be more suitable to their characteristics.

I found that although Dow's founder, Dr. Herbert Dow, had died some seventeen years before, his beliefs were held in such respect that one or another of his sayings was frequently quoted to me. While his comments were directed primarily at matters within Dow, I decided that at least two of them were equally appropriate to my own business, in that they could be applied at least as well as to optimizing the selection of investments as to matters internal to the Dow Chemical Company. One of these was "Never promote someone who hasn't made some bad mistakes, because if you do, you are promoting someone who has never done anything." The failure to understand this element by so many in the investment community has time and again created unusual investment opportunities in the stock market.

The truly worthwhile accomplishment in the business world nearly always requires a considerable degree of pioneering, in which ingenuity has to be seasoned with practicality. This is particularly true when the gains are sought through leading edge technological research. No matter how able the people are and no matter how good may be most of their ideas, there are times when such efforts are bound to fail, and fail dismally. When this happens and the current year's earnings drop sharply below previous estimates as the costs of the failure are added up, time and again the investment community's immediate consensus is to downgrade the quality of the management. As a result, the immediate year's lower earnings produce a lower than the historic price earnings ratio to magnify the effect of reduced earnings. The shares often reach truly bargain prices. Yet if this is the same management that in other years has been so successful, the chances are the same ratio of average success to average failure will continue on in the future. For this reason, the shares of companies run by abnormally capable people can be tremendous bargains at the time one particular bad mistake comes to light. In contrast, the company that doesn't pioneer, doesn't take chances, and merely goes along with the crowd is liable to prove a rather mediocre investment in this highly competitive age.

The other of Dr. Dow's comments which I have tried to apply to the process of investment selection is "If you can't do a thing better than others are doing it, don't do it at all." In this day of heavy-handed government intervention in so many types of business activities, of high taxes and labor unions, and of rapid shifts in public taste from one product to another, it seems to me that the risk of common stock ownership is seldom warranted unless it is confined to companies with enough competitive spirit constantly to be trying and frequently succeeding in doing things in a manner superior to industry in general. In no other way are profit margins usually broad enough to meet the demands of growth. This is, of course, particularly true during periods when inflation is having a significant effect in eating away at reported profits.

HISTORY VERSUS OPPORTUNITY

There were some remarkable parallels between the period when I was starting my business at the depths of the Great Depression and during the years 1947 through the very early 1950's, when I was restarting it after a military service interlude of three and a half years. Both periods were times when it was unusually hard to obtain immediate results for clients in the face of overwhelming general pessimism. Both were times that were to prove spectacularly rewarding for those who had the patience. In the earlier period, stocks were driven to perhaps the lowest level in relation to real value seen in the Twentieth Century, not just because of the economic havoc wrought by the Great Depression, but also because prices were discounting the worry of many investors as to whether the American system of private enterprise would itself survive. It survived, and in the ensuing years the rewards of those able and willing to invest in the right stocks were fabulous.

Just a few years after World War II, another fear kept stocks at levels almost as low in relation to intrinsic value as those seen at the depths of the Great Depression. This time, business was good and corporate earnings were steadily rising. Nevertheless, almost the entire investment community were mesmerized by a simple comparison. A relatively few years after the Civil War, a period of immediate prosperity was followed by the Panic of 1873, and almost six years of deep depression. A somewhat similar period of prosperity after World War I was followed by the Crash of 1929 and the even deeper depression of about the same length. In World War II, the costs of war had run on a per diem basis about ten times that of World War I. "Therefore," reasoned the dominant investment view of this period, "current excellent earnings don't mean anything." They will be followed by a horrendous crash and a period of extreme adversity when all would suffer.

Year after year went by, and the per share earnings of more corporations rose. Along about 1949, this period became known as the era in which "American business is worth more dead than alive," because as soon as word spread that a publicly owned company was about to go out of business, its shares would rise dramatically. The liquidating value of many a company was so much more than its current market valuation. Year followed year, and slowly it began dawning on the investment public that perhaps stocks were being held back because of a myth. The expected business decline never did arrive and, excepting for two relatively minor recessions in the 1950's, the stage was being set for the great rewards to long-term investors that were to follow.

As I write these words in the closing weeks before the decade of the 80's is about to start, it amazes me that more attention has not been paid to restudying the few years of stock market history that started in the second half of 1946 to see whether true parallels may actually exist between that period and the present. Now, for the third time in my lifetime, many stocks are again at prices which, by historic standards, are spectacularly low. In relation to reported book value, they may not be quite as cheap as they were in the post-World War II period. However, if that reported book value is adjusted for replacement value in real dollars, they may perhaps be cheaper than in either of the two prior, bargain value periods. The question arises: are the worries that are holding back stock values in the present period, such matters as the high cost of energy or the dangers from the political left or of overextended credit, with the inevitable resulting drain on the level of business activity as liquidity is restored, more serious and more apt to stop the future growth in this country than the fears that held back stock prices in these two prior periods? If not, once the problems of overextended credit have been solved, it might be logical to assume that the 1980's and period beyond may offer the same sort of rewarding opportunities that characterized the two former periods of abnormally low prices.

LESSONS FROM THE VINTAGE YEARS

From a business standpoint, the fifteen years from 1954 through 1969 were a magnificent time for me, as most of the relatively few stocks I was holding advanced significantly more than did the market as a whole. Even so, I managed to make some bad mistakes. Successes came from diligent application of the approaches I have already spelled out. It is the mistakes that are more noteworthy. Each brought its own new lesson.

Good fortune can breed laxness. The mistake which now embarrassed me the most, although it was not the most costly, arose from the careless application of a sound principle.

In the early 1960's, I had technological investments that were proving quite pleasing in the electronic, chemical, metallurgical, and machinery industries. I did not have a comparable investment in the promising drug field, and started seeking one. Along the way, I talked to a medical specialist who was preeminent in his field. At the time, he was tremendously excited about a new drug family about to be introduced by a small Midwestern manufacturer. These drugs he felt could have quite favorable impact on the future earnings of this firm relative to others in this field. The potential market seemed very, very exciting.

I then talked to just one of the officers of this company and to only a few other investment people all of whom were equally excited about the potentials of this new drug. Unfortunately, I did not pursue my standard checks either with other drug companies or with other experts knowledgeable in this particular specialty to see if they might have contrary evidence to offer. Regretfully, I subsequently learned, none of the proponents had made a thorough investigation either.

The stock was selling at a price well above its worth before considering the benefits of this new family of drugs, but at a price which could have been but a minor fraction of potential value if the new drugs were all their supporters imagined. I bought the shares only to see them drop, at first a mere 20 percent and then over 50 percent. Ultimately the whole company was sold for cash at this low price to a large non-pharmaceutical corporation seeking to enter the drug field. Even at this price, now somewhat less than half of what I had paid for the shares, I subsequently learned that the acquiring company lost money on the deal. Not only did this new family of drugs fail to measure up to the extensive hopes that had been enthusiastically projected by my friend, the medical specialist, but also on painful "post-mortem" reexamination of the situation, I found that there were management problems in this small drug manufacturer. With a more thorough investigation both failings would, I believe, have become apparent to me.

From that embarrassing time forward, I have tried to be particularly thorough in making investigations in periods when things were going well. The only reason this particular investment folly wasn't more costly stemmed from my caution. Since I had had only a slight contact with the management, I made only a small initial investment, planning to buy more as I got to know the company better. Their troubles overtook me before I had a chance to compound my original folly.

As the long bull market was reaching its final peak in 1969 another mistake occurred. To understand what happened it is necessary to recreate the psychological fever which gripped most investors in technological and scientific stocks at that time. Shares of these companies, particularly many of the smaller ones, had enjoyed advances far greater than the market as a whole. During 1968 and 1969 only one's imagination seemed to cap the dreams of imminent success for many of these companies. Some of these situations did have genuine potential, of course. Discrimination was at a low ebb. For example, any company serving the computer industry in any way promised a future, many believed, that was almost limitless. This contagion spread into instrument and other scientific companies as well.

Up to this time, I resisted the temptation to go into any of the similar companies that had just "gone public" at very high prices in the previous year or two. Yet, being in frequent contact with those who were sponsoring these excitement inducing companies, I kept looking for a few that might be genuinely attractive. In 1969 I did find an equipment company working in an extremely interesting new frontier of technology; one that had a real basis for its existence. The firm was run by a brilliant and honest president. I can remember still, after a long luncheon session with this man, my pacing up and down the airport awaiting my airplane home and trying to determine whether I should buy this company's shares at the prevailing market. After considerable deliberation, I decided to go ahead.

I was right in diagnosing the potential of this company for it did grow in the years that followed. Nevertheless, it was a poor investment. My mistake lay in the price I paid to participate in the promise. Some years later, after the company had shown rather respectable growth, I sold these shares, but at a price very little different from my original cost. While I believe I was right in selling when I thought the company had reached a point where its future growth was considerably more uncertain, nevertheless selling an investment at a meager profit after it has been held for a number of years is not the way to make capital grow or even protect it against inflation. In this case, disappointing performance was the result of being seduced by the excitement of the times into paying an unrealistic initiation price.

DO FEW THINGS WELL

A policy judgment that was wrong for me engendered quite a different kind of mistake, and one which did cost a significant amount of dollars. My mistake was to project my skill beyond the limits of experience. I began investing outside the industries which I believe I thoroughly understood, in completely different spheres of activity; situations where I did not have comparable background knowledge.

When it comes to manufacturing companies that serve industrial markets or to companies on the leading edge of technology that are serving manufacturers, I believe that I know what to look for—where both the strong points and pitfalls may lie. However, different skills proved important in evaluating companies making and selling consumer-type products. When the products of competitive companies are essentially rather similar to one another, and when changes in market share depend largely on shifting public tastes or on fashions greatly influenced by the effectiveness of advertising, I learned that the abilities which I had in selecting outstanding technological companies did not extrapolate to the point where I could identify what produces unusual success in real estate operations.

Others may do well in quite diverse investment arenas. Perhaps, unlike the other types of mistakes I have made during my business career, this one should properly be ignored by others. Nevertheless, an analyst must learn the limits of his or her competence and tend well the sheep at hand.

STAY OR SELL IN ANTICIPATION OF POSSIBLE MARKET DOWNTURNS?

Should an investor sell a good stock in the face of a potentially bad market? On this subject, I fear I hold a minority view given the investment psychology prevalent today. Now more than ever, the actions of those who control the vast bulk of equity investments in this country appear to reflect the belief that when an investor has achieved a good profit in a stock and fears the stock might well go down, he should grab his profit and get out. My view is rather different. Even if the stock of a particular company seems at or near a temporary peak and that a sizable decline may strike in the near future, I will not sell the firm's shares provided I believe that its longer term future is sufficiently attractive. When I estimate that the price of these shares will rise to a peak quite considerably higher than the current levels in a few years time, I prefer to hold. My belief stems from some rather fundamental considerations about the nature of the investment process. Companies with truly unusual prospects for appreciation are quite hard to find for there are not too many of them. However, for someone who understands and applies sound fundamentals, I believe that a truly outstanding company can be differentiated from a run-of-the-mill company with perhaps 90 percent precision.

It is vastly more difficult to forecast what a particular stock is going to do in the next six months. Estimates of short-term performance start with economic estimates of the coming level of general business. Yet the forecasting record of seers predicting changes in the business cycle has generally been abysmal. They can seriously misjudge if and when recessions may occur, and are worse in predicting their severity and duration. Furthermore, neither the stock market as a whole nor the course of any particular stock tends to move in close parallel with the business climate. Changes in mass psychology and in how the financial community as a whole decided to appraise the outlook either for business in general or for a particular stock can have overriding importance and can vary almost unpredictably. For these reasons, I believe that it is hard to be correct in forecasting the short-term movement of stocks more than 60 percent of the time no matter how diligently the skill is cultivated. This may well be too optimistic an estimate. On the face of it, it doesn't make good sense to step out of a position where you have a 90 percent probability of being right because of an influence about which you might at best have a 60 percent chance of being right.

Moreover, for those seeking major gains through long-term investments, the odds of winning are not the only consideration. If the investment is in a well-run company with sufficient financial strength, even the greatest bear market will not erase the value of holding. In contrast, time after time, truly unusual stocks have subsequent peaks many hundreds of percent above their previous peaks. Thus, risk/reward considerations favor long-term investment.

So, putting it in the simplest mathematical terms, both the odds and the risk/reward considerations favor holding. There is a much greater chance of being wrong in estimating adverse short-term changes for a good stock than in projecting its strong, long-term price appreciation potential. If you stay with the right stocks through even a major temporary market drop, you are at most going to be temporarily behind 40 percent of the former peak at the very worst point and will ultimately be ahead; whereas if you sell *and don't buy back* you will have missed long-term profits many times the short-term gains from having sold the stock in anticipation at a short-term reversal. It has been my observation that it is so difficult to time correctly the near-term price movements of an attractive stock that the profits made in the few instances when this stock is sold and subsequently replaced at significantly lower prices are dwarfed by the profits lost when timing is wrong. Many have sold too soon and have either never gotten back in or have postponed reinvestment too long to recapture the profits possible.

The example I will use to illustrate this point is the weakest one I have experienced. In 1962, two of the major electronics investments I had made had risen to heights that made the outlook for near-term price movement extremely dangerous. Texas Instruments was selling at over fifteen times the price I had paid for it seven years before. Another company which I bought a year or so later, and which I shall call by the fictitious name of "Central California Electronics," had enjoyed a similar percentage rise. Prices had gone too far. I consequently informed each of my clients that the prices of these two stocks were unrealistically high and discouraged them from using these prices in measuring their current net worth. This is a practice I have rarely followed, and then only when I had an unusually strong conviction that the next important move for one or more of my stocks would be sharply downward. Nevertheless, in the face of this conviction, I urged my clients to maintain their holdings, in the belief that some years ahead both stocks would rise to very much higher levels. When the correction in values came for these two stocks, it proved even more severe than I had anticipated. Texas Instruments at its subsequent bottom sold off 80 percent from its 1962 peak. Central California Electronics did not perform quite so badly, but still sold off by almost 60 percent. My beliefs were being tested in the extreme!

However, within a few years Texas Instruments was once again selling at new high levels more than double its 1962 high. Patience had paid off here. Central California Electronics' performance was not a happy one. As the general stock market started to recover, problems within the management of Central California Electronics became apparent. Changes in personnel occurred. I became quite worried and made what I believe was a thorough investigation. I reached two conclusions and neither one pleased me. One was that I had misjudged the former management. I should have been more aware of its deficiencies, yet wasn't. Neither could I be sufficiently enthusiastic about the new management to warrant continuing to hold the shares. I consequently sold these holdings in the following twelve-month period at a price only slightly better than half of the 1962 peak. Even so, my clients, depending on the applicable purchase price, gained from seven to ten times the original cost.

As I have already indicated, I am deliberately citing a weak example rather than a dramatic one to illustrate why I believe it pays to ignore near-term fluctuations in situations that hold real promise. My error in the Central California Electronics instance was not in holding the shares through a temporary decline, but in something far more important. I had grown too complacent as a result of the enormous success of my investments in this company. I began paying too much attention to what I was hearing from top management and not doing sufficient checking with people at lower levels and with customers. When I recognized the situation and acted upon it, I was then able to make the same kind of gains I had expected to make in Central California Electronics by switching these funds to other electronic companies, chiefly Motorola, which fortunately rose in the next few years to a value several times higher than the prior peak of Central California Electronics.

IN AND OUT MAY BE OUT OF THE MONEY

There is more to learn from the Texas Instruments and Central California Electronics situations. When I originally acquired these Texas Instruments shares in the summer of 1955, they were bought for the longest type of long-range investment. It seemed to me the company fully warranted this degree of confidence. About a year later, the stock had doubled. With one exception, the various owners of the funds I managed, familiar as they were with my method of operations, showed no more interest in taking a profit than did I. However, at that time I had one relatively new account owned by people who, in their own business, were used to building up inventory when markets were low and cutting it back sharply when they were high. Now that Texas Instruments had doubled, they brought strong pressure to sell, which for a time I was able to resist. When the stock rose an additional 25 percent to give them a profit of 125 percent of their cost, the pressure to sell became even stronger. They explained, "We agree with you. We like the company, but we can always buy it back at a better price on a decline." I finally compromised with them by persuading them to keep part of their holding and sell the rest. Yet when the big drop occurred several years later and the shares fell 80 percent from their peak, this new bottom was still almost 40 percent higher than the price at which this particular holder was so eager to sell!

After a very sharp advance, a stock nearly always looks too high to the financially untrained. This client demonstrated another risk to those who follow the practice of selling shares that still have unusual growth prospects simply because they have realized a good gain and the stock appears temporarily overpriced. These investors seldom buy back at higher prices when they are wrong and lose further gains of dramatic proportions.

At the risk of being repetitious, let me underscore my belief that the short-term price movements are so inherently tricky to predict that I do not believe it possible to play the in and out game and still make the enormous profits that have accrued again and again to the truly long-term holder of the right stocks.

THE LONG SHADOW OF DIVIDENDS

In these comments I have tried to show how, as the years have passed, various experiences gradually helped to shape my investment philosophy. However, looking back, I find no specific event, either a mistake or a favorable opportunity, which caused me to reach the conclusions I have on the matter of dividends. Many observations over a long period of years gradually crystallized my views. I started out taking for granted the belief, as widely accepted forty years ago as it is today, that dividends were something highly favorable to the stockholder and something which should be welcomed enthusiastically. Then I began seeing companies that had so many exciting looking new ideas flowing from their research departments that they could not capitalize upon them all. Resources were too scarce or too expensive. I began thinking how much better it might be for some stockholders if, instead of paying dividends, more of the company's resources were retained and invested in more of these innovative products.

I began increasingly to recognize that the interests of all stockholders were not identical. Some investors needed dividend income to support their lifestyle. These stockholders would undoubtedly prefer current dividends to greater future profits and increased value for their shares resulting from increased investment in promising products and technologies. These investors could find investments in firms whose needs and opportunities for productive use of capital were not too demanding.

But how about the stockholder whose earning power or other income sources exceeded needs and who was regularly saving money anyway? Would it not be better for this investor if the company passed up its dividends, which would often be subject to a fairly high income tax rate, and instead reinvested the funds, tax-free, in future growth?

Shortly after World War II, when I started concentrating my investment activities almost solely on the attainment of major, long-range capital appreciation, another aspect of the dividend payout issue became even more apparent. The companies with the greatest growth prospects were under tremendous pressure to pay no dividends at all. Their need for funds and their ability to use funds productively was too large. The cost of developing these new products was just the first heavy drain on capital needed to finance growth. There followed the heavy marketing expense needed to introduce them to the customer. With success, plant expansion was needed to service a growing volume. Once the new line was on its way, there were further capital requirements for the increased inventories and accounts receivable which, in most cases, grow almost in direct proportion to the volume of the business.

There seemed a natural fit of interest between those firms with bountiful investment opportunities and certain investors who sought to make the greatest possible profit in relation to the risk involved and who neither needed additional income nor wanted to pay unnecessary taxes. Such investors should, I believe, mainly confine investments to nondividend paying companies with strong earning power and with attractive places to reinvest their earnings. These were the clients I sought to serve.

Recently, however, the situation has become less clear-cut. Institutional holders have become an increasingly dominant force in day to day stock transactions. Institutions such as pension and profit sharing funds pay no income tax on their dividends. Many of them as a matter of policy will not invest in a company unless it pays some dividend, no matter how small. Attracting and holding these buyers have caused many companies with unusual prospects to initiate modest dividend payments of rather small percentage total annual earnings. Managers of some would-be growth companies have concurrently reduced their payout dramatically. Today, the skill in investing retained earnings wisely has become a more critical factor in separating the unusual company from the pack.

For these reasons, I have come to believe that the most that can be said on this subject of dividends is that it is an influence that should be downgraded very sharply by those who do not need the income. In general, more attractive opportunities will be found among stocks with a low dividend payout or none at all. However, so general is the feeling among those who determine dividend policies that paying out dividends is beneficial to the investor (as it is for some) that occasionally I have found truly attractive opportunities among higher dividend payout companies, although this has not happened very often.

4

IS THE MARKET EFFICIENT?

B y the coming of the 1970's nearly all of my investment philosophy was firmly in place, molded by my experience of four prior decades. It is not coincidence that with only one exception all of both the wise and the foolish actions I have mentioned as examples that helped form the background of this philosophy were incidents that occurred during these four prior decades. This does not mean that I have made no mistakes in the 1970's. Unfortunately, it seems that no matter how much I try, sometimes I must stub my toe more than once in the same way before I truly learn. However, in the examples I have used I usually took the first instance when a particular type of event happens to illustrate my point, which explains why all but one of the examples I used occurred during these earlier periods.

It might be helpful to notice the striking parallels in each of these past ten-year periods. With the possible exception of the 1960's, there has not been a single decade in which there was not some period of time when the prevailing view was that external influences were so great and so much beyond the control of individual corporate managements that even the wisest common stock investments were foolhardy and perhaps not for the prudent. In the 1930's there were years when this view, influenced by the Great Depression, was at its most extreme, but perhaps not any more than the fear of what the German war machine and World War II might do in the 1940's, or the certainty that another major depression would hit in the 1950's, or fear of inflation, hostile government actions, etc. in the 1970's. Yet every one of these periods created investment opportunities that seemed almost incredible with all the advantages of hindsight. In each of these five decades there were not a few, but many common stock opportunities that ten years later yielded profits running to many hundreds of percent for those who had bought and stayed with the shares. In some instances profits ran well into the thousands of percent. Again in every one of these five decades some stocks which were the speculative darlings of the moment were to prove the most dangerous kind of trap for those who blindly followed the crowd rather than who really knew what they were doing. All of these ten-year periods essentially resembled the others in that the greatest opportunities came from finding situations that were extremely attractive but that were undervalued because at that particular moment the financial community had significantly misjudged the situation. As I look back on the various forces that buffeted the securities market over this fifty-year period and at the great waves of public optimism and pessimism that succeeded each other over this time span, the old French proverb, "Plus ca change, plus c'est la meme chose" (the more things change, the more they remain the same), comes to mind. I have not the slightest doubt that as we enter the emerging decade of the 1980's, with all the problems and the prospects that it now offers, the same will continue to hold true.

THE FALLACY OF THE EFFICIENT MARKET

In the last few years, too much attention has been paid to a concept that I believe is quite fallacious. I refer to the notion that the market is perfectly efficient. Like other false beliefs in other periods, a contrary view may open up opportunities for the discerning.

For those unfamiliar with "efficient" market theory, the adjective "efficient" does not refer to the obvious mechanical efficiency of the market. A potential buyer or seller can get his order to the market where a transaction can be executed very effectively within a matter of a couple of minutes. Neither does "efficiency" refer to the delicate adjustment mechanism which causes stock prices to move up or down by fractions of a point in response to modest changes in the relative pressure of buyers and sellers. Rather, this concept holds that at any one time the market "efficient" prices are assumed to reflect fully and realistically all that is known about the company. Unless someone has some significant, illicit inside information, there is no way genuine bargains can be found, since the favorable influences that make a potential buyer believe that an attractive situation exists are already reflected in the price of stock!

If the market was as efficient as it has become fashionable to believe, and if important opportunities to buy or significant reasons to sell were not constantly occurring, stock returns should not subsequently have the huge variations that they do. By variation, I am not referring to changes in prices for the market as a whole, but rather the dispersion of relative price changes of one stock against another. If the market is efficient in prospect, then the nexus of analysis that leads to this efficiency must be collectively poor.

Efficient market theory grew out of the academic School of Random Walkers. These people found that it was difficult to identify technical trading strategies that worked well enough after transactions costs to provide an attractive profit relative to the risks taken. I don't disagree with this. As you have seen, I believe that it is very, very tough to make money with in and out trading based on short-term market forecasts. Perhaps the market is efficient in this narrow sense of the word.

Most of us are or should be investors, not traders. We should be seeking investment opportunities with unusual prospects over the long run and avoiding investment opportunities with poorer prospects. This has always been the central tenet of my approach to investments in any case. I do not believe that prices are efficient for the diligent, knowledgeable, long-term investor.

Directly applicable to this is an experience I had in 1961. In the fall of that year, as in the spring of 1963, I undertook the stimulating duty of substituting for the regular finance professor in teaching the senior course of investments at Stanford University's Graduate School of Business. The concept of the "efficient" market was not to see the light of day for many years to come and had nothing to do with my motivation in the exercise I am about to describe. Rather, I wanted to show these students in a way they would never forget that the fluctuations of the market as a whole were insignificant compared to the differences between the changes in price of some stocks in relation to others.

I divided the class into two groups. The first group took the alphabetical list of stocks on the New York Stock Exchange, starting with the letter A; the second group, those starting with the letter T. Every stock was included in alphabetical order (except preferreds and utilities, which

I consider to be a different breed of cats). Each student was assigned four stocks. Each student looked up the closing price as of the last day of business of 1956, adjusted the stock dividends and stock splits (rights were ignored as not having sufficient impact to be worthy of the additional calculations), and compared this price with the price as of Friday, October 13th (if nothing else, a colorful closing date!). The percentage increase or decrease that occurred in each stock over this period of almost five years was noted. The Dow Jones averages rose from 499 to 703, or by 41 percent in this period. Altogether, there were 140 stocks in this sample. The results are displayed in the following table:

Percentage Capital Gain or Loss	No. of Stocks in Group	Percentage of Total Group
200% to 1020% gain	15 stocks	11%
100% to 199% gain	18 stocks	13%
50% to 99% gain	14 stocks	10%
25% to 49% gain	21 stocks	15%
1% to 24% gain	31 stocks	22%
Unchanged	3 stocks	2%
1% to 49% loss	32 stocks	23%
50% to 74% loss	6 stocks	4%
	140 stocks	100%

These data are quite insightful. In a period when the Dow Jones averages rose 41 percent, 38 stocks, or 27 percent of the total, showed a capital loss. Six of them, or 4 percent of the total, recorded a loss of over 50 percent of their total value. In contrast, roughly one quarter of the stocks realized capital gains that would have been considered spectacular.

To drive the point home, I noted that if a person invested $10,000 in equal amounts in the five best stocks on this list, at the outset of this four and three-quarter year period, his capital would now be worth $70,260. On the other hand, if he had invested the $10,000 in the five worst stocks, his capital would have shrunk to $3,180. These extreme results were most unlikely. It would take luck, either good or bad, as well as skill, to hit either of these extremes. It would not be so implausible for a person with real investment judgment to have picked five out of the ten best stocks for his $10,000 investment, in which case his net worth on Friday the 13th would have been $52,070. Similarly, some investors consistently select stocks for the wrong reasons and manage to pick lemons. For them selecting five out of the ten poorest in performance is also not an entirely unrealistic expectation of results. In that case, the $10,000 investment would have shrunk to $4,270. On the basis of this comparison, there might be, in less than five years, a difference of $48,000 between a wise and an unwise investment program.

A year and a half later, when I also taught this same course, I repeated the exact same exercise, with the exception that instead of using the letters A and T, I selected two different letters in the alphabet from which to form the sample of stocks. Again, over a five-year time frame, but with a different starting and a different closing date, the degree of variation was almost exactly the same.

Looking back on most markets of five-year duration, I believe that one can find stock performance results that are about as disparate. Some of this dispersion may come as the result of surprises—important new information about a stock's prospects that could not be reasonably foreseen at the outset of the period. Most of the differences, however, can be anticipated at least roughly both in terms of direction and general magnitude of gains and losses relative to the market.

THE RAYCHEM CORPORATION

In view of this kind of evidence, it is hard for me to see how anyone can consider the stock market efficient, again using the word "efficient" as it is used by the proponents of this theory. But to belabor the point further, let me take a stock market situation of just a very few years ago. In the early years of the 1970's, the shares of the Raychem Corporation had considerable prestige in the market place and were accordingly selling at a relatively high price earnings ratio. Some of the reasons warranting this prestige may be perceived by some comments made by the company's Executive Vice President, Robert M. Halperin. In outlining what he called the four cardinal points to Raychem's operating philosophy, he stated:

1. Raychem will not do anything technically simple (i.e., something that would be easy for potential competitors to copy).
2. Raychem won't do anything unless it can be vertically integrated;

that is, Raychem must conceive the product, manufacture it, and sell it to the customer.

3. Raychem won't do anything unless there is a substantial opportunity for real proprietary protection, which generally means patent protection. Unless this occurs, research and development energies will not be employed on a project, even though otherwise it might fit into Raychem's skills.

4. Raychem will only go into new products when it believes it can become the market leader in whatever niche, sometimes smaller, sometimes larger, that product attempts to capture.

By the mid-1970's, awareness of these unusual strengths was sufficiently prevalent among those who controlled large institutional funds so that sizable blocks of shares had been taken out of the market by people who believed that Raychem was a situation of unusual competitive strength and attractiveness. However, it was another aspect of this company that gave Raychem its greatest appeal to these holders and was probably the cause of the high price earnings ratio at which it was then selling. Many considered that Raychem, which was spending an above average percentage of sales on new project development, had perfected a research organization capable of producing an important enough stream of new products so that the company could be depended on to show an uninterrupted upward trend in sales and profits. These research products had quite justifiably a special appeal to the financial community because many of the newer ones only indirectly competed with older products of other companies. Primarily, the new products enabled high-priced labor to do the same job in considerably less time than had previously been required. There were enough savings offered to the ultimate customer of these products to justify a price which should afford Raychem a pleasing profit margin. All this caused the stock toward the end of 1975 to reach a high of over $42½ (price adjusted for subsequent stock splits)—a level about 25 times the estimated earnings for the fiscal year ending June 30, 1976.

RAYCHEM, DASHED EXPECTATIONS, AND THE CRASH

Toward the close of the June 30, 1976 fiscal year, Raychem was hit by two hammer blows, which were to play havoc with the price of the stock and with the company's reputation in the financial community. The financial community had become very excited about a proprietary polymer, Stilan, which enjoyed unique advantages over other compounds used by the airplane industry for coating wire and which was then in the final research stages. Furthermore, the polymer was to be the first product in which Raychem would go basic, that is, make the original chemicals in its own plant rather than buying raw materials from others and compounding them. Because of the appeal of the product, Raychem had allocated by a considerable margin more funds to this research product than to any other in its history. The financial community assumed this product was already on its way to success, and after passing through the usual "learning curve" experienced by all new products it would become highly profitable.

Actually, quite the opposite was occurring. In the words of the Raychem management, Stilan was "a scientific success but a commercial failure." Improved products of an able competitor, while technically not as desirable as Stilan, proved adequate for the job and were far cheaper. Raychem management recognized this. In the course of a relatively few weeks, management reached the painful decision to abandon the product and write off the heavy investments made in it. The resulting charge to earnings for that fiscal year was some $9.3 million. This charge-off caused earnings, exclusive of some offsetting special gains, to drop to $.08 a share from $7.95 the previous fiscal year.

The financial community was as much upset by the erosion of the great confidence in the company's research ability as by the precipitous drop in earnings. Largely ignored was the basic rule that some new product developments are bound to fail in all companies. This is inherent in all industrial research activity and in a well-run company is far more than offset in the long run by other successful new products. It may have been just bad luck that the particular project on which the most money had been spent had been the one to fail. At any rate, the effect on the stock price was dramatic. By the fourth quarter of 1976, the stock had dropped to a low of approximately $14¾ (again adjusted for subsequent splits amounting to six to one) or to approximately one-third its former high. Of course, only a tiny amount of stock could be bought or sold at the low point for the year. Of greater impact, the stock was available at prices only moderately above this low level for months thereafter.

Another development also affected the profits of the company at this moment and contributed to Raychem's fall from favor. One of the most difficult tasks for those responsible for the success of any growing company is to change the management structure appropriately as the company grows to allow for the difference between what is needed for proper control of small companies and optimum control of big companies. Until the end of the 1976 fiscal year, Raychem management had been set up along divisional lines based largely on manufacturing techniques; that is, on the basis of the products produced. This worked well when the company was smaller, but was not conducive to serving the customer most efficiently as the company was growing. Therefore, at about the end of 1975 fiscal year, top Raychem management started working on a "big company" management concept. The firm restructured the divisions by the industry served rather than by the physical and chemical composition of the products being manufactured. The target date to make the change was set at the end of the 1976 fiscal year. This was done at a time when there was not the least thought within the management that this date would coincide with the time of the huge write-off for the abandonment of Stilan.

Everyone in Raychem knew that when the organizational change was to occur there would be at least one quarter and probably a minimum of two of substantially reduced earnings. While making these changes caused almost no change in the individuals on the Raychem management payroll, so many people now had different superiors, different subordinates, and different co-workers with whom they had to interface their activities that a time of inefficiency and adjustment was bound to occur until Raychem employees learned how best to coordinate their work with the new faces with whom they were now dealing. Perhaps no stronger indication could have existed to justify long-range confidence in this company or to indicate that management was not concerned with short-term results than its decision to go ahead with this project as planned rather than to postpone what was bound to be a second blow to Raychem's current earnings.

Actually, this significant change worked with considerably less difficulty than had been anticipated. As expected, the first quarter earnings of the new fiscal year were much lower than would have been the case if the change had not been made. However, the change was working so well that as the second quarter progressed, the short-term costs of what had been done had largely been eliminated. Fundamentally these developments should have been considered bullish by analysts. Raychem was now in a position to handle growth properly in a way that could not have been done before. It had successfully hurdled a barrier of the type that is most apt to dull the luster of otherwise attractive growth companies. By and large, the financial community did not seem to recognize this, however, and instead the temporary further shrinkage of earnings was just one more factor holding the stock at the low levels to which it had fallen.

Making these price levels even more attractive to potential investors was another influence that I have seen happen in other companies shortly after they had abandoned a major research project that had proved unsuccessful. One financial effect of the abandonment of Stilan was that a sizable amount of money that had heretofore been devoted to that project was now free to be allocated elsewhere. Even more important, it had similarly freed the time of key research people for other endeavors. Within a year or two much like a field of flowers starting to bloom when rain follows drought, the company began to enjoy what was possibly a greater number of attractive research projects in relation to its size than had ever before been experienced.

RAYCHEM AND THE EFFICIENT MARKET

Now what has Raychem's situation to do with this theory of an "efficient market" that has recently gained such a following in certain financial quarters? According to that theory, stocks automatically and instantly adjust to whatever is known about a company, so that only those who might possess illicit "inside information" that is not known to others could benefit from what might lie ahead for a particular stock. In this instance, at the drop of a hat, the Raychem management would and did explain to anyone interested all the facts I have just cited and explained how temporary they believed was the period of poor earnings.

Actually, well after all this had happened and when profits were climbing to a new all-time high level, the Raychem management went even further. On January 26, 1978, they held a long one-day meeting at their headquarters which I had the privilege of attending. Raychem management invited to this meeting the representatives of all institutions, brokerage houses, and investment advisors who either had any interest in Raychem or they thought might have. At this meeting the ten most senior executives of Raychem explained with what I believe was extreme frankness and in detail, such as I have only occasionally seen at similar meetings of other companies, the prospects, the problems, and the current status of Raychem matters under their jurisdiction.

In the year or two following this meeting, Raychem's earnings growth developed exactly as might have been inferred from what was said there. During that period, the stock was to much more than double from the price of $23¼ at which it was selling that day. Yet in the weeks immediately following this meeting, there was no particular effect on the stock whatsoever. Some of those present were obviously impressed by the picture being presented. Too many, however, were still under the influence of the double shock that they had experienced a year or two before. They obviously mistrusted what was being told them then. So much for the theory of an efficient market.

What kind of conclusion does the investor or the investment professional reach from experiences like Raychem? By and large, those who have accepted and been influenced by this theory of the "efficient market" fall into two groups. One is students, who have had a minimum of practical experience. The other, strangely enough, seems to be many managers of large institutional funds. The individual private investor, by and large, has paid relatively little attention to this theory.

From this experience gained in applying my personal investment philosophy, I would conclude that in my field of technological stocks, as the decade of the 1970's comes to an end, there would therefore be more attractive opportunities among the larger companies, the market for which is dominated by the institutions, than among the small technological companies where the individual private investor plays a considerably bigger role. Just as some ten years earlier those who recognized the folly of the then prevailing concept of the two-tier market benefited from recognizing that particular nonsense for what it was, so in each decade false ideas arise creating opportunities for those with investment discernment.

CONCLUSION

This then is my investment philosophy as it has emerged over a half century of business experience. Perhaps the heart of it may be summarized in the following eight points:

1. Buy into companies that have disciplined plans for achieving dramatic long-range growth in profits and that have inherent qualities making it difficult for newcomers to share in that growth. There are so many details, both favorable and unfavorable, that should also be considered in selecting one of these companies that it is obviously impossible in a monograph of this length to cover them adequately. For those interested, I have attempted to summarize this subject as concisely as I could in the first three chapters of *Conservative Investors Sleep Well.** A brief outline appears in the Appendix.

2. Focus on buying these companies when they are out of favor; that is, when, either because of general market conditions or because the financial community at the moment has misconceptions of its true worth, the stock is selling at prices well under what it will be when its true merit is better understood.

3. Hold the stock until either (a) there has been a fundamental change in its nature (such as a weakening of management through changed personnel), or (b) it has grown to a point where it no longer will be growing faster than the economy as a whole. Only in the most exceptional circumstances, if ever, sell because of forecasts as to what the economy or the stock market is going to do, because these changes are too difficult to predict. Never sell the most attractive stocks you own for short-term reasons. However, as companies grow, remember that many companies that are quite efficiently run when they are small fail to change management style to meet the different requirements of skill big companies need. When management fails to grow as companies grow, shares should be sold.

4. For those primarily seeking major appreciation of their capital, de-emphasize the importance of dividends. The most attractive opportunities are most likely to occur in the profitable, but low or no dividend payout groups. Unusual opportunities are much less likely to be found in situations where high percentage of profits is paid to stockholders.

5. Making some mistakes is as much an inherent cost of investing for major gains as making some bad loans is inevitable in even

---

Conservative Investors Sleep Well, Harper & Row, 1975.

the best run and most profitable lending institution. The important thing is to recognize them as soon as possible, to understand their causes, and to learn how to keep from repeating the mistakes. Willingness to take small losses in some stocks and to let profits grow bigger and bigger in the more promising stocks is a sign of good investment management. Taking small profits in good investments and letting losses grow in bad ones is a sign of abominable investment judgment. A profit should never be taken just for the satisfaction of taking it.

6. There are a relatively small number of truly outstanding companies. Their shares frequently can't be bought at attractive prices. Therefore, when favorable prices exist, full advantage should be taken of the situation. Funds should be concentrated in the most desirable opportunities. For those involved in venture capital and quite small companies, say with annual sales of under $25,000,000, more diversification may be necessary. For larger companies, proper diversification requires investing in a variety of industries with different economic characteristics. For individuals (in possible contrast to institutions and certain types of funds), any holding of over twenty different stocks is a sign of financial incompetence. Ten or twelve is usually a better number. Sometimes the costs of the capital gains tax may justify taking several years to complete a move toward concentration. As an individual's holdings climb toward as many as twenty stocks, it nearly always is desirable to switch from the least attractive of these stocks to more of the attractive. It should be remembered that ERISA stands for Emasculated Results: Insufficient Sophisticated Action.

7. A basic ingredient of outstanding common stock management is the ability neither to accept blindly whatever may be the dominant opinion in the financial community at the moment nor to reject the prevailing view just to be contrary for the sake of being contrary. Rather, it is to have more knowledge and to apply better judgment, in thorough evaluation of specific situations, and the moral courage to act "in opposition to the crowd" when your judgment tells you you are right.

8. In handling common stocks, as in most other fields of human

activity, success greatly depends on a combination of hard work, intelligence, and honesty.

Some of us may be born with a greater or lesser degree of each of these traits than others. However, I believe all of us can "grow" our capabilities in each of these areas if we discipline ourselves and make the effort.

While good fortune will always play some part in managing common stock portfolios, luck tends to even out. Sustained success requires skill and consistent application of sound principles. Within the framework of my eight guidelines, I believe that the future will largely belong to those who, through self-discipline, make the effort to achieve it.

APPENDIX

KEY FACTORS IN EVALUTATING PROMISING FIRMS*

M y philosophy calls for making a relatively small number of investments but only in unusually promising companies. Obviously, I am looking for signs of growth potential in the companies I study. As important, I am trying, through my analysis, to avoid risk. I want to make sure that the firm's management has the wherewithal to capitalize on the potential and to minimize my investment risks in the process. Summarized below are some of the defensive characteristics that I search for in the companies that are to meet my standards of unusual promise when I undertake financial analysis, interviews with management, and discussions with informed people associated with the industry.

FUNCTIONAL FACTORS

1. The firm must be one of the lowest-cost producers of its products or services relative to its competition, and must promise to remain so.
   a. A comparatively low breakeven will enable this firm to survive depressed market conditions and to strengthen its market and

---

*Excerpts from Fisher, *Conservative Investors Sleep Well*, Harper & Row, 1975. Chapters 1–3.

pricing position when weaker competitors are driven out of the market.

b. A higher than average profit margin enables the firm to generate more funds internally to sustain growth without as much dilution caused by equity sales or strain caused by overdependence on fixed-income financing.

2. A firm must have a strong enough customer orientation to recognize changes in customer needs and interests and then to react promptly to those changes in an appropriate manner. This capability should lead to generating a flow of new products that more than offset lines maturing or becoming obsolete.

3. Effective marketing requires not only understanding of what customers want, but also explaining to them (through advertising, selling or other means) in terms the customer will understand. Close control and constant monitoring of the cost/effectiveness of market efforts are required.

4. Even nontechnical firms today require a strong and well-directed research capability to (a) produce newer and better products, and (b) perform services in a more effective or efficient way.

5. There are wide differences in the effectiveness of research. Two important elements of more productive research are (a) market/profit consciousness, and (b) the ability to pool necessary talent into an effective working team.

6. A firm with a strong financial team has several important advantages:

a. Good cost information enables management to direct its energies toward those products with the highest potential for profit contribution.

b. The cost system should pinpoint where production, marketing, and research costs are inefficient even in sub-parts of the operation.

c. Capital conservation through tight control of fixed and working capital investments.

7. A critical finance function is to provide an early warning system to identify influences that could threaten the profit plan sufficiently ahead of time to devise remedial plans to minimize adverse surprises.

PEOPLE FACTORS

1. To become more successful, a firm needs a leader with a determined entrepreneurial personality combining the drive, the original ideas, and the skills necessary to build the fortunes of the firm.

2. A growth-oriented chief executive must surround himself with an extremely competent team and to delegate considerable authority to them to run the activities of the firm. Teamwork, as distinct from dysfunction struggles for power, is critical.

3. Attention must be paid to attracting competent managers at lower levels and to training them for larger responsibilities. Succession should largely be from the available talent pool. The need to recruit the chief executive from outside is a particularly dangerous sign.

4. The entrepreneurial spirit must permeate the organization.

5. More successful firms usually have some unique personality traits—some special ways of doing things that are particularly effective for their management team. This is a positive not a negative sign.

6. Management must recognize and be attuned to the fact that the world in which they are operating is changing at an ever increasing rate.

    a. Every accepted way of doing things must be reexamined periodically, and new, better ways sought.

    b. Changes in managerial approaches involve necessary risks, which must be recognized, minimized and taken.

7. There must be a genuine, realistic, conscious and continuous effort to have employees at every level, including the blue collar workers, believe that their company is really a good place to work.

    a. Employees must be treated with reasonable dignity and decency.

    b. The firm's work environment and benefits programs should be supportive of motivation.

    c. People must feel they can express grievances without fear and with reasonable expectation of appropriate attention and action.

    d. Participatory programs seem to work well and be an important source of good ideas.
8. Management must be willing to submit to the disciplines required of sound growth. Growth requires some sacrifice of current profits to lay the foundation for worthwhile future improvement.

BUSINESS CHARACTERISTICS

1. Although managers rely heavily on return of assets in considering new investments, investors must recognize that historic assets stated at historic costs distort comparisons of firms' performance. Favorable profit to sales ratios, notwithstanding differences in turnover ratios, may be a better indicator of the safety of an investment, particularly in an inflationary environment.
2. High margins attract competition, and competition erodes profit opportunities. The best way to mute competition is to operate so efficiently that there is no incentive left for the potential entrant.
3. Efficiencies of scale are often counterbalanced by the inefficiencies of bureaucratic layers of middle management. In a well-run firm, however, the industry leadership position creates a strong competitive advantage that should be attractive to investors.
4. Getting there first in a new product market is a long step toward becoming first. Some firms are better geared to be there first.
5. Products are not islands. There is an indirect competition, for example, for consumers' dollars. As prices change, some products may lose attractiveness even in well-run, low cost companies.
6. It is hard to introduce new, superior products in market arenas where established competitors already have a strong position. While the new entrant is building the production, marketing power, and reputation to be competitive, existing competitors can take strong defensive actions to regain the market threatened. Innovators have a better chance of success if they combine technology disciplines, e.g. electronics and nucleonics in a way that is novel relative to existing competitive competencies.

7. Technology is just one avenue to industry leadership. Developing a consumer "franchise" is another. Service excellence is still another. Whatever the case, a strong ability to defend established markets against new competitors is essential for a sound investment.

INDEX